Read this book online today:

With SAP PRESS BooksOnline we offer you online access to knowledge from
the leading SAP experts. Whether you use it as a beneficial supplement or as
an alternative to the printed book, with SAP PRESS BooksOnline you can:

- Access your book anywhere, at any time. All you need is an Internet connection.
- Perform full text searches on your book and on the entire SAP PRESS library.
- Build your own personalized SAP library.

The SAP PRESS customer advantage:

Register this book today at *www.sap-press.com* and obtain exclusive free trial
access to its online version. If you like it (and we think you will), you can choose to
purchase permanent, unrestricted access to the online edition at a very special price!

Here's how to get started:

1. Visit *www.sap-press.com*.
2. Click on the link for SAP PRESS BooksOnline and login (or create an account).
3. Enter your free trial license key, shown below in the corner of the page.
4. Try out your online book with full, unrestricted access for a limited time!

Your personal free trial **license key**
for this online book is:

aruq-stfc-z97h-ekpd

Global Available-to-Promise with SAP®

SAP® Essentials

Expert SAP knowledge for your day-to-day work

Whether you wish to expand your SAP knowledge, deepen it, or master a use case, SAP Essentials provide you with targeted expert knowledge that helps support you in your day-to-day work. To the point, detailed, and ready to use.

SAP PRESS is a joint initiative of SAP and Galileo Press. The know-how offered by SAP specialists combined with the expertise of the Galileo Press publishing house offers the reader expert books in the field. SAP PRESS features first-hand information and expert advice, and provides useful skills for professional decision-making.

SAP PRESS offers a variety of books on technical and business related topics for the SAP user. For further information, please visit our website: *www.sap-press.com.*

Shaun Snapp
Discover SAP SCM
2010, 384 pp.
978-1-59229-305-6

Carter et al.
SAP Extended Warehouse Management: Processes, Functionality, and Configuration
2010, 847 pp.
978-1-59229-304-9

Balaji Gaddam
Capable to Match (CTM) with SAP APO
2009, 273 pp.
978-1-59229-244-8

Jochen Balla and Frank Layer
Production Planning with SAP APO (2nd Edition)
2011, 402 pp.
978-1-59229-354-4

Sandeep Pradhan and Pavan Verma

Global Available-to-Promise with SAP®

Functionality and Configuration

Galileo Press

Bonn • Boston

Galileo Press is named after the Italian physicist, mathematician and philosopher Galileo Galilei (1564–1642). He is known as one of the founders of modern science and an advocate of our contemporary, heliocentric worldview. His words *Eppur si muove* (And yet it moves) have become legendary. The Galileo Press logo depicts Jupiter orbited by the four Galilean moons, which were discovered by Galileo in 1610.

Editor Laura Korslund
Technical Reviewer Susanti Chandra
Copyeditor Julie McNamee
Cover Design Graham Geary
Photo Credit iStockphoto.com/melhij
Layout Design Vera Brauner
Production Kelly O'Callaghan, Graham Geary
Typesetting Publishers' Design and Production Services, Inc.
Printed and bound in the United States of America

ISBN 978-1-59229-385-8

© 2012 by Galileo Press Inc., Boston (MA)

1st edition 2012

Library of Congress Cataloging-in-Publication Data
Pradhan, Sandeep.
Global available to promise with SAP : functionality and configuration /
Sandeep Pradhan, Pavan Verma. — 1st ed.
p. cm.
Includes bibliographical references and index.
ISBN-13: 978-1-59229-385-8
ISBN-10: 1-59229-385-9
1. SAP ERP. 2. Sales management—Computer programs.
3. Inventory control—
Data processing. 4. Business logistics—Data processing.
I. Verma, Pavan. II. Title.
HF5438.35.P73 2012
658.00285'53—dc23
2011031667

SUSTAINABLE FORESTRY INITIATIVE Certified Fiber Sourcing
Label applies to the text stock www.sfiprogram.org

Contents at a Glance

Dear Reader,

In an ever-changing and often precarious market, companies are constantly searching for ways to increase their delivery reliability, and thus keep their customer base. Your goal is to help a company get ahead of the pack in terms of delivering their goods and services to customers in a timely manner and as promised (and maybe even scoop up new business!). While you know that the SAP provided functionality of global available-to-promise is the solution to meet this goal, the *whys* and *hows* of implementing and configuring this functionality to meet your company's unique situations and needs are not always quite as clear.

In this book, you will benefit from the combined expertise of two authors who are highly experienced in the field. Sandeep Pradhan and Pavan Verma provide you with a reference guide for your implementation or maintenance project to understand how to configure global AIP to fit your business needs. By the end of the book, you will have a firm grasp on how to bridge the integration gap between planning procedures and your company's order fulfillment processes with ATP, capable-to-match, variant configuration, and much more.

We appreciate your business, and welcome your feedback. Your comments and suggestions are our most useful tools to help us improve our books for you, the reader. We encourage you to visit our website at *www.sap-press.com* and share your feedback about this work.

Thank you for purchasing a book from SAP PRESS!

Laura Korslund
Editor, SAP PRESS

Galileo Press
Boston, MA

laura.korslund@galileo-press.com
www.sap-press.com

Contents

11 Integrating Global ATP with Supply Planning 257

12 Integrating the SAP Customer Relationship Management System with Global ATP 273

13 Accelerate Your Global ATP Implementation with Service-Oriented Architecture (SOA) Packages 289

14 Maintenance and Monitoring Procedure for Global ATP 303

Contents

Appendices 323

Preface

Companies face constant challenges in their order-fulfillment cycle to meet customer order delivery dates. The goal of any company is to increase the reliability of delivery and also ensure the correct product availability to an exclusive customer base. With the introduction of the global available-to-promise (which we will refer to as global ATP) functionality in SAP, companies are moving forward from a traditional manufacturing push-based supply chain to a market demand pull-based principle. Global ATP introduces many innovative concepts for order-management processes to fulfill market demand on time, increase delivery reliability, and keep inventory levels low at the warehouse.

The objective of this book is to explain how the global ATP functionality within the SAP Supply Chain Management (SAP SCM) suite can be configured and implemented to meet a company's order-fulfillment cycle. This book serves as a functional and technical guide in explaining how global ATP from SAP can be integrated into supply chain business process improvement initiatives.

Target Audience

The target audience for this book is the supply chain practitioners who are considering or are already involved in the implementation of global ATP—whether as a project manager, a project member, or a consultant. The book assumes that the reader has a basic knowledge of the order-to-cash (OTC) business process and an understanding of the logistics process in supply chain management.

What Will I Learn?

The book provides comprehensive guidelines not only for implementing the ATP solution within the order fulfillment business process, but also to maintain the production environment. The book is based on functionalities available in SAP ERP (ECC 6.0) and SAP SCM 7.0 versions. Each chapter explains global ATP functionality, configuration, master data, and testing steps to fulfill customer business requirements while integrating a specific business case. Most of the business examples you will see are based on the authors' project experiences.

The book starts with an introduction to the order-to-cash (OTC) business process and explains how available-to-promise (ATP) fits in the overall process (**Chapter 1**). Then the global ATP functionality and its core features are introduced in **Chapter 2**. The next couple of chapters focus on global ATP technology (**Chapter 3**) and basic configuration, along with master data requirements for global ATP (**Chapter 4**).

After this preliminary introduction, the book dives into the core capabilities functionality within global ATP. Starting with transportation shipment and scheduling to derive a correct availability date, based on logistics lead time (**Chapter 5**), the book next introduces the rule-based mechanism for the ATP check. The rule-based functionality (**Chapter 6**) allows a company to formulate its business rules to be based on product and/or location substitution during the ATP check. Setting up business priorities during order processing and proper product allocation (**Chapter 7**) is critical for a company to make a profit from sales. Due to constant changes in the supply chain situation, the backorder processing (BOP) (**Chapter 8**) provides the latest ATP corrections.

For some of the manufacturing scenario (make-to-order) variants, global ATP directly integrates with production (**Chapters 9** and **10**) to calculate the capacity and critical component checks necessary to derive the material availability check, against which the ATP check needs to be performed. The integration with supply chain planning (**Chapter 11**) and SAP Customer Relationship Management (SAP CRM) (**Chapter 12**) provides a foundation for global ATP to improve the current business processes in OTC and planning function areas.

The closing section of the book provides an overview for how the global ATP business process can be mapped in the service-oriented architecture (SOA) environment (**Chapter 13**). Last, we explain in **Chapter 14** how a good housekeeping of the global ATP system is imperative for monitoring and maintenance in the production environment.

The Appendix section contains some valuable information about the minor and major technical enhancement possibilities in global ATP, and also lists some of important SAP OSS developer notes.

Acknowledgements

I would like to offer very special thanks to my wife Imelda Linggawidjaja, daughter Jessica Anna, and my parents for giving me the time and encouragement to write this book.
Sandeep Pradhan

I would like to thank my parents for my existence and blessings; my wife Monika Verma, and sons Aditya and Akshat for giving me the time and encouragement to write this book.
Pavan Verma

Finally, we would like to thank Laura Korslund and Meg Dunkerley from Galileo Press, as well as the production team, for helping us in all phases of the project and providing encouragement. Also, a special thanks to Susanti Chandra for becoming our technical reviewer and providing valuable corrections and comments on the book.

Cash is the lifeblood of any company, and it flows through an order-to-cash cycle—the heart of any company's supply chain. This chapter reviews the different order fulfillment models, identifies business challenges, and highlights key performance indicators for ways to improve the process.

1   Order-to-Cash Business Process

In today's competitive environment, one way to deliver greater value to stakeholders is to improve the order-to-cash (OTC) process. The OTC process is integral in any business and touches many other processes, including order management; accounts; revenue reporting; and management, sales, and customer relationship management. Industry research indicates that improving the performance of the order-fulfillment process translates into better business performance and competitive industry advantage. Ensuring the smooth flow of the OTC business processes (receiving the order, fulfilling the order, billing, and getting paid) is vitally important, yet companies face significant challenges in controlling orders as they progress through the entire fulfillment process.

In this chapter, we'll look at the different OTC business models, identify the business challenges, and recommend key performance indicators (KPIs) for process improvements. The chapter also explains how available-to-promise (ATP) fits in with the overall OTC business process and supply chain architecture.

1.1   Order-to-Cash Overview

Order-to-cash (OTC) is the business process where goods are ordered, delivered and received, invoiced, and paid for. Whether your company's primary business is manufacturing, distribution, or retail, this process is critical for business performance. Recent advanced manufacturing research (AMR) supply chain studies show that OTC performance is closely linked to overall business performance, both for cost containment and sustainable growth. Although every company has a unique OTC business model, most companies face similar challenges related to inventory accuracy, on-time delivery, freight costs, and labor productivity.

Let's look at a typical business example for a consumer goods company, which supports the entire OTC process chain for a typical sales process from sales order to delivery to billing:

1. A sales order is created for finished goods based on a customer quotation (optional). The stock availability of the finished goods in the warehouse is checked for confirmation of quantity and date based on the customer-requested quantity and delivery date. The consumer goods company allows for a credit limit threshold for the customer based on the partner payment history.

2. A credit check for the customer might be executed, which might block the further handling of the sales document. In this scenario, the order-management representative will need to release the sales order for further processing.

3. In delivery processing, the delivery is created; the goods are picked, kitted, packed, and shipped from the warehouse; and the goods issue is posted to trigger the invoice process. In the billing process that follows, an invoice is created by the finance department and sent to the customer.

4. To complete the OTC process, the customer payment is posted to clear accounts receivable.

This business process shown in Figure 1.1 requires tight integration of the order-management team with transportation, logistics, and finance for delivering orders as promised.

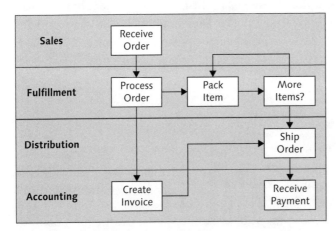

Figure 1.1 Order-to-Cash Business Process

An ineffective OTC process can impact a company's financials through the following:

▶ High order-taking error rates

▶ High order-fulfillment error rates

▶ High days sales outstanding (DSO) rates

▶ High cost of dispute resolutions

▶ Inefficient/ineffective collection processes

▶ Long-term losses due to customer defections

The OTC business process requires that all of the sub-processes be executed with a high percentage of reliability to maintain the commitment given to customers on delivery dates. This aligns with the corporate strategy of *perfect order* fulfillment, which is defined as the percentage of orders that are delivered in full and on time to the initial request and/or commit date and match the customer documentation (invoice, purchase order, receipt).

A recent study by consulting company Software AG of supply chain business and IT executives revealed the top five priorities that companies have regarding the OTC process:

▶ Customer service is a priority; customer delivery time is the top improvement area.

▶ Accommodating new product introduction in the OTC cycle is the top business challenge.

▶ Visibility is a top priority, but challenges remain with IT and business alignment around visibility.

▶ Unifying the supply chain environment is the top goal for IT.

▶ The ability to monitor and respond to customer order changes needs improvement.

Companies are looking at innovative ways to implement these priorities and increase their sales revenues and profit margins. However, any business transformation initiatives come with business challenges, which we will explain next.

Business Challenges

The OTC business process touches every customer experience with the company. Ensuring that the business transaction flows smoothly with the customer is important, yet many companies face challenges during the order-fulfillment lifecycle. In today's business environment, a company's order-management team faces many business challenges, including the following:

▸ **Multiple distribution channels**
Distributing products through various channels such as retailers, wholesalers, and directly to consumers poses challenges in managing product demand, customer service, and fulfillment.

▸ **Complex orders with distributed line items**
Multiple sourcing points in an order make delivering an order on time as requested challenging. Companies struggle with awareness, such as knowing when each item for that order is expected to arrive; lack of notification of any item that may not arrive with others; and then being unable to respond most effectively to maintain customer satisfaction levels.

▸ **Increased need to consolidate customer orders**
In an effort to reduce transportation costs, shippers consolidate goods while shipping to multiple customers. Maintaining visibility and being able to coordinate final delivery is becoming a more frequent requirement.

▸ **International logistics variability**
Huge numbers of products are built in low-cost manufacturing locations. The management of international inbound logistics is crucial in maintaining the fluidity of a company's supply chain.

▸ **Poor perfect order metrics**
Lack of proper business integration between order management and procurement, manufacturing, and logistics leads to silos of information that affect customer service levels.

▸ **Poor order fulfillment visibility**
Business users lack near real-time visibility of the steps involved in this end-to-end process. Business users are constantly challenged by an inability to sense upstream and downstream changes, and the relevant data is not easily linked back to the OTC process.

▶ **Lack of business process synergy within business units in a company**
Process synergy is diminished by a lack of coordination and collaborative joint effort from different business units within a company toward a single customer-facing business process.

▶ **Adapting to regulatory legal changes in business environment**
Difficulty in complying with changes in trade regulations that affect OTC business process puts the business at risk.

▶ **Increased expedited freight costs**
Unpredictable events, such as increased demand, can cause companies to panic and start expediting freight.

▶ **Increased charge-backs from customers**
Supply chains today are extended, and although order sourcing no longer occurs at a single point, customer deliveries still must be on time and complete. The lack of a business process to synchronize consolidation of shipments from multiple origins onto a single order and react quickly to customer order changes increase the possibility of late deliveries. These incomplete or delayed orders increase charge-backs from customers.

To improve their OTC business process, companies need to constantly find ways to address these challenges, enabling full visibility and automation of the process and thereby gaining access to the key levers that control the process from initial order taking through the invoice settlement process.

Next, we will explore the industry best practices in OTC processes using Supply Chain Operation Reference Model (SCOR), and learn how available-to-promise connects different business scenarios.

1.2   Supply Chain Operation Reference Model

The Supply Chain Operations Reference (SCOR) model is a process reference model developed by the management consulting firm PRTM and AMR Research. SCOR is endorsed by the Supply Chain Council (*www.supply-chain.org*) as the cross-industry de facto standard diagnostic tool for supply chain management. SCOR enables users to address, improve, and communicate supply chain practices within and between all interested parties in an extended enterprise. The SCOR management tool spans from customer to supplier that describes the business activities associated with all phases of satisfying a customer demand.

SCOR provides standard business process definitions, terminology, and metrics. It enables companies to benchmark themselves against others and influence future application development to improve business processes in five distinct functional areas (as shown in Figure 1.2):

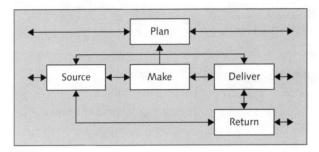

Figure 1.2   Functional Areas of the SCOR Model

▸ **Plan**
Processes that balance aggregate demand and supply to develop a course of action that best meets sourcing, production, and delivery requirements.

▸ **Source**
Processes that procure goods and services to meet planned or actual demand.

▸ **Make**
Processes that transform a product to a finished state to meet planned or actual demand.

▸ **Deliver**
Processes that provide finished goods and services to meet planned or actual demand, typically including order management, transportation management, and distribution management.

▸ **Return**
Processes associated with returning or receiving returned products for any reason. These processes extend into post-delivery customer support.

SCOR provides three levels of process detail, which are illustrated in Figure 1.3. Each level of detail assists a company in defining scope (level 1), configuration or type of supply chain (level 2), and process element details, including performance attributes (level 3). Below level 3, companies break down core and sub-process elements into operational activities and tasks and start implementing specific supply chain management practices. At this stage, companies define practices to achieve a competitive advantage and adapt to changing business conditions.

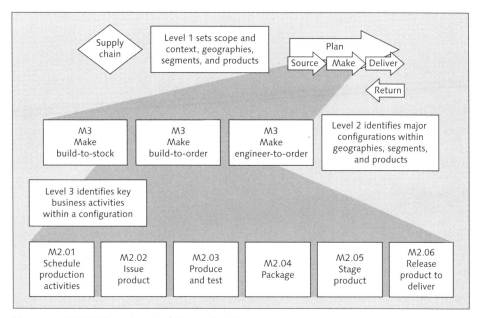

Figure 1.3 SCOR: Three Levels of Process Details

The next four subsections of this section detail the SCOR OTC business models under different business scenarios of make-to-stock (MTS), make-to-order (MTO), engineer-to-order (ETO), and retail products. This will help you to understand the core business activities within the end-to-end OTC business process.

1.2.1 SCOR Order-to-Cash Model for Stocked Product

Businesses primarily use a stocked product or make-to-stock (MTS) inventory mechanism to match their consumer demand with the production forecast. The SCOR OTC definition for this model is the process of delivering product that is maintained in a finished goods state prior to the receipt of a firm customer order (source: Supply Chain Council, SCOR). Figure 1.4 illustrates the business activities within this model, which touches the order management, logistics planning, warehouse, and accounts receivable business teams.

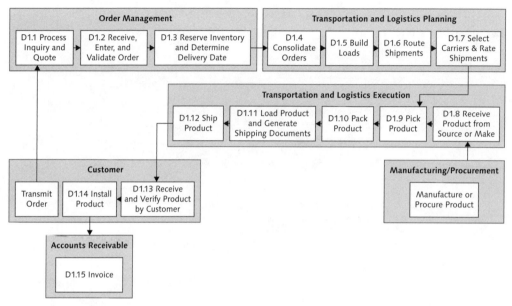

Figure 1.4 Order-to-Cash Model for Stocked Product

During the order commitment to customer, timely and informed decision making is required between the upstream (order receipt) and downstream (order fulfillment) to provide the correct delivery date on orders. This business scenario is typical in the manufacturing and distribution industry. For example, in a computer manufacturing business, the fast-moving computer goods inventory is stored in a warehouse for fulfilling market demands. Because the goods inventory turn is fast, the replenishment cycle is based on the lead time from the manufacturing plant to the warehouse. After the goods are manufactured in-house or procured externally, the goods are sent to the warehouse to fulfill the customer's orders.

The major business objective of order management in MTS environment (as shown in Table 1.1) is to receive the order and provide commitment to the customer when the order will be fulfilled. Note that the business process references correspond to Figure 1.4.

Functional Area	Business Process	Process Description	Best Practices
Order management	D1.1 Process inquiry and quote.	Receive and respond to general customer inquiries and requests for quotes.	▶ Without reserving inventory, convert a quote into an order in a single step. ▶ Use single point of contact for all order inquires (including order entry).
	D1.2 Receive, enter, and validate order.	▶ Receive orders from the customer and enter them into a company's order-processing system. Orders can be received through phone, fax, or electronic media. ▶ When order is input in the system, examine orders to ensure an orderable configuration and provide accurate price. ▶ Check the customer's credit; optionally, accept payment.	▶ Use electronic commerce (customer visibility of stock availability, and use of hand-held terminals for direct order entry, confirmation, credit approval), and check stock and reserve inventory online. ▶ Enable real-time visibility into backlog, order status, shipments, scheduled material receipts, customer credit history, and current inventory positions.
	D1.3 Reserve inventory and determine delivery date.	Identify and reserve inventory (both on hand and scheduled) for specific orders, and commit to and schedule a delivery date.	▶ Provide EDI links between manufacturing and distributor to achieve visibility of complete finished goods inventory and expected shipments. ▶ Automatically reserve inventory and dynamic sourcing of product for single shipment to customer. ▶ Clearly define the inventory allocation exception process, which is jointly owned by manufacturing and sales.

Table 1.1 Order Management Business Activities

The objective of Transportation and Logistics Planning (Table 1.2) is to optimize the effective use of resources with the goal of cost savings during order fulfillment.

Functional Area	Business Process	Process Description	Best Practices
Transportation and logistics planning	D1.4 Consolidate orders.	Analyze orders to determine the groupings that result in least-cost/best-service fulfillment and transportation.	▶ Consolidate orders by customer, source, traffic lane, carrier, and so on. ▶ Combine consolidation needs with other divisions/companies.
	D1.5 Build loads.	Select transportation modes, and build efficient loads.	▶ Consolidate inbound and outbound requirements. ▶ Build load in stop sequence (i.e., first truck destination loaded last, etc.).
	D1.6 Route shipments.	Consolidate loads and route them by mode, lane, and location.	▶ Optimize carrier/route based on continuous movement and consolidation/pooling.
	D1.7 Select carriers and rate shipments.	Select specific carriers by lowest cost per route, and rate and tender shipments.	▶ Select carriers by least cost per shipment and rate using actual rates prior to release to billing.

Table 1.2 Transportation and Logistics Planning Business Activities

The goal of transportation and logistics execution (Table 1.3) is to pick, pack, and ship the ordered products from the warehouse facility.

Functional Area	Business Process	Process Description	Best Practices
Transportation and logistics execution	D1.8 Receive product from source or make.	Perform the following activities: receiving product, verifying, recording product receipt, determining putaway location, and putting away and recording the location that a company performs at its own warehouses. This may include quality inspection.	▸ Use automatic identification. ▸ Download PO and advanced ship notifications (ASNs) for automated receiving and putaway. ▸ Assign dynamic locations, including lot control, zoned putaway, quality assurance, and Activity-Based Costing (ABC) frequency of access.
	D1.9 Pick product.	Perform the following series of activities: retrieving orders to pick, determining inventory availability, building the pick wave, picking the product, recording the pick, and delivering product to shipping in response to an order.	▸ Use dynamic simulation of picking requirements optimized for labor, cost, and time. ▸ Use dynamic location assignment, including lot control, zoned picking, and quality assurance.
	D1.10 Pack product.	Perform the series of activities necessary for packing the product in the warehouse.	▸ Configure the packaging to provide the product in the best condition to customer.
	D1.11 Load products and generate shipping documents. D1.12 Ship product.	Perform the following series of tasks: placing product onto vehicles; generating the documentation necessary to meet internal, customer, carrier, and government needs; and sending the product to the customer.	▸ Use ASNs and UCC128 container labeling. ▸ Electronically generate and download shipping documents.

Table 1.3 Transportation and Logistics Execution Business Activities

Upon receipt of the goods at the customer (shown in Table 1.4), the goods are verified for the correct delivery and installation (if required) for the product to be fully functional.

Functional Area	Business Process	Process Description
Customer	D1.13 Receive and verify product by customer.	Customer receives the shipment and verifies that the order was shipped complete and that the product is of sufficient quality.
	D1.14 Install product.	When necessary, prepare and install the product at the customer site. The product is fully functional upon completion.

Table 1.4 Customer Business Activities

The last process within the OTC process (shown in Table 1.5) is the invoicing to the customer and payment receipt within the agreed payment terms.

Functional Area	Business Process	Process Description	Best Practices
Accounts receivable	D1.5 Invoice.	Send a signal to the financial organization that the order has been shipped and that the billing process should begin and payment be received or be closed out if payment has already been received. Payment is received from the customer within the payment terms of the invoice.	▶ Use Electronic Data Interchange (EDI) and electronic funds transfer (EFT) for payment to speed closing of receivables and to reduce processing costs. ▶ Provide visibility to and quickly escalate delinquent accounts for resolution. ▶ Electronically transfer shipment information to the finance department.

Table 1.5 Accounts Receivable Business Activities

Now that you understand the OTC process decomposition of the MTS business model, let's move on to the second business scenario of make-to-order (MTO) in which the manufacturer only produces the product after a customer has placed a sales order. This scenario is explained next with the industry best practices for its business processes.

1.2.2   SCOR Order-to-Cash Model for Make-to-Order Product

Make-to-order (MTO) is a business production strategy that typically allows consumers to purchase products that are customized to their specifications. The SCOR OTC definition for this model is the process of delivering products that are manufactured, assembled, or configured from standard parts or subassemblies (source: Supply Chain Council, SCOR). Manufacturing, assembly, or configuration begins only after the receipt and validation of a firm customer order. Figure 1.5 illustrates the business activities within this OTC model.

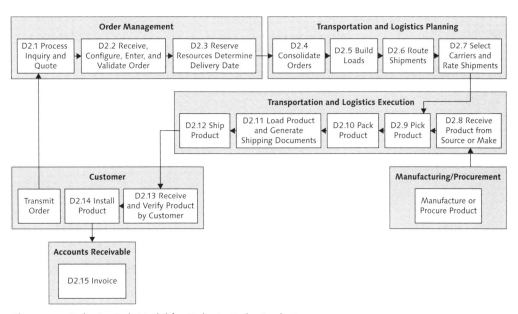

Figure 1.5   Order-to-Cash Model for Make-to-Order Product

You will find the business activities, which are different from the MTS OTC model, in Table 1.6. To better understand the MTO scenario, let's consider a business example where a computer manufacturing company only begins finished goods assembly after a customer order provides the assembly specification. This scenario ensures tight inventory for its key component. The business process of MTO does create additional wait time for the consumer to receive the product but allows for more flexible customization compared to purchasing from retailers' shelves.

Functional Area	Business Process	Process Description	Best Practices
Order management	Process inquiry and quote.	Receive and respond to general customer inquiries and requests for quotes.	▶ Without reserving inventory, convert a quote into an order in a single step. ▶ Without reserving inventory, convert a quote into an order but do not generate a build signal or reserve inventory capacity. ▶ Use a single point of contact for all order inquiries (including order entry).
	Receive, configure, enter, and validate order.	▶ Receive orders from the customer and enter them into a company's order-processing system. Orders can be received through phone, fax, or through electronic media. ▶ Configure the product to the customer's specific needs, based on standard available parts or options. ▶ When order is input in the system, examine orders to ensure an orderable configuration and provide accurate price.	▶ Use electronic commerce (customer visibility of stock availability, use of hand-held terminals for direct order entry, confirmation, and credit approval), and check stock and reserve inventory online. ▶ Organize order entry by customer segment. ▶ Provide differentiated service to customers based on volume of business. ▶ Empower the customer team to fully service customer requests, including formal orders and ad hoc requests.

Table 1.6 Order Management Business Activities for the Make-to-Order Model

Functional Area	Business Process	Process Description	Best Practices
		▸ Check the customer's credit. ▸ Optionally, accept payment.	▸ Provide customers with one point of contact for all products. ▸ Enable real-time visibility into backlog, order status, shipments, scheduled material receipts, customer credit history, and current inventory positions.
	Reserve resources and determine delivery date.	Identify and reserve inventory and/or planned capacity for specific orders, and commit to and schedule a delivery date.	▸ Use dynamic deployment based on constraint-based planning and optimal scheduling. ▸ Automatically reserve inventory and dynamically source products for single shipment to customer.

Table 1.6 Order Management Business Activities for the Make-to-Order Model (Cont.)

1.2.3 SCOR Order-to-Cash Model for Engineer-to-Order

Engineer-to-order (ETO) is a manufacturing philosophy in which finished goods are built to unique customer specifications. For example, in an industrial machinery company, the company has a long waiting lead time for its component assembly. The customer order drives the specification of the industrial machinery requested.

ETO companies (e.g., industrial machinery, construction, engineering) build unique products designed to customer specifications. Each product requires a unique set of item numbers, bill of materials (BOM), and routings. Estimates and quotations are required to win business. Products are complex with long lead times, typically months or even years.

Unlike standard products, the customer is heavily involved throughout the entire design and manufacturing process. Assemblies and raw materials may be stocked but are not assembled into the finished good until a customer order is received and the part is designed. The SCOR OTC definition for this model is the process of delivering a product that is designed, manufactured, and assembled from a BOM that includes one or more custom parts (source: Supply Chain Council, SCOR). Design will begin only after the receipt and validation of a firm customer order. The ATP check is done on critical assembly items that have a long lead-time. Figure 1.6 illustrates the OTC business model within this process.

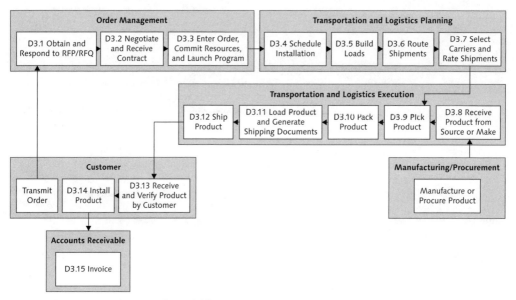

Figure 1.6 Order-to-Cash Model for an Engineer-to-Order Product

Table 1.7 highlights the business activities within ETO business scenarios, which are different from MTS and MTO business scenarios.

Functional Area	Business Process	Process Description	Best Practices
Order management	Obtain and respond to request for proposal (RFP) or request for quote (RFQ).	Receive a request for proposal or request for quote, evaluate the request (estimating the schedule, developing costs estimates, establishing price), and respond to the potential customer.	▸ Use computer aided design & engineering (CAD/CAE) applications to simulate design, cost, and manufacturing processes. ▸ Partner with outside design firms to provide skills and capacity, as needed.
	Negotiate and receive contract.	Negotiate order details with the customer (e.g., price, schedule, product performance) and finalize the contract. Optionally, accept payment.	
	Enter order, commit resources, and launch program.	Enter/finalize the customer order, approve the planned resources (e.g., engineering, manufacturing, etc.), and officially launch the program.	
Logistics planning	Schedule installation.	Evaluate the design and build schedules relative to the customer-requested installation date to determine the installation schedule.	

Table 1.7 Business Activities within the Order-to-Cash Process for Engineer-to-Order

Now that we've covered the OTC process decomposition of the ETO business model, let's consider the third business scenario of retail in which the distribution and merchandising of finished goods are core business processes. The retail business model is different from other business models because it is closer to the direct consumer base.

1.2.4 SCOR Order-to-Cash Model for Retail

The OTC model for retail products refers to the processes used to acquire merchandise and sell finished goods at a retail store (source: Supply Chain Council, SCOR). A retail store is a physical location that sells products (and services) directly to the consumer using a point-of-sale (POS) process (manual or automated) to collect payment. Merchandising at a store level refers to the stocking and restocking of products (based on ATP results in designated storage locations) to generate sales in a retail store. The ATP results help in the replenishment process within the retail industry.

Table 1.8 summarizes the business activities associated with OTC for retail in delivering the products to customers or consumers. The retail business focuses on keeping the right product in the correct quantity to meet the consumer demand. Today, besides the traditional retail shop, consumers are purchasing goods online as well, so the business model must work for different distribution models.

Business Process	Process Description	Best Practices
Generate stocking schedule	Schedule resources to support item-stocking requirements.	▶ Use automated pick list. ▶ Push product on trailer arrival.
Receive product at the store	Perform warehouse activities such as receiving product, verifying, recording product receipt, determining putaway location, putting away, and recording the location at the retail stores. This may include quality inspection.	▶ Schedule labor that matches product flow.
Pick product from backroom	Retrieve restocking orders to pick, determine inventory availability, build a pick wave, pick item and quantity from a designated backroom warehouse location, record the resulting inventory transaction, and deliver the product to point of stock.	▶ Use automated directed picking. ▶ Base staging on in-store zones. ▶ Automatically replenish back stock based on minimum stocking levels. ▶ Define stocking levels and criteria.

Table 1.8 Business Activities within the Order-to-Cash Process for Retail

Business Process	Process Description	Best Practices
Stock shelf	For restocks, identify the item location, stock the shelf according to merchandise plans, and record the appropriate inventory transaction. For promotional items and stock repositioning, prepare shelves and POS, place stock, and perform end-of-sale activities.	▸ Complete stocking in zones. ▸ Perform off-peak stocking. ▸ Perform item/shelf scanning upon putaway. ▸ Provide proof of performance (promotion management). ▸ Scan displays for promo conformance.
Fill shopping cart	Typically: select products, store products, and move through to checkout.	▸ Relieve items from inventory when item is removed from shelf. ▸ Provide multiple locations throughout store. ▸ Measure and compare with same activity of the previous period (e.g., a year ago, a period ago, etc.). ▸ Use loyalty card data.
Checkout	Perform the processes and tasks associated with product checkout, including scanning, method of payment, credit application and approval, service agreement, order confirmation, and/or invoice or receipt.	▸ Enable automatic customer payment. ▸ Use profiles to drive customer recognition upon checkout. ▸ Notify customer of existing/future events or promotions.
Deliver and/or install	Prepare and install the product at the customer site. The product is fully functional upon completion.	▸ Provide product or service training to employees or FAQs online. ▸ Measure, monitor, and adjust service or product installation.

Table 1.8 Business Activities within the Order-to-Cash Process for Retail (Cont.)

Now that we've discussed the different OTC business models for MTS, MTO, ETO, and retail, let's look at the key performance indicators (KPIs). KPIs are used to measure business performance; they indicate how well companies are operating their business processes and what the bottleneck areas are.

1.3   Key Performance Indicators for Order-to-Cash

Key performance indicators are used to measure an organization's performance relationship to its own historical data or to other organizations. OTC KPIs are primarily customer-facing, and they focus on accurate, complete, and timely fulfillment of customer orders. The following illustrate the most commonly used KPIs in OTC:

► **Perfect order fulfillment**
A perfect order meets all of the following five standards:

- ► An order is considered complete if the products ordered are the products provided and the quantities ordered match the quantities provided (% order delivered in full).

- ► An order is considered on time if the location, specified customer entity, and delivery time are met upon receipt (delivery performance to customer by commit date).

- ► An order is considered to be in perfect condition if the products delivered have no manufacturing or packaging errors and are accepted by the customer (perfect condition).

- ► An order is considered to have shipment transaction accuracy if all the shipment documentation related to the order is accurate, complete (with the correct price and quantity) and on time (shipment transaction accuracy).

- ► An order is considered to have Electronic Data Interchange (EDI) transaction accuracy if the customer-facing EDIs mentioned in the list run error free (EDI 859, 855, 810) (EDI transaction accuracy).

► **Order fulfillment cycle time**
Order fulfillment cycle time is the time taken from customer authorization of a sales order to customer receipt of the product. The major segments of time include order entry, manufacturing, distribution, and transportation.

► **Cash-to-cash cycle time**
Cash-to-cash cycle time is a continuous measure defined by adding the number of days of inventory to the number of days of receivables outstanding and then subtracting the number of days of payables outstanding. The result is the number of days of working capital your organization has tied up in managing your supply chain.

▸ **Shipping accuracy**
Shipping accuracy information comes from the customer, who lodges complaints about incorrect order fulfillment. This information becomes the numerator in the shipping accuracy measurement when subtracted from total order lines shipped. Dividing by the total order lines shipped measures the metric percentage.

▸ **Delivery performance to customer request date**
The delivery performance refers to the percentage of orders delivered on the customer's requested date.

▸ **Order fulfillment costs**
The order fulfillment costs include those for processing the order, allocating inventory, ordering from the internal or external supplier, scheduling the shipment, reporting order status, and initiating shipment.

As seen from various KPIs for OTC, the accuracy of promising the delivery date is crucial for business performance and increasing customer satisfaction. Within the order-promising process, product availability check, or available-to-promise (ATP), forms an important functionality. The next section explains where ATP fits in the overall end-to-end OTC business process.

1.4   Available-to-Promise in Order-to-Cash

The available-to-promise (ATP) business function provides a response to customer order inquiries based on resource availability. It generates available quantities of the requested product and delivery due dates. Classifying ATP into either a push-based or pull-based supply chain is primarily done to support a specific business scenario.

A business example can be incorporated from computer manufacturing for both the scenarios. A push-based ATP based on forecasts regarding future demand can be applied to matured and stable computer products. Based on anticipation of demand, ATP quantities and availability dates are computed. For example, the traditional determination of ATP is based on Master Production Scheduling (MPS). Pull-based models, on the other hand, apply to computer products that are customized per customer specifics to dynamically allocate resources in response to actual customer orders. This means that pull-based ATP can balance forecast-driven resource replenishment with order-triggered resource utilization.

ATP functions can be executed in real time, driven by each individual order, or in batch-mode, which means that at a certain time interval, the system checks availability for orders piled up in that period of time. The process is triggered by the need to check resource availability before making a commitment to deliver an order. For example, ATP calculation in SAP ERP depends on the level of stock, planned receipts (e.g., production orders, purchase orders, planned orders), and planned requirements (e.g., sales orders, deliveries, reservations).

For accurate order promising and good delivery performance to the customer, it is imperative to take account of the ordering lead times and supply chain bottlenecks during the ATP checks. The order-promising process for MTS differs from MTO or the ETO business model. In the MTS model, the major bottleneck for demand fulfillment is the available stocks of finished goods. In the MTO or ETO, manufacturing resources such as materials and capacity needs to be considered and allocated before giving delivery commitment to customer orders.

Table 1.9 shows, based on the specific company business model, how granular we need to perform ATP checks to give accurate delivery commitment to customer orders.

Business Model	Order Lead Time	Bottleneck/Restriction	ATP Granularity
MTS	Transportation time	Available stocks of finished goods	Finished goods
MTO	Production time + Transportation time	Available stocks of components and capacity of the production process	Components; production capacity
ETO	Assembly time + Transportation time	Available stocks of components and capacity of the assembly process	Components; assembly capacity

Table 1.9 ATP Granularity Levels Based on Order-to-Cash Business Model

ATP is a critical component in the supply chain operation for delivery confirmation on the customer orders. Companies can provide better order commitment when the supply chain processes of demand allocation, order promising, master scheduling, capacity planning, and delivery performance are all integrated in one business application architecture, as shown in Figure 1.7.

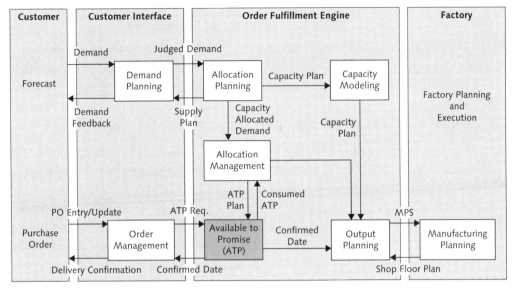

Figure 1.7 Order Fulfillment Engine in the Supply Chain System Architecture

The supply chain architecture can be broadly divided into three end-to-end business process areas based on above overall schematic diagram in Figure 1.7:

▶ **Demand-to-support process**
  The process is built around collaboration between the company and customers. Besides the demand-forecast process, there is the product allocation process of distributing inventory to customers based on a defined quota or percentage. The result of supply-demand netting is feedback to customer account managers to inform customers of their schedule accordingly. The forecast demand feedback helps the customer in long-term product planning and short-term purchase order placement.

▶ **Order-to-confirm process**
  This is a critical process that measures the responsiveness and accuracy of customer purchase orders. The main mechanism of this process lies in the order-fulfillment engine that includes ATP and capacity modeling. Various business rules can be configured within the ATP model and combined with capacity and lead-time constraints during the ATP check. Proper ATP results help to formulate a realistic plan (in the form of MPS) to be given to the manufacturing plant for production. The combination of reliable ATP result and MPS plan provides a confirmed delivery date to customer orders.

▸ **Order-to-ship process**
The process focuses on delivering the goods to the customer on the committed date. The major challenge this process faces is balancing the customer orders with current inventory levels, taking account of frequent changes in the customer order (upstream), and the impact on MPS (downstream).

1.5 Summary

Every customer wants a reliable promise that they will receive their product orders in the promised quantity and promised date. Order promising is quickly becoming important for companies who are building their core competencies to retain customers and increase market share. This chapter defined the OTC process and highlighted business challenges surrounding this process in today's competitive supply chain environment. Using the Supply Chain Reference Model (SCOR) framework, the chapter illustrated different OTC business models, namely in make-to-stock (MTS), make-to-order (MTO), engineer-to-order (ETO), and retail environments. The chapter also identified the critical KPIs to measure the OTC supply chain performance. The chapter concluded by explaining available to promise (ATP) and how it fits in the overall supply chain business process architecture and provides a critical function in the order-fulfillment engine.

The next chapter introduces the SAP SCM technology *global available-to-promise* (global ATP). The chapter explains the SAP SCM product capabilities that support different business scenarios, and how they meet customer ATP-specific requirements.

The global available-to-promise functions are used with order promising and fulfillment checking across the entire supply chain. This chapter explains the SAP SCM global available-to-promise capabilities for use with order fulfillment and checking methods in the order-commitment process.

2 Introduction to Global Available-to-Promise

The need to provide commitment back to customers is called the available-to-promise (ATP) capability, which is offered by a supply chain operations team to a sales team. A strong ATP functionality is important to any manufacturing or distribution company's credibility with its customers. The truth is that often manufacturing and distribution companies make promises to customers without knowing if they can actually meet the demand.

This chapter introduces the global available-to-promise (global ATP) functionality and its core capabilities that you can use to solve the complexities that arise during the order-promising process. Besides explaining the basic differences of performing ATP in SAP ERP versus that of global ATP, the chapter highlights the basic and advanced ATP check methods. We also outline a recommendation for a global ATP implementation approach.

2.1 Global Available-to-Promise Overview

The aim of available-to-promise (ATP) is to determine if an incoming order can be promised for a specified customer request date. ATP enhances the response time for order promising and reliability of order fulfillment. It directly links the available resources, including both material and capacity, to customer orders and enhances the supply chain performance. The process helps by improving on-time delivery performance, allocating sufficient inventory to buffer inventories, and planning system integration.

With SAP global available-to-promise (global ATP), an application within the SAP Supply Chain Management (SAP SCM) suite, global ATP not only provides basic ATP checks, but also enhanced and extended flexible user decision-support features to model different supply chain order-fulfillment business scenarios.

Global ATP, one of the core functionalities within SAP Advance Planning & Optimization (SAP APO), provides an integrated planning and execution system. Figure 2.1 illustrates the five different functionalities within the SAP APO suite. The first three functionalities in the figure (Demand Planning, Supply Network Planning, and Production Planning/Detailed Scheduling) focus on aligning demand and supply planning, whereas the other two (global ATP and Transportation Planning/Vehicle Scheduling) are involved with order execution and fulfillment.

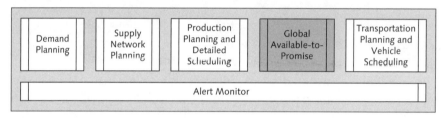

Figure 2.1 SAP Advanced Planning & Optimization Suite

Global ATP leverages an SAP APO technology of SAP liveCache, which is a robust tool that processes a large volume of transactional data and enables data sharing across several applications. The technology offers fast planning, simulation, and what-if analysis. The SAP APO objective is to synchronize supply with demand in the global supply chain by balancing demand and supply with management of demand, distribution, and manufacturing planning. The SAP APO modules shown in the figure are described here:

- **Demand planning (DP):** Improves the forecast quality and planning accuracy.

- **Supply Network Planning (SNP):** Improves visibility across the supply chain and lowers inventory.

- **Production planning and detailed scheduling (PP/DS):** Supports the creation of optimized production plans.

- **Global ATP:** Offers capabilities that support responding to customer order requests.

▶ **Transportation planning and vehicle scheduling (TP/VS):** Optimizes transportation loads and minimizes transportation costs.

▶ **Alert Monitor:** Powerful exception management tool integrated with all SAP APO functionalities.

A company's ability to provide an accurate delivery commitment on a customer order is important for maintaining a strong relationship with its customer. Giving reliable and accurate information concerning when customer orders will be delivered increases customer satisfaction and creates repeat business. SAP SCM provides technology in the form of global ATP to meet the challenge of providing product availability information across a company's local and global supply chain.

2.2   Global ATP Capabilities

Global ATP provides a set of capabilities that support a company's ability to respond to customer order requests on a real-time basis. Global ATP offers the following key features in its portfolio:

▶ **Seamless integration with other SAP ERP applications and components**
Global ATP can be integrated with SAP ERP 6.0 or SAP CRM where the order-processing business process takes place. It can also be integrated with other SAP APO functionalities (DP, SNP, PP/DS) for providing inputs to supply planning. This offers seamless integration of business processes.

▶ **Availability checks on various SAP ERP documents with defined scope**
Global ATP can be used for various documents (sales order, delivery, stock transfers, component check for production order, goods issue check). However, the main use of global ATP lies more in the sales and distribution area than in the manufacturing process. The ATP check can also be performed for replenishment stock transport orders.

▶ **Rule-based ATP for product or location substitution strategies**
In a branched supply chain network, rules-based ATP allows manufacturing and distribution companies to take advantage of shipping goods from alternative sites. It also offers the flexibility of shipping substituted products as required to successfully satisfy customer demands.

▶ **Product allocation to control commitment to key customers**
This feature allows distribution companies to distribute and sell their products

that are in short supply. Allocations for distribution can be defined on various criteria such as distribution channels, geographic region, customer groups, or key customers.

▸ **Backorder processing (BOP) to manage the order portfolio**
As a critical step in order confirmation to customer orders, this feature allows distribution companies to prioritize their order fulfillment to align with business goals. BOP also helps in performing re-ATP checks on customer orders, based on current inventory situation.

▸ **Multilevel ATP to trigger bill of materials (BOM) explosion and perform component checks**
This feature is helpful for business scenarios that require products to be configured for individual customers. It is commonly used in the make-to-order business scenario.

▸ **Capable-to-promise (CTP)**
Enables the business to call SAP APO production planning to produce the remaining quantity from an ATP check or procure the item externally. This is commonly used in the make-to-order scenario where the sales orders is pegged with the production order for order fulfillment.

▸ **Transportation and shipment scheduling**
Involves backward scheduling to determine the requested material availability date based on the customer-requested delivery date and then forward scheduling to determine the committed delivery date based on the committed material availability date. This feature helps business determine reliable loading and delivery dates for the customer orders.

All of these global ATP functionalities offer the following key benefits to customers:

▸ Less time to give reliable availability check results on the current supply chain situation

▸ Prevention of over-commitment to customer orders

▸ Ability to search supply in multiple locations to reduce overall supply chain costs

▸ Effective management of backlog to process all the sales orders

▸ Opportunity to prioritize customers and realign order commitments during constraint supply chain situations

Now that we have seen the capabilities of global ATP, let's see how it compares with the ATP functionality available in SAP ERP.

2.3   ATP in SAP ERP versus Global ATP

The concept of ATP is not new in SAP ERP because the functionality is available in Sales & Distribution (SD) and Production Planning (PP). The ATP check capabilities in SAP ERP deliver great results for basic business scenarios, but they have some functionality limitations in complex business scenarios when compared to global ATP. The main functionality comparisons between the standard ATP in SAP ERP and global ATP are highlighted in Table 2.1.

Business Process Requirement	ATP in SAP ERP	Global ATP
Availability check across supply chain network locations.	The ATP check is done on a single plant/product combination.	With rules-based ATP, global ATP offers the functionality to perform availability checks across multiple locations to minimize supply chain cost and maintain customer-service levels. Global ATP can also create stock transfer orders between the two locations during the substitution process.
Product substitution in case of product shortage situations.	Only manual product substitution is possible.	With rules-based ATP, the requirement can be modeled for a defined list of product substitutions during the online availability checks.
During production capacity constraint or product launch, the business needs to allocate supply based on various criteria.	The feature is available in SAP ERP with the use of a standard or self-defined info structure in the flexible planning module.	With product allocation, different characteristics combinations can be defined for the allocation of constraint supply.

Table 2.1   ATP Functionality Comparison between SAP ERP and Global ATP

Business Process Requirement	ATP in SAP ERP	Global ATP
Reallocation of supply and sales orders are required to better align with current inventory situations.	SAP ERP offers BOP on fixed criteria.	Global ATP offers more flexibility when filtering, sorting, and scheduling the sales document using the BOP feature.
Integrate production and ATP check functionality.	Not available.	Available in capable-to-promise (CTP) functionality.
Check the availability of lower-level components during the ATP check.	Not available.	Available in multilevel ATP functionality.
Consideration of reverse logistics in the availability check.	Not available.	Global ATP supports reverse logistics by considering customer returns as planned receipts, increasing the ATP quantity.
Continuous flow output consideration in process industries where the products are available in different stages with long-running manufacturing process orders.	Not available.	Global ATP offers the feature to consider material availability by taking account of the continuous flow of production output with proportional distribution of ATP quantity in different time buckets.
Product availability simulation.	SAP ERP offers a simple simulation feature.	Global ATP simulation extends to both product availability checks based on the method designed and also on the back-order processing.

Table 2.1 ATP Functionality Comparison between SAP ERP and Global ATP (Cont.)

Business Process Requirement	ATP in SAP ERP	Global ATP
Integration with transportation during the product availability check.	SAP ERP offers delivery and transportation scheduling feature.	Global ATP can be integrated with the transportation planning and vehicle scheduling (TP/VS) module to consider the transportation constraints so that the system checks on product availability and delivery route simultaneously.
Scope of check (receipts, requirements, stocks) elements during the ATP check.	Available for defined material requirements planning (MRP) elements.	More granular than SAP ERP and allows the business to choose more firm and reliable ATP categories.

Table 2.1 ATP Functionality Comparison between SAP ERP and Global ATP (Cont.)

SAP ERP does offer basic business requirements in performing ATP checks, but lacks the ability to model complex business variants and rules. If the company has a simple distribution network, the ATP functionality should suffice. The next section explains the basic method in global ATP, which offers more flexibility than standard ATP features in SAP ERP.

2.4   Global ATP Basic Methods

The basic methods for ATP generate good results if the ATP quantity is available on the requested date. If the ATP quantity is not available, global ATP will propose a new delayed delivery date. As shown in Figure 2.2, after the sales orders are created, the ATP check is performed for product availability, which proposes partial or full delivery proposals based on the receipt element's availability. If the quantity cannot be confirmed fully in the same date, separate partial confirmations will be proposed on different dates. The communication between SAP ERP and global ATP is managed by the Core Interface (CIF) (you can find a detailed explanation of this in Chapter 3).

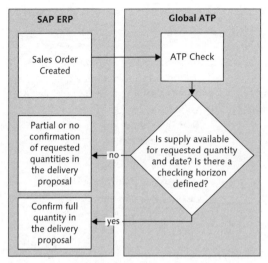

Figure 2.2 Flow Between Order Processing in SAP ERP and ATP Check in Global ATP

The ATP check performed on customer orders can be using basic and/or advanced ATP methods. We will look at the basic ATP method in this section. The following three different basic ATP methods are explained in the following sections:

▶ Product availability check

▶ Product allocation

▶ Forecast

2.4.1 Product Availability Check

This availability check is one of the time-phased simplest checks in global ATP and partially behaves in a similar manner to the SAP ERP availability check. This method can be used in any industry using the make-to-order (MTO) scenario. The ATP result is a simple calculation of the following:

Stock + Total receipts – Confirmed requirements elements

The scope of check can be defined for the business event and ATP group combination (explained later in Chapter 3) by following the menu path IMG • ADVANCED PLANNING AND OPTIMIZATION • GLOBAL AVAILABLE-TO-PROMISE • GENERAL SETTINGS • PRODUCT AVAILABILITY CHECK • MAINTAIN CHECK CONTROL, or by using Transaction /SAPAPO/AC03 (see Figure 2.3). The scope of check not only defines which elements or categories are considered in the availability check, but also a company's degree of risk conservativeness toward the customer order confirmation. The scope of check defines the requirements, receipts, and stock categories to be used in ATP quantity determination.

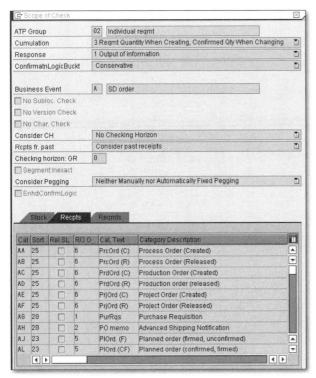

Figure 2.3 Scope of Check

The ATP result in SAP ERP can be adapted to customers' different business requirements with the help of enhancement (user exits), which are called before or after the ATP functionality to better reflect the results. Similarly, global ATP uses SAP liveCache and time series to give better results. SAP APO time series enables you to combine characteristics during the availability check. A good example is in the steel or pharmaceutical industries, where the products are configured with characteristics-based planning. For these products, the product properties are stored at the batch level where the ATP check can be performed.

Global ATP also supports transportation and shipment scheduling to determine material availability date (backward and forward, see Figure 2.4) based on which ATP check is performed for the customer orders. This functionality allows for proper determination of the requested material availability date (MAD) using transportation and loading lead times. The ATP check is then performed on this MAD to commit a confirmed delivery date to customer orders.

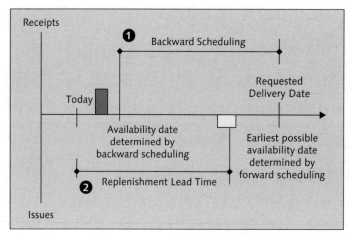

Figure 2.4 Date Scheduling Logic in Global ATP

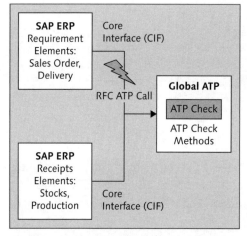

Figure 2.5 Technical Architecture for Global Consolidation of SAP ERP and Global ATP Systems

On the technical architecture capability side, it's possible to have one global ATP communicating with consolidation of multiple SAP ERP environments. An example of technical architecture is shown in Figure 2.5, where two SAP ERP systems are connected with a single instance of global ATP. While the requirement and receipts elements reside in a different SAP ERP system, these elements can be consolidated in the global ATP environment for performing the availability check. This form of technical architecture is commonly adapted for global consolidation and minimizes the cost implication on hardware and maintenance.

2.4.2   Product Allocation

Product allocation is the second basic method, which is widely used by firms to make decisions on how to distribute and sell products that are in supply shortage. Distribution decisions are made based on distribution channels, geographic regions, customer groups, or strategic customers. This method is widely used in high-tech, steel manufacturing, chemical, automotive, oil and gas, and pharmaceutical sectors. The strategy has gained business acceptance in environments where high-volume items, high-value items, or products with long manufacturing lead times need to be distributed on a consistent basis.

When a product is in short supply, distribution companies want to make sure that each customer receives a proportional allocation of inventory and that the ATP check isn't reserving the entire inventory for one customer with a large order. This situation is usually encountered during material or capacity constraint, seasonal sales, good promotions, price changes, or new product launches where the supply chain may encounter supply shortages. Product allocation planning addresses these business situations by restricting the first in, first out (FIFO) method of order confirmation in SD. Allocation planning addresses the problem by restricting the allocation to specific customers or other criteria such as customer groups or regions. The restriction criteria are flexible to your company's needs.

Global ATP integrates with SAP DP to deliver the allocation capabilities based on characteristics combinations replicating marketing hierarchies for allocating the supply. The availability check with product allocations primarily follows two steps:

1. Perform the availability check.
2. Perform the product allocation check.

The lesser of the ATP and available allocation will be confirmed in the sales order item. Table 2.2 provides an example of how the confirmed quantity is placed for this business scenario.

Order Quantity	ATP Quantity	Allocation Quantity	Confirmed Quantity	Comments
100	150	120	100	Totally confirmed
100	60	120	60	Partially confirmed (due to ATP quantity)
100	150	80	80	Partially confirmed (due to allocation quantity)
100	80	60	60	Partially confirmed (due to ATP + allocation quantity)
100	60	80	60	Partially confirmed (due to ATP + allocation quantity)

Table 2.2 Combination of Product Availability with Product Allocation

The allocation quantity for the preceding table is derived from the allocation object (see Figure 2.6) in global ATP, which defines the quota allocation per the hierarchy. The characteristic combinations are populated to define the hierarchy allocations and serve as master data for the quota allocation maintenance. The sales order is checked against the characteristic combination criteria for an existing product allocation quantity. The quota allocation is entered in the SAP APO DP book (Transaction /SAPAPOAPO/SDP94) based on the characteristics combination master data.

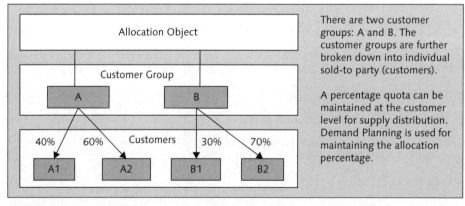

Figure 2.6 Allocation Object in the Global ATP Product Allocation Functionality

Another important feature is the allocation sequence that allows the system to check for alternate allocation procedures when the first one cannot fully confirm the quantity. This feature is part of the product allocation in the global ATP.

2.4.3   Forecast

The third check method is important for the MTO industries (e.g., a computer manufacturer) where no physical inventory is available to confirm the customers' orders. For a typical industry such as a PC manufacturing company, which is market-pull driven, the primary production commences after the sales order is received from the customer. During the initial ATP check, the quantity confirmation is performed against the forecast or planned independent requirements. Similar to product allocation, this check method can be integrated with SAP DP for getting the consensus forecast, or SAP Demand Management for getting the planned independent requirements.

2.5   Global ATP Advanced Methods

The global ATP basic methods form the baseline for the product availability check. Building on these basic methods, we can introduce additional advanced ATP checks to model supply chain constraints. For example, you can perform ATP checks across multiple locations for fulfilling customer orders. The advanced availability check methods include the following:

▶ **Combination of basic methods**
  To distribute its products proportionally in the market, the company wants to perform product allocation first, and then an availability check on its products. The check sequence of either method is done via the check instruction configuration. The product allocation first determines the resulting confirmed quantity, which is checked against the relevant ATP quantity from the product availability check, or vice versa.

▶ **Rules-based ATP check**
  Establish rules to determine what, where, and when to deliver products using location substitutions, product substitution, production process model (PPM) substitution, and characteristics substitution.

▶ **Production capable-to-promise (CTP)**
  Integrates manufacturing and ATP check functionality. During sales order

processing, CTP triggers product planning at the manufacturing plant and determines the delivery date based on the schedule of production capacity.

▶ **Production multilevel ATP**
Checks the availability of components and proposes substitutions. It is based on the BOM explosion at the end item level to check ATP for each component.

▶ **Availability check for kits**
Kits are BOMs that are always shipped in complete and assembled form (e.g., palletized products). This process corresponds to the production process but without any production resource to combine the components as a complete kit.

▶ **Third-party order processing**
This method is helpful when the goods are shipped directly from the supplier to the customer. The company takes the sales order and ships the products directly from the external partner or supplier to the customer warehouse. Using the source determination and product allocation method, this check enables the company to ensure the requirements can be confirmed without having to take into account backorders or cancellations.

In the following subsections, we will discuss three of the commonly used advanced check methods in depth: rules-based ATP, CTP, and multilevel ATP checks.

2.5.1 Rules-Based ATP Check

The rules-based ATP check method was primarily designed for the consumer goods industry and distributors, which have a complex distribution supply chain. The business scenario supported by this feature allows the goods to be shipped to a customer from different sources or with alternative product options. The rule maintenance master data drives the predetermined sequence for alternative locations and alternative products. The substitution rules are the iterative availability check process based on business rules. The check can be processed in several business dimensions: product, location, batch characteristics, or production process model for manufacturing.

A typical example for location substitution (see Figure 2.7) is the replenishment of inventory for satellite warehouses from a regional hub warehouse based on market demand. The business process steps include a sales order coming into distribution center A, whereby the global ATP check confirms the order based on available stock at warehouse A and balance ATP replenishment from warehouse B. Global

ATP also creates a stock transport order for shipping the products between the two locations. You can also use location substitution to always replenish a customer from a specific warehouse.

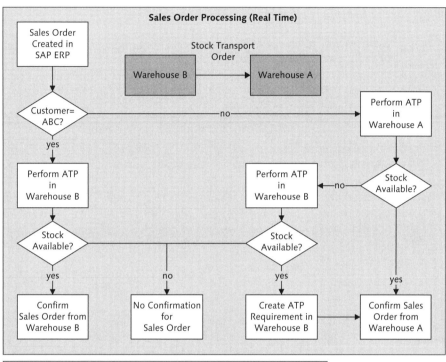

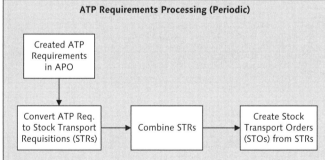

Figure 2.7 Location Substitution Scenario Modeled in Global ATP Rules-Based ATP

The basis of the rules-based ATP check is formed by multiple rules that are executed sequentially. The condition technique, which is commonly used in SD in pricing determination, can be used to define business rules. A typical use of the condition technique in a business scenario is to define different order fulfillment locations for different customers. A rule maintenance is a master data created in global ATP that primarily consists of below four elements:

▶ **Product Substitution List/procedure:** Defines the sequential list of substitution products and the validity period.

▶ **Location Substitution List/procedure:** Defines the sequential list of substitution locations and the validity period.

▶ **Product/Location rule control parameter:** Defines whether to use location or product or a combination of both procedures.

▶ **Calculation profile:** User setting to define how the system should confirm the order when the desired delivery date is not met. Defines allowed delay or early confirmation days.

Figure 2.8 shows a Rule Maintenance screen (accessed via Transaction /SAPAPO/ RBA04), where we define the business rule for the sequence of the product locations where the ATP check needs to be performed. The figure shows that the same product is checked across multiple locations first and then substituted by a different product if the ATP check is still not successful.

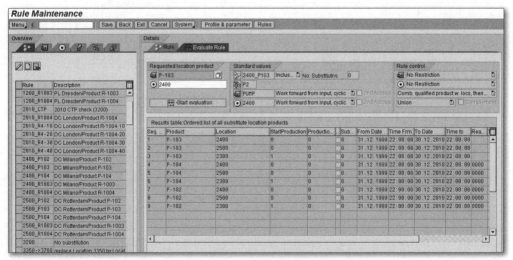

Figure 2.8 Rule Maintenance for Location and Product Substitution

2.5.2 Multi-Item Single Delivery

Multi-Item Single Delivery (MISL), also known as complete delivery, provides the functionality of shipping all the items in sales orders from a single location. This is useful when a company wants to consolidate its products for to reduce costs (e.g., transportation costs). During the sales order processing, global ATP uses the MISL functionality (built via rules-based ATP) to determine whether all the items requested in the sales orders are available in a single location. If the single location is not found, the items remain partially confirmed or unconfirmed. During the global ATP MISL process as seen in Figure 2.9 (accessed via Transaction /SAPAPO/AC04), the multiple items are not confirmed in the primary location, but are confirmed in a secondary location. The system automatically updates the location in the sales order by creating an additional item that shows where the order is confirmed.

Figure 2.9 Multi-Item Single Delivery Using Rules-Based ATP

2.5.3 Production Capable-to-Promise

Working in conjunction with the SAP APO PP/DS functionality, this check method integrates the ATP check and production functionality. This global ATP solution is ideal for industries with configured products (steel, paper) or companies with constrained production due to bottlenecks (chemical).

During the sales order processing, if the existing supply cannot cover the demand, the PP/DS functionality is called in real time as a part of the ATP check to determine the manufacturing plant capacity (see Figure 2.10). It then creates a simulation production plan to find the best possible date for delivering the goods while considering the capacity of the manufacturing resources. If the plan is accepted, global ATP generates supply elements that can stock the transport order for nonmanufacturing sites or the production plan for manufacturing sites.

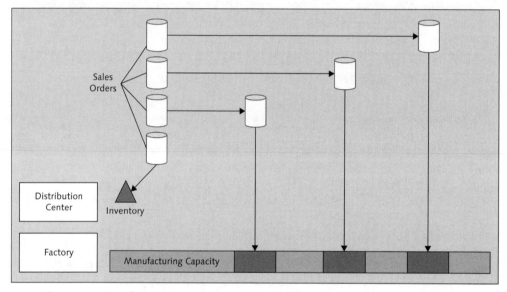

Figure 2.10 Manufacturing Capacity-Based Order Fulfillment

2.5.4 Production Multilevel ATP Check

The multilevel ATP check method is designed for discrete industries that engage in multilevel assembly for configured products (e.g., PCs). This method is useful in industries where the assembly items are stocked and only when a customer sales order is received, the assembly items are assembled for the final product. The method checks the availability of the components (via BOM explosion of the primary product) before committing to the delivery date of the order. The differences between CTP and multilevel ATP are shown in Table 2.3.

Business Process Requirement	Multilevel ATP	CTP
Availability check on component level	Checks on component product availability as defined in the scope of check; supports rules-based ATP	Uses the PP/DS pegging functionality and primarily checks the end item product availability
Characteristics-dependent planning	Does not support	Supports characteristics planning
Scheduling of finished goods	Cumulated in daily bucket	Plans until lowest level of time (seconds)
Result	ATP tree structure	PP/DS planned orders
Display of check results	ATP result overview	Provides planning log
Performance	Better	Needs close monitoring
Capacity restrictions	Daily production rate	Finite scheduling on resource
Scheduling of components	Lead-time scheduling	Detailed scheduling as the production order
Lot size	Lot-for-lot	Fixed/min/max
Block planning	Does not support	Supports

Table 2.3 Differences between Multilevel ATP and CTP

One major difference between CTP and Multilevel ATP is the use of the ATP tree. The ATP tree structure is a new object created during multilevel ATP, which prevents the online creation of the receipt generated by global ATP for system-performance reasons. The conversion to receipt elements for the confirmed orders can be done later as a background job.

An example of multilevel ATP is shown in Figure 2.11 and Figure 2.12, where the order confirmation is done in two dates. The first date is based on the stock availability, while the balance quantity is based on the planned orders availability date, taking into account component lead time and resource capacity.

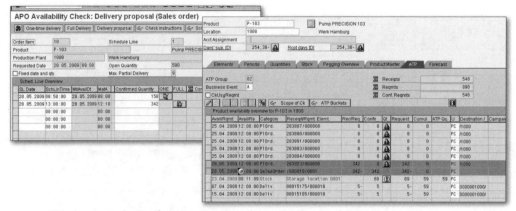

Figure 2.11 Order Confirmation Based on the Production Availability Date

Figure 2.12 shows how the BOM is exploded for the parent item, and the component's availability is checked before the final confirmation of the order.

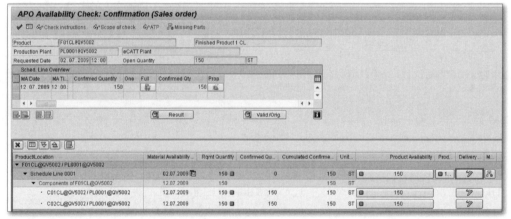

Figure 2.12 Bill of Materials Explosion in a Multilevel ATP Check

2.6 Global ATP Extended Functions

Besides the basic and advanced methods, there are two extended features that are invariably implemented with any global ATP check methods and across all industries. The first method is backorder processing (BOP), which is used primarily for resolving backorder conflicts and re-ATP of the sales orders to reconfirm the delivery dates based on the latest inventory after the MRP run. The second method is the scheduling function, which is used for determining the correct material availability date (MAD) for shipping the goods.

2.6.1   Backorder Processing

BOP is a critical step in sales order confirmations. It aligns the confirmation process with business goals by prioritizing the sales orders to determine which orders to ship first. BOP is also critical when the supply is constrained and you must decide which sales orders to prioritize for shipping. As a reallocation process, BOP aligns the supply plan and the open sales orders.

The BOP process consists of defining the order processing scope through master data, and executing the BOP in the following four steps:

1. Identify the business criteria important for prioritization. For example, this could be the document creation date or material availability date.

2. Filter the scope of BOP by selecting the orders that will be included in the processing.

3. The user defines the sort profile for defining the sequence to allocate the available stocks to the customer orders.

4. Execute the BOP either interactively (manually reconfirming the sales documents) or as a background job. The *BOP monitor* provides the tool to analyze the changes and result of BOP.

In a business scenario, BOP is essential in the following situations:

▶ Unexpected goods receipts (creates more ATP quantity as a result). This will help a business confirm customer orders that were not confirmed when orders were first received.

▶ Unexpected goods issues (creates less [negative] ATP quantity as a result). This helps businesses prioritize orders during supply shortage.

▶ High-priority order (to fulfill the demand, the confirmation of some low-priority orders must be cancelled). This will help businesses increase the profit margin by serving important customer sales orders.

The functionality of BOP is enhanced with the event-driven quantity assignment (EDQA) feature (see Figure 2.13) where BOP occurs automatically if sales orders/ stock inventory is changed. As you can see, when a goods receipt is performed in the warehouse, global ATP automatically confirms the orders from the order due list.

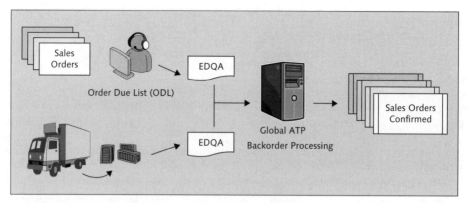

Figure 2.13 Event-Driven Quantity Assignment in Backorder Processing

2.6.2 Time and Scheduling Functions

Transportation and shipment scheduling is an integral part of global ATP and serves as a scheduling tool for proposing a material availability date, loading date, and delivery date during the sales order processing. The scheduling (see Figure 2.14) works backward from the requested date to arrive at the MAD. MAD is the date for checking product availability. Master data will be required in SAP APO in the form of lead times between plants/vendors and transportation zones (ship-to party, state).

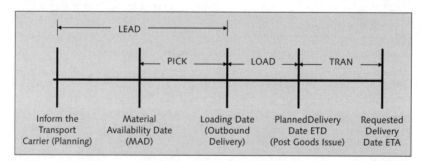

Figure 2.14 Transportation and Shipment Scheduling Lead Time in Global ATP

The feature helps customers with the following functions:

- Schedule the correct ETA for supply availability
- Properly calculate the lead time between supplier and customer points
- Increase the customer-service level and sales based on supply availability at the committed date

Global ATP also provides configurable process scheduling (CPS) as an enhanced scheduling feature to map the logistics function of the company. CPS uses business processes that have activities, and these activities have a start date and end date. CPS should be used in scenarios where transportation and shipment scheduling cannot be achieved using the condition technique. The only difference is that CPS is a lot more flexible where instead of fixed activities for shipment scheduling (e.g., pick, tran), you can add more activities (hold). In addition to duration determination, CPS can also do calendar determination, time zone determination, and location determination using the condition technique.

2.6.3   Global ATP Exception Management Alerts

The exception management process identifies issues (*exceptions*) that will lead to changes/adjustments in the operational demand and supply plans and improvements in the order-fulfillment process in general. Global ATP provides the SAP APO Alert Monitor alert management tool (shown in Figure 2.15), which can be used to model ATP alerts. Custom alerts can also be defined per business requirements (e.g., product allocation alerts can be triggered via custom macros defined in SAP APO DP).

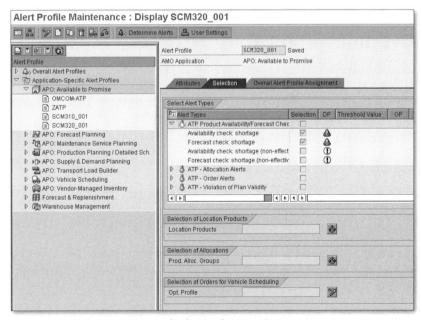

Figure 2.15   Global ATP Alert Profile for Configuring Alerts

2.6.4 Global ATP Implementation Approach

A clear implementation methodology is recommended for successful deployment of the global ATP functionality. The methodology can be divided into five areas, leading toward the production of global ATP functionality.

1. **Implementation scenarios**
   The implementation of global ATP can be combined either with other modules of SAP APO or implemented as a standalone with SAP ERP integration. The viable combinations are listed here:

   ▶ *DP + global ATP*: Combining the forecasting process and allocation process with ATP.

   ▶ *DP + SNP + global ATP*: Integrating demand and supply planning with order fulfillment.

   ▶ *PP/DS + global ATP*: Integrating manufacturing directly with the order-fulfillment process.

   ▶ *Global ATP*: Leveraging on advanced check methods capabilities for complex business scenarios.

2. **Big-bang versus phased approach**
   The majority of global ATP implementations primarily start with a proof of concept (POC) and develop into a project following business acceptance. The project implementation times are usually short—spanning three to five months—and the phased approach is best suited to minimize any business risk and better understand the global ATP behavior in the productive environment. To mitigate the business impact of the ATP check running in two environments—legacy and global ATP—it is recommended to roll out the global ATP solution by customer and distribution center. This also requires activating the CIF model by distribution centers.

3. **Global ATP check methods selection**
   It is imperative to map global ATP functionalities according to business-specific needs to solve order-fulfillment issues. The advantage of global ATP is that you do not need a single global approach, and each global ATP functionality can be implemented separately to solve the business problem. The basic and advanced methods can also be combined to deliver two-step ATP checks on customer orders.

4. **Business value versus implementation effort**

A matrix (see Figure 2.16) that shows the global ATP functionality ease of implementation versus business value can accelerate the change management and
business readiness process.

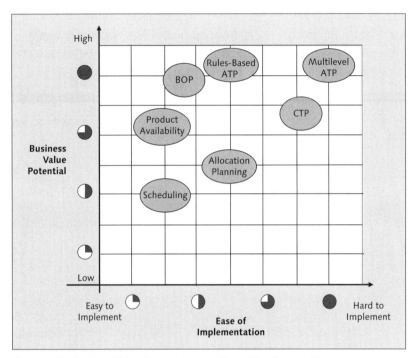

Figure 2.16 Business Value Potential versus Ease of Implementation

5. **Performance testing**

Global ATP can be technically challenging due to the volume of transaction
processing. It is always advisable to perform scalability/stress testing before
going to production up to a scale of 120% sales-order volume. The stress testing
should focus on the Remote Function Call (RFC) communication between SAP
ERP and global ATP to fine-tune SAP Basis settings with parallel processing, and
also look at options for a disaster recovery plan if the global ATP system is
down.

2.7 Summary

This chapter provided an overview of the global ATP capabilities and how different check methods can solve complex business scenarios related to order promising. A comparison between the traditional ATP in SAP ERP and global ATP shows the advantages a company can harvest by implementing the advanced feature to model its supply chain constraints during the ATP check. Global ATP offers seamless integration with other SAP ERP modules to support the order-to-cash (OTC) end-to-end business process. We also discussed the key global ATP functionalities.

The next chapter introduces the global ATP technical architecture, the integration between the execution system (SAP ERP) and the ATP system (global ATP) using the Core Interface, and the basic configurations to make it work.

This chapter explains the technical architecture side of global ATP, which involves execution and planning system integration. You will learn the basic configuration for setting up the Core Interface required to make the availability check work seamlessly across multiple systems.

3   How SAP APO Global ATP Technology Works

Global available-to-promise (global ATP) uses the advantage of SAP APO technology to process availability checks during order processing. This technology enables a real-time optimized decision-support tool via online searches to determine if the customer-requested product, quantity, and date/time can be satisfied on time. The technology runs in SAP APO time-series objects, which are able to handle large volumes of customer orders and shares information across several SAP ERP applications.

This chapter focuses on the technical side of global ATP. The chapter explains the technology and technical landscape between SAP ERP and global ATP. We will also cover the Core Interface (CIF) in depth, which is used for communicating master data and transactional data between SAP ERP and global ATP.

3.1   Global ATP Time Series

SAP liveCache has a large memory and behaves like both an object-oriented and relational database. SAP liveCache can store time-series data in structures, and it allows concurrent data access by several applications. A time series represents requirement and receipts elements for product and location in aggregation form. Each element is aggregated (see Figure 3.1) per time bucket and category. The diagram shows the ATP time series for both requirements and receipt elements, which are bucketed from the actual dates.

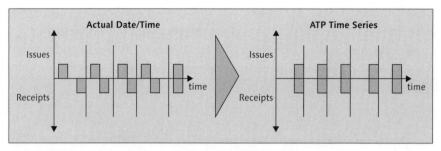

Figure 3.1 Aggregation of Receipts and Requirements in a Time Series

A time series is managed separately for each planning object, which includes a combination of product, location, account assignment, and planning segment. Each time series is identified by a unique key consisting of a category, sub-location, version, and characteristics combination for characteristics product availability. The sub-location and version correspond to the storage location and the physical batch (stock) in SAP ERP. The time series can be modified per customer requirements to define the suitable ATP time buckets. The time series has the following features (see Figure 3.2):

▶ Receipts and issue buckets are defined separately (e.g., receipts to be available at the beginning or end of the bucket).

▶ A daytime availability check is performed with several buckets defined for a day.

▶ The ATP GROUP configuration controls the logic used to evaluate the ATP time series in the product availability check. The following options are available for evaluation:

  ▶ **Conservative logic:** ATP valuates receipt data at the end of the receipt bucket as stored in the time series. Results confirmed by ATP do not trigger any production planning and detailed scheduling (PP/DS) alerts. This is a widely used method during the ATP check.

  ▶ **Totally conservative logic:** ATP valuates data according to the conservative logic but cannot confirm between the start of the issue bucket and the end of the receipt bucket. All issues are confirmed at the end of the receipt bucket at the earliest.

  ▶ **Progressive logic:** ATP valuates the receipt data at the start of the bucket, which is one day earlier than specified in the time series. Pegging relationships are confirmed by ATP but can trigger PP/DS alerts.

▶ ATP time bucket limits can be managed in UTC or the local time zone for respective locations.

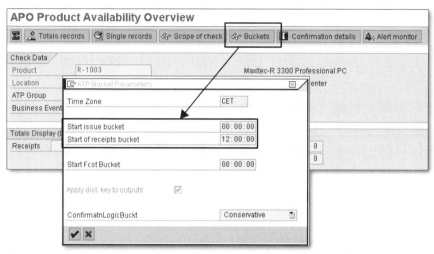

Figure 3.2 ATP Time Series Buckets Definitions during the Availability Check

Now that we've covered the ATP time-series concept, let's look at the technical landscape for global ATP. The landscape integrates different application systems using different interface technology.

3.2 Global ATP Technical Landscape

Application integration plays a major role in successful online processing of customer orders. These interfaces, which come in the form of IDocs or remote function call (RFC) queues, require constant monitoring and troubleshooting of errors (if any). Figure 3.3 shows an overview of the technical landscape for order fulfillment in relation to global ATP.

A particular company might have deployed multiple SAP and non-SAP application systems to support its business functions. The following list describes how different application landscapes can be combined with global ATP:

▶ **Integration with SAP ERP via CIF for both master and transactional data**
The CIF provides the technology platform to synchronize the data between SAP ERP and global ATP to near real time.

▶ **Integration with non-SAP ERP via BAPI (Business Application Programming Interface) for transactional data**
A BAPI provides a communication interface for both master and transactional data. SAP provides a standard BAPI for creation, update, and deletion of different business objects from non-SAP environments.

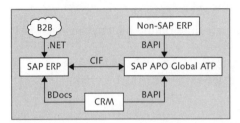

Figure 3.3 Technical Landscape with SAP APO Global ATP

▶ **Integration with SAP CRM via BAPI and BDoc (business document)**
A business document (BDoc) is a set of transaction statements that represents a logical object. It is an envelope of all the business data necessary to run a business process (e.g., a sales document).

▶ **Integration with the business-to-business (B2B) portal via IDoc**
Many companies are leveraging on .NET technology to build customer portals. The SAP .NET Connector is a development environment that enables communication between the Microsoft .NET platform and SAP ERP systems. This connector supports RFCs and Web services, and it allows customers to write different applications such as Web forms, Windows forms, or console applications in the Microsoft Visual Studio .NET.

Of all these interfaces, the CIF serves as the important communication channel between SAP ERP and global ATP. In the next section, we will look at the CIF transactions you need to use to set up the interface between SAP ERP and global ATP.

3.3 Core Interface (CIF)

SAP APO Core Interface (CIF) is the communication layer to be applied to SAP ERP to enable an exchange of data between SAP APO and SAP ERP. CIF forms a part of the SAP ERP plug-in, ensuring compatibility between different SAP ERP components installed in a single system. Using RFC technology, CIF provides the following:

▸ Integration models to specify which master and transaction data need to be exchanged between SAP ERP and SAP APO systems.

▸ Techniques for initial, incremental, or real-time data transfers between SAP ERP and SAP APO systems.

▸ Error-handling alerts and monitoring to ensure data transfer consistency between execution (SAP ERP) and planning systems (SAP APO).

▸ Synchronous communication mode for real-time online updates between SAP ERP and SAP APO (e.g., global ATP).

▸ Asynchronous communication mode for processing data in the background between SAP ERP and SAP APO (e.g., SNP).

Let's now look at the configuration steps in SAP ERP and global ATP to set up the core interface communication between the two systems.

3.3.1 Core Interface Configuration Steps

The setup and running of distributed SAP ERP applications is based on Application Link Enabling (ALE) technology. ALE includes the exchange of messages with consistent data retention in linked SAP ERP systems, controlled by the business. Because data is distributed between systems, you need to identify each system within a network. The *logical system* is used for this purpose, and it serves as the identity for an application running on that specific server. Various applications that run on a common database are grouped together in a logical system. The logical system is set up by the SAP Basis team.

A business scenario may exist whereby the company has global and regional ERP systems connecting with one global ATP system. In this business scenario, we have to integrate master and transactional data from different logical systems that reference the same object in SAP APO. For this purpose, a *business system group* (BSG) helps integrate different physical systems into a super-ordinate logical unit. BSG is commonly used in distributed system landscapes, and set up is done by the SAP Basis team. A mapping structure for maintaining and activating *user enhancements* may also be required. Table 3.1 lists important configuration steps in SAP ERP for setting up CIF communication between SAP ERP and SAP APO.

Steps	Transaction	Remarks
Define logical systems for SAP ERP and SAP APO.	SALE or BD54	Different applications in common database.
Assign SAP ERP client to logical SAP ERP.	SCC4	Before two or more systems can communicate with each other, the technical coupling between them must be set up. The target address for the data transfer is determined during the setup of an RFC destination in SAP ERP. The name of the corresponding RFC destination must be identical to the name of the logical target system (SAP APO). One RFC destination is required for each target client (e.g., 001).
Define SAP APO release.	NDV2	The table controls the downward compatibility of the SAP APO CIF.
Set target system and queue type.	CFC1	To enable the successful setup of communication between SAP ERP and SAP APO, the appropriate target system for this data channel must be installed in the definition of the RFC destination.
Define RFC connection to SAP APO.	SM59	Connection is defined to source system via a communication user (CPIC) with proper authorization.
Register inbound queues.	SMQR	Register for CF* queues communication flow.
Register outbound queues.	SMQS	Register for CF* queues communication flow.
Define transfer parameters.	CFC2	Detailed error messages are stored in the destination system's application log.
Filter and select block size.	CFC3	Parameters: Block-Sizes for initial transfer (setting).

Table 3.1 Configuration Steps in SAP ERP for the Core Interface

Similar configuration activities are required in the SAP APO system for the CIF communication between SAP ERP and SAP APO. Table 3.2 lists the important configuration steps in SAP APO for setting up CIF communication between SAP ERP and SAP APO.

Steps	Transaction	Remarks
Define the logical system for SAP ERP and SAP APO.	SALE or BD54	
Assign the SAP APO client to the logical SAP APO system.	SCC4	
Define the BSG.	/SAPSAP APO/C1	We recommend that you assign the SAP APO system to the same BSG as the logical system or SAP ERP instances that contain the master data server.
Assign the logical system for SAP APO and SAP ERP to BSGs.	/SAPAPO/ C2	To provide for correct communication on the SAP APO side as well, every source system (SAP ERP) must be assigned to a BSG (a BSG can consist of one or more source systems). This means that the current BSG must be linked to at least one SAP ERP source system.
Define the RFC connection to SAP ERP.	SM59	The connection is defined to the source system via communication user (CPIC) with proper authorization.
Register inbound queues.	SMQR	Register for CF* queues communication flow.
Register outbound queues.	SMQS	Register for CF* queues communication flow.
Define transfer parameters.	/SAPAPO/ C4	Display/set user parameters (debugging, logging).
Define runtime information.	/SAPAPO/ CP3	Object specific setting for publication.
Define distribution per publication type.	/SAPAPO/ CP1	Define the publication object (planning result) per locations (plant) and logical system.
Generate and publish the distribution definition.	/SAPAPO/ CP2	Generation and deletion of distribution definitions.

Table 3.2 Configuration Steps in SAP APO for the Core Interface

3.3.2 Core Interface Enhancements

Enhancements refer to customer code added to SAP ERP objects to include additional custom functionalities to meet business requirements that are not supported in standard SAP ERP functionality. Different types of enhancements can be implemented. The common ones are source-code modifications (user exits), customer exits, business add-ins (BAdIs), business transaction events (BTEs), screen enhancements, and menu exits.

An example of a CIF enhancement is a requirement to transfer additional material master data from SAP ERP to SAP APO to influence planning result or global ATP allocation determination. This can be easily achieved by using EXIT_SAPLCMAT_001 during the CIF outbound from SAP ERP to SAP APO. Similarly, EXIT_/SAPAPO/ SAPLCIF_PROD_001 is available in SAP APO CIF inbound. The list of available CIF enhancements can be identified by using Transaction SMOD (as shown in Figure 3.4), which lists all available user exits provided by SAP ERP. The enhancement can be further implemented by using Transaction CMOD for creating a project and assigning the enhancement to your project. Another way to identify the user exits is to identify the function module (FM) in Transaction SE37.

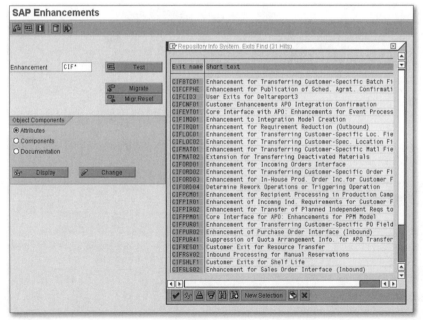

Figure 3.4 CIF Enhancements Available in SAP ERP

Now that we have set up the configuration for CIF, we need to build the integration models in SAP ERP. The integration models define the scope of the objects (master and transaction data) we want to transfer between SAP ERP and SAP SCM.

3.4   Building Integration Models for Global ATP in SAP ERP

The datasets (master and transactional) required for global ATP are selected in the integration model. The integration model is set up in two steps:

1. *The generation* step selects the object based on the selection criteria. Filter selection restricts the object volume further.

2. *The activation* step transfers the data across the systems.

For performance reasons, you should use separate integration models for master data and transaction data. Table 3.3 lists the important transactions you will need to set up in the CIF integration model.

Steps	Transaction	Remarks
Create the integration model.	CFM1	No change integration model available. Use the same variant to make object changes and save the variant. The model needs to be regenerated to include the new objects.
Activate the integration model.	CFM2	
Search objects for CIF models.	CFM5	Filter object search.
Change the transfer for master data.	CFP1	
Transfer master data online.	CFC5	Online delta transfer of master data.
Transfer the production process model (PPM).	CFP3	Online delta transfer of PPM.
Display application logs.	SLG1	Display entries in the application log (outbound from SAP ERP).
Display application logs.	CFG1	Display entries in the application log (inbound to SAP ERP).
Deleted entries in application logs.	CFGD	Periodic deletion of entries in application logs.

Table 3.3   CIF Integration Model Transactions in SAP ERP

Four integration models are required for global ATP. The following list details the setup steps for the master data (accessed via Transaction CFM1 and CFM2 in SAP ERP):

▶ ATP CUSTOMIZING
Checking this box initiates a one-time transfer (shown in Figure 3.5), which brings all the ATP customization to SAP APO.

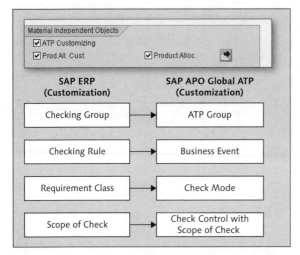

Figure 3.5 Integration Model Selection to Bring SAP ERP ATP customizing to SAP APO

▶ ATP CHECK
Setting the ATP CHECK box (see Figure 3.6) opens the ATP check channel between SAP ERP and SAP APO for order promising.

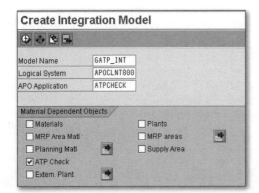

Figure 3.6 Integration Model Selection to Activate the ATP Check in Global ATP

▶ **Master data**

The master data for which the ATP check needs to be performed should be available in SAP APO. Set up integration models for the location and product combinations in the ATP check scope using Transaction CFM1 in SAP ERP. Once the integration model is created and generated, use Transaction CFM2 to activate the model. We recommend keeping the integration models separate for each plant (location) in SAP ERP so that a master data issue for one plant does not hold other plant data.

▶ **Transactional data**

You also need to set up integration models for transactional data, which will include an ATP check in global ATP. Use Transaction CFM1 to create and generate the integration model. Once generated use Transaction CFM2 to activate the model. All ATP receipt and requirement elements defined in scope of check for transaction data need to be in global ATP. These elements include stocks, sales orders, manufacturing orders, and other forms of transaction data.

After the CIF integration models are generated and activated, the data flow between the two systems—SAP ERP and SAP SCM—needs to be monitored for any functional or technical issue failures.

The next section explains the monitoring process for CIF in SAP APO.

3.5   Monitoring Core Interface Processing in Global ATP (SAP APO)

Monitoring how the master and transactional data queues are processed successfully between SAP ERP and global ATP (SAP APO) requires you to understand the error that has been encountered. Two forms of errors are possible during the communication:

▶ Communication errors; for example, network errors or a nonexistent RFC destination.

▶ Application errors; for example, program errors, locking of objects, missing master data for transactional data, and non-posting of data to the target system.

Table 3.4 lists all the necessary CIF-related transactions in SAP APO for monitoring and routine processing of master and transaction data.

Steps	Transaction	Remarks
Monitor the CIF queues using the CIF cockpit.	/SAPAPO/CC	CIF cockpit is a container for CIF background jobs, qRFC (queued remote function call; the CIF is a way of setting up RFCs), and CIF comparisons.
Rectify the SAP ERP and APO transaction data inconsistencies.	/SAPAPO/CCR	CIF Delta Report to detect transactional data inconsistencies that can be corrected by suitable measures.
Monitor CIF using the queue manager.	/SAPAPO/CQ	SCM Queue Manager to manage the inbound and outbound queues in SAP APO.
Trigger CIF queue alert when queue is stuck.	/SAPAPO/CW	qRFC monitoring for outbound queues.
Run consistency report between SAP liveCache and database.	/SAPAPO/ OM17	Inconsistencies may occur if the SAP APO database data or the SAP liveCache data can no longer be completely restored due to system crashes and inappropriate backup strategies. Because there is currently no logging for demand planning (DP) data, inconsistencies can still occur in this area following a recovery. If necessary, use this transaction to check the external consistency between the SAP APO database and SAP liveCache and to set it up again.
Display outbound application logs.	SLG1	Display entries in the application log (outbound from SAP APO).
Display inbound application logs.	/SAPAPO/C3	Display entries in the application log (inbound to SAP APO).
Delete application logs.	/SAPAPO/C6	Routine deletion of application logs.
Monitor outbound queues processing.	SMQ1	qRFC-monitor (outbound-queue).
Monitor inbound queues processing.	SMQ2	qRFC-monitor (inbound-queue).

Table 3.4 CIF Processing Transactions in SAP APO

3.6   Summary

Core Interface (CIF) is a major communication interface between SAP ERP and global ATP that provides real-time online processing of customer orders. This becomes even more important when transferring large data volumes requiring good data consistency. CIF has effective built-in monitoring tools to assist in management and troubleshooting. This chapter gave an overview of how CIF can be set up between SAP ERP and SAP APO (global ATP) using integration models.

The next chapter introduces the basic configuration and master data requirements to make global ATP work. You will learn the different basic configuration settings and the SAP ERP and global ATP master data mapping influence for global ATP results.

This chapter examines the basic configuration in SAP ERP and global ATP that is required for different availability checks. We also present the basic master data that drives the product availability check in global ATP.

4   Basic Configuration and Master Data Required for Global ATP

Understanding the basic global ATP configuration and master data settings in SAP ERP and global ATP is an important step toward setting up global ATP. The configuration defines the type of ATP check to be performed for the master data in scope. Global ATP offers a technical feature that allows you to transfer/import the basic SAP ERP customization to the global ATP environment via CIF. This ability to import settings provides consistency in the customization in both SAP ERP and global ATP, which ensures that the ATP check can be performed in SAP ERP when the global ATP system is not available. Additionally, the master data integration between the two systems ensures data consistency.

This chapter provides an overview of the basic configuration of global ATP and supporting master data to perform ATP checks in global ATP. The basic configuration is similar to the SAP ERP product availability check, and the configuration primarily can be CIFed (transferred) from the SAP ERP to the global ATP system, along with all of the ATP-related master data maintained in SAP ERP.

4.1   Basic Global ATP Configuration

In the previous chapter, you learned how to use the integration model to transfer basic SAP ERP customization into global ATP. These customization settings help you perform the product availability check in global ATP, similar to SAP ERP. In this section, we will list all the basic configuration objects and their purposes.

The basic global ATP configuration objects shown in Figure 4.1 seek to answer two basic questions during the product availability check:

1. **What type of global ATP check are you performing (basic or advanced methods)?**
   The configuration object that answers this question is *Check Instruction*, which is derived by a combination of a business event and check mode. The business event helps you identify the business transaction you are performing. An example of a business event is the creation of a sales order or delivery. The check mode mentions the type of ATP check you are performing. An example of ATP type is capable-to-promise (CTP), which triggers production during the sales order ATP check directly.

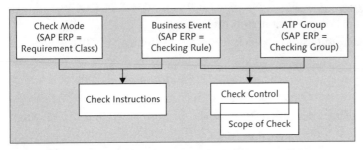

Figure 4.1 Basic Configuration objects in Global ATP

2. **What ATP categories are you committing/confirming against during the check?**
   The configuration object that answers this question is *Check Control,* which is comprised of the checking horizon and scope of check. The Check Control is derived from a combination of the business event and ATP group. This way, the product availability check can be controlled individually depending on the transaction and product.

The checking horizon defines the time horizon for which we would like to perform the ATP check. Let's say a business decides that the checking horizon can be 30 days, for which the business wants to perform the ATP checks. The scope of check defines the requirements, receipts, and stocks elements, which need to be included during the ATP check. Examples of elements are sales orders (requirements), planned orders (receipts), and unrestricted stock (stock), which can be used in the ATP calculation.

To answer these two questions, the basic global ATP configuration objects are explained next. We have also highlighted the basic configuration steps for each object in the logical sequence for which the configuration needs to be performed.

4.1.1 Business Event

The business event identifies the type of business transaction that initiates the ATP check. Business events can be sales orders or deliveries, which are transferred from SAP ERP to global ATP as events during order processing. The business event is used with other ATP settings to determine the entire check control (scope of check) and check instruction (type of check). The business event can be displayed by following the menu path SPRO • Advanced Planning and Optimization • Global Available-to-Promise (Global ATP) • General Settings • Maintain business event.

4.1.2 Check Mode

Check mode is primarily used to forecast consumption and identify the type of ATP check method that the business should use. The check mode is maintained in the menu path SPRO • Advanced Planning and Optimization • Global Available-to-Promise (Global ATP) • General Settings • Maintain Check mode. Check mode (see Figure 4.2) is derived from the SAP ERP requirement class. An example of a check mode as shown in the figure is the Production Type, which determines whether production needs to be triggered or not during the ATP check. Check mode is used to do the following in the ATP process:

▶ Determine how sales orders consume forecast in assignment mode. The No Allocation option causes forecast not to be used, and the Allocation option causes forecast to drive supply planning so that the sales order consumes the forecast.

▶ Determine the type of check for production. There are options of capable-to-promise ("Standard"), "Multilevel ATP," or "Characteristics evaluation-based."

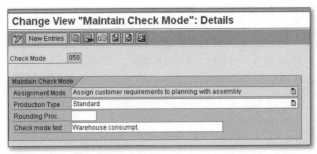

Figure 4.2 Check Mode in ATP

4.1.3 Check Instructions

Check instruction is a key configuration step to determine the ATP type (basic or advanced) and scope of the availability check, which can be controlled depending on the calling process and product master maintenance. During the simulation run for the product availability check (Transaction /SAPAPO/AC04), the user can find the check instruction settings. Settings for determining the check instruction can exist in the basic configuration, product master, and in the location-determination activity (rules-based ATP).

The settings in the location-determination activity (integrated rule maintenance) are used in the location substitution method. To maintain check instructions as shown in Figure 4.3, follow the IMG menu path SPRO • ADVANCED PLANNING AND OPTIMIZATION • GLOBAL AVAILABLE-TO-PROMISE (GLOBAL ATP) • GENERAL SETTINGS • MAINTAIN CHECK INSTRUCTION. In the check instruction configuration, maintain the following parameters:

1. In the MAINTAIN CHECK INSTRUCTION section, define the basic check method (product availability or product allocation or forecast). You can either maintain one of the basic methods or a combination, based on the business scenario.

2. If the rules-based ATP check is applicable, maintain the advanced check method in the form of rules-based ATP for location and/or product substitution where the network inventory needs to be consumed before giving new net requirements to the sourcing factory location. Check the field ACTIVATE RBA TO TRIGGER RULES-BASED ATP.

3. Define the advanced check method in the form of capable-to-promise (CTP) or multilevel ATP check method in the PRODUCTION and MULTILEVEL ATP CHECK sections. This method triggers production during the ATP check.

4. Activate third-party order processing in the THIRD-PARTY ORDER PROCESSING section.

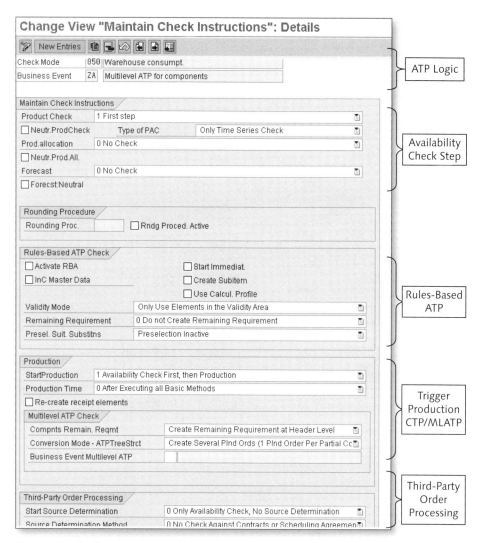

Figure 4.3 Check Instruction Configuration

4.1.4   ATP Group

The ATP group (see Figure 4.4 for the configuration screen) is a grouping at product level. The ATP group is derived from the SAP ERP checking group. The SAP ERP checking group can be configured in the IMG path SPRO • LOGISTICS EXECUTION • SHIPPING • AVAILABILITY CHECK • DEFINE CHECKING GROUP. The configuration is transferred via the integration model to global ATP. This checking group controls the following elements:

▸ Scope of the ATP check in conjunction with the business event

▸ Cumulative ATP check processing for supply shortage check

▸ Logic to evaluate the ATP time series during the availability check

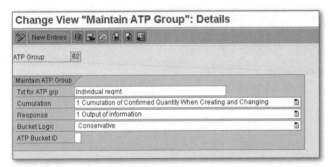

Figure 4.4 ATP Group Configuration

The cumulative ATP check maintained performs two different shortage checks:

▸ **Check taking account of the cumulated confirmed quantities**
During the calculation of the cumulated ATP quantity, global ATP takes the summation of all confirmed quantities into account. A new sales order can only be confirmed if the total receipts exceed the total confirmed quantities.

▸ **Check taking account of the cumulated requirement quantities**
During the calculation of the cumulated ATP quantity, global ATP takes the summation of all open requirement quantities into account. New sales orders can only be confirmed if the total receipts exceed the total requirement quantities.

> **Note**
>
> Refer to Chapter 3, Section 3.1, for a reminder about bucket logic for ATP time-series evaluation.

4.1.5 Check Control (Check Horizon, Categories, Scope of Check)

Check control identifies the categories for the scope of check during ATP. These categories are a combination of SAP ERP material resource planning (MRP) elements, SAP APO categories, and/or legacy categories. Also defined within check control is the checking horizon activation configuration. Check horizon limits the ATP time-series check and is equivalent to the replenishment lead time. Maintained at the ATP group and business event combination level, the configuration is maintained at the GENERAL and SCOPE OF CHECK levels (as shown in the DIALOG STRUCTURE area of see Figure 4.5). For the GENERAL tab, the following checks are performed:

▶ Whether the check needs to be restricted within a certain level (e.g., storage location or batches of material)

▶ Whether to consider check horizon during the ATP

▶ Whether past receipts need to factor in (open purchase order not delivered on scheduled date)

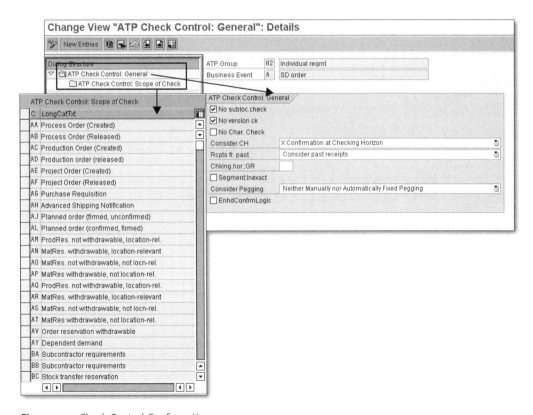

Figure 4.5 Check Control Configuration

A detailed list of the allowable ATP categories for the combination of ATP group and business event is maintained in the SCOPE OF CHECK tab (as shown in Figure 4.5).

4.2 Master Data Requirement for Global ATP

Now that the basic configuration is completed for global ATP, you need to maintain the master data in SAP ERP and global ATP to perform the product availability check in global ATP. This section explains how the SAP ERP master data is integrated via CIF with the global ATP master data. Any changes in the master data need to be done directly in SAP ERP, which will then be transferred by CIF in a nightly batch job as global ATP master data.

SAP ERP serves as the central master data maintenance and needs to have data consistency with the fields mapped in the global ATP system to avoid any transactional data failures. The following subsections explain the combination master data maintained in SAP ERP and global ATP for performing the ATP check.

4.2.1 Check Mode Determination

The global ATP Check Mode is derived from the SAP ERP customer requirement class. Every material needs to have a planning strategy maintained for defining forecast consumption. The planning strategy represents the business procedure for planning production quantities and dates, and it also defines whether and how customer requirements consume planning independent requirements.

A planning strategy is assigned to a material master using a strategy group in SAP ERP. Various requirement types are defined for each strategy, and each requirement type is assigned to a requirement class. In SAP ERP, the requirements class is usually determined by the strategy group of the material but can also be a result of the schedule line category in the sales order. Based on the requirement class, the check mode is transferred to SAP APO. The requirement class, as shown in Figure 4.6, can be determined in two ways: via the material master data or via the sales order document item category.

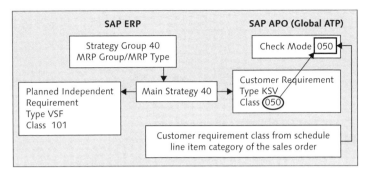

Figure 4.6 Determination of Check Mode

Following is the determination logic for both methods:

▶ **Determination using material master**
The check mode can be determined in SAP ERP using a combination of strategy group and MRP group fields (or MRP type). Using the strategy group and the customer requirement type, the requirement class is identified, which is transferred as a check mode to global ATP.

▶ **Determination using transaction**
Alternatively, the check mode is derived from the combination of the sales order document item category (e.g., TAN) and material master MRP type (which is used to derive the requirement type and requirement class for the material).

4.2.2 Checking Horizon

The checking horizon defines the time horizon in which a product availability check can be carried out. If the requirement date is outside the checking horizon, the ATP check is not carried out, and the sales order requested quantity is not confirmed in full.

The checking horizon can also be used to model the replenishment lead time in the order-promising process. To make the checking horizon work, activate the customizing in check control and master data (CHECKG HORIZON and CHECKING HORIZON CALENDAR fields shown in Figure 4.7).

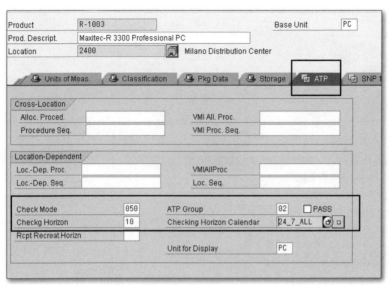

Figure 4.7 Checking Horizon in Global ATP—Product Location Master Data

Figure 4.8 illustrates how the checking horizon can be derived from SAP ERP master data.

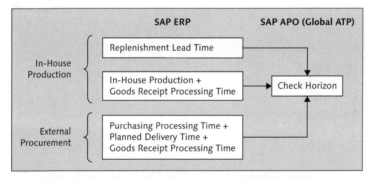

Figure 4.8 Check Horizon Derivation from SAP ERP Master Data

The checking horizon (time period window the ATP check needs to be performed) in global ATP is derived from the SAP ERP material master data. For an in-house production scenario where the company manufactures its own products, the checking horizon is identified by either replenishment lead time or a combination of the in-house manufacturing processing time plus the goods receipt time for quality inspection at the warehouse. For external procurement, where the company procures the finished goods and distributes to markets, the checking horizon is a summation of purchasing lead time, planned delivery time from the vendor, and goods receipt time at the warehouse.

4.2.3 ATP Group

The ATP group combines groups of settings by defining the scope of check in conjunction with the business event, ATP time-series bucket logic, and shortage check during the availability check. As shown in Figure 4.9, the SAP ERP material master data field—AVAILABILITY CHECK—is transferred via CIF as ATP GROUP in the SAP APO product location master data. The ATP group can be seen under scope of check in the SAP APO product availability overview (Transaction /SAPAPO/AC03).

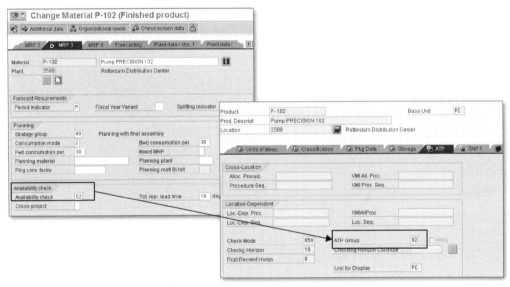

Figure 4.9 ATP Group Mapping from SAP ERP Material Master Data

4.3 Summary

This chapter explored how the basic global ATP configuration and master data relevant to the product availability check in global ATP is integrated between the SAP ERP and global ATP systems. Understanding these basic configurations and master data is important to build the foundation to set up global ATP in SAP APO.

These basic configurations define the type of ATP (basic or advanced) the company needs to model to solve its specific order-processing business scenarios.

The next chapter introduces important concepts in logistics scheduling to derive correct and accurate dates for material availability and delivery dates to customers. The chapter shows how companies can achieve accuracy on their order-promising business process using the global ATP functionality of condition technique and configurable process scheduling.

Transportation and shipment scheduling is an integral part of the global ATP process because it helps to calculate all the lead times to arrive at the material availability date correctly. This chapter explains two options available in global ATP: the condition technique and the configurable process scheduling method.

5 Integrating Transportation Shipment and Scheduling with Global ATP

The globalization of the economy has led companies to manufacture and source goods from various worldwide locations. This in turn has provided challenges to the order-management team to accurately estimate the delivery dates of finished goods for customer order fulfillment. Additionally, if your company uses SAP APO for a global ATP check, it becomes mandatory to use the transportation shipment and scheduling feature in global ATP. The SAP APO component may already have the various lead times defined, which can be integrated along with scheduling function of global ATP.

The scheduling function is primarily used to calculate the lead time between the material availability date (MAD) at the sourcing location and the requested delivery date on customer orders at customer sites. This functionality ensures accuracy on the order delivery dates and lays down a plan for the execution team to fulfill. Most of the order management KPIs are based on these date calculations.

This chapter presents the basic and advanced form of shipment scheduling techniques available in global ATP.

5.1 Transportation and Shipment Scheduling Overview

Transportation and shipment scheduling is an integral submodule of global ATP and a suggested scheduling tool for sales-order processing. For instance, manufacturing companies who ship to global customers need to determine the loading date and delivery date for customer orders. The backwards scheduling of the shipment based on the estimated date of arrival at the customer determines the activities for the manufacturing company to plan the MAD and production date accordingly. The scheduling feature used for processing customer orders helps companies with the following:

▶ Scheduling the correct estimated time of arrival regarding supply availability

▶ Proper calculation of lead time between supplier and customer points

▶ Increased customer-service level and sales based on supply availability at the committed date

The process of transportation and shipment scheduling occurs during order processing. As shown in Figure 5.1, upon the sales order creation in SAP ERP, the sales order performs an online remote function call (RFC) to the SAP Supply Chain Management (SAP SCM) system to perform the transportation and shipment scheduling calculation. After the scheduling calculation is completed, the calculated MAD forms the baseline against which the global ATP is checked. Global ATP provides the delivery proposal for the confirmation dates and quantities for each sales order schedule line item. Upon acceptance or rejection of the delivery proposal, the sales order can be saved.

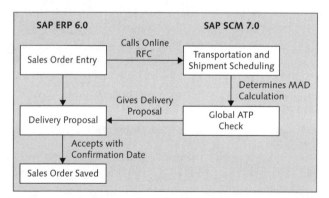

Figure 5.1 Sales Order Processing Involving Scheduling Function

Also, using the sales order's requested date, the scheduling process determines the MAD, which becomes input to the global ATP process for conducting the product availability check. If the product is not available, or the MAD calculation results in a date in the past, the system performs forward scheduling to best determine the committed delivery date based on the committed material availability before giving the confirmation date back to SAP ERP sales orders.

The scheduling function consists of business process activities. The planning and execution business activities lead-time are calculated backwards from the customer's delivery date. The key activities, which are shown in Figure 5.2, consist of picking/ packing, loading, shipping, and unloading the shipments.

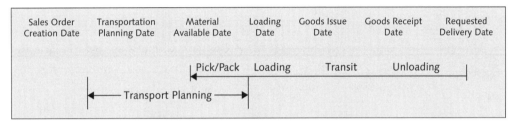

Figure 5.2 Transportation and Shipment Scheduling—Key Business Activities

Typically, these business activities are common in every manufacturing and distribution company where the warehouse performs the transportation planning a couple of days before the actual shipment date.

Business Example

Let's say a paper company wants to ship bulk customer orders. The company needs to reserve truck capacity with the transporter company days earlier than the physical loading date for the goods. Based on the scheduling performed in SAP SCM, the transporter is given an estimated arrival time at the warehouse. On the execution day, the paper goods are physically picked from the warehouse storage space, packed, and moved in the warehouse outbound space. The paper goods are then physically loaded on the truck and shipped to customers. On the customer side, the transporter informs the customer regarding the goods arrival and unloads the paper goods for a proof of delivery receipt.

All of these physical goods movements are modeled in the transportation planning and scheduling for accurate delivery date estimation during order processing.

In global ATP, the scheduling function can be done either by using the condition technique or by using configurable process scheduling (CPS). The former is recommended for business scenarios where the lead times are well defined for different order-processing scenarios. The latter is good when shipping constraints are built on the execution. The condition technique method consists of modeling the various warehouses and shipping lead times in the system. The CPS method builds on the condition technique and includes additional supply chain constraints. For example, a paper manufacturing company that ships its paper goods only on specific calendar days to key specific customers is using constraint.

If neither of the scheduling functions is built in the system, the sales order shipping schedule gives the impression that all the business activities can be performed in the same date and completed. Figure 5.3 (access this screen via Transaction VA03) depicts an example where the MAD and customer requirement dates are the same, and no scheduling function is modeled. In this example, no warehouse or transportation lead time is defined.

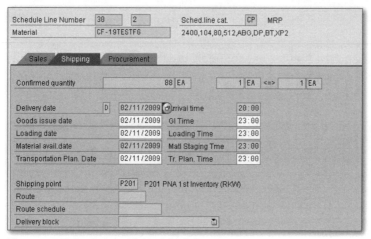

Figure 5.3 Sales Order with No Scheduling Function

5.1.1 Transportation and Shipment Scheduling using the Condition Technique

The condition technique method solves the problem of various lead-time definitions on the order-fulfillment activities. Various lead times, which are displayed in Figure 5.4, can be modeled in the condition technique for a specific business variant (e.g., shipping point for a plant).

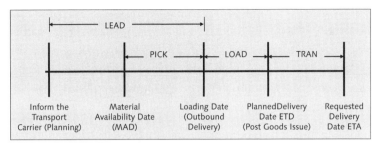

Figure 5.4 Condition Technique Models the Business Activities

For instance, the paper manufacturing company may have various shipping points configured in the SAP ERP system as the dispatch locations to fulfill different customer orders. The shipping point in turn is determined by the shipping condition (customer master data), loading group (material master data), and plant combination. The business driver may be that the paper manufacturing company wants to separate its truck loading spaces based on vehicle size and capacity. Therefore, in the condition technique, various shipping points per plant can be modeled with different scheduling lead times.

The business activities for a paper manufacturing company's theoretical calculation are as follows for better understanding on how the dates are derived by system:

▶ Transportation lead time from the paper company warehouse to the customer warehouse. Transit time is determined by activity TRAN:

Goods Issue Date = Delivery Date – TRAN

▶ Physical loading activities of paper products in the truck. Loading time is determined by activity LOAD:

Loading Date = Goods Issue Date – LOAD

▶ Lead time to inform the transporter in advance to book and reserve the truck capacity. Planning time is determined by activity LEAD:

Transportation Planning Date = Loading Date – LEAD

▶ Physical picking and packing of the paper products in the warehouse. Pick/pack time is determined by activity PICK:

  ▶ The date where the goods is available in the manufacturing warehouse for shipping to customer.

  MAD = Loading Date – PICK

Now we will walk through each of the specific configuration steps. The only prerequisite for the company is a clear direction of how the company wants to model the business activities and data gathering. The configurations we discuss in the following sections provide steps for modeling how the paper manufacturing company ships the goods to its customers and plans its warehouse and transportation activities using condition techniques.

5.1.2 Condition Technique Configuration

The first step in the configuration is that the transportation scheduling should be active for the sales document type in scope in SAP ERP. This is done by following the path IMG • Sales and Distribution • Basic Functions • Delivery Scheduling and Transportation Scheduling • Define Scheduling by Sales Document Type. (An example of this configuration in SAP ERP is shown in Figure 5.14, later in this chapter.) The configuration involves maintaining the relevant sales order type and activating the transportation scheduling feature.

The majority of the other configurations are done in SAP SCM. Figure 5.5 shows the complete picture of the configuration objects, including how these objects are connected and the sequence of the customization to be followed.

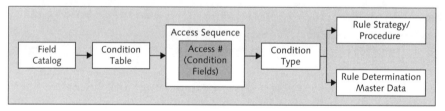

Figure 5.5 Configuration Objects for Condition Technique

Now access Transaction /SAPCND/AU01 and set up the field catalog for the characteristics combinations for which scheduling function lead-time will be defined (see Figure 5.6). These tables display SAP ERP standard fields available for defining the characteristics combination. If the table contains all the characteristics fields that match the business requirement for condition technique, then no further configuration is required. For our paper manufacturing example, we select Shipping Point and Plant as our combination for defining the condition technique. The shipping points per plant are configured in the SAP ERP system as the dispatch locations to fulfill different customer orders from various manufacturing plants.

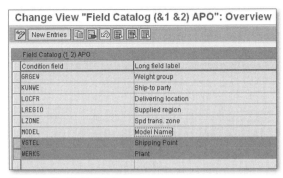

Figure 5.6 Field Catalog

You can also set up additional fields for the condition table by adding fields in the structure /SAPAPO/KOMGU.

Go to Transaction /SAPCND/AU03 to define the condition table. Double-click the fields, and click the GENERATE icon to create a condition table.

Next, define the access sequence with the condition table combination by accessing Transaction /SAPCND/AU07, as shown in Figure 5.7. Click the NEW ENTRIES button, and define the access sequence for transportation activity (TRAN). Include the condition table generated earlier in the access sequence definition.

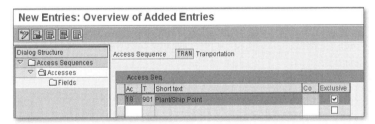

Figure 5.7 Access Sequence

Now you can go to Transaction /SAPCND/AU06 to define the condition type (Figure 5.8). Again, click the NEW ENTRIES button, and define the condition type with the earlier configuration of access sequence.

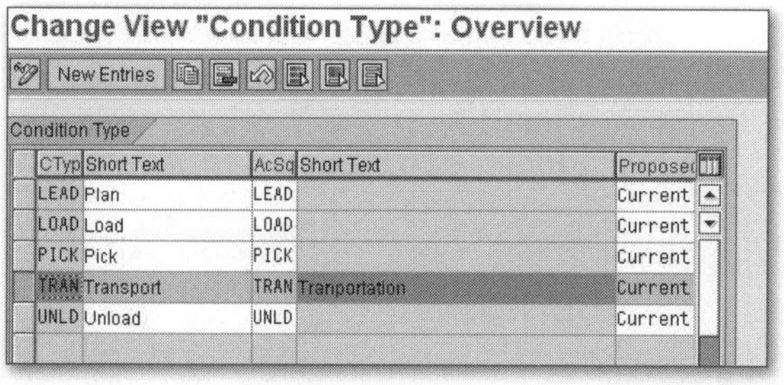

Figure 5.8 Condition Type

Define the rule strategy/procedure in Transaction /SAPCND/AU08 as shown in Figure 5.9. The user will need to list all of the warehouse and transportation activities that need to be factored in the scheduling function. Figure 5.9 displays the SAP SCM standard scheduling procedure, and you can view the complete list for the calculation of the lead time across all the maintained condition types.

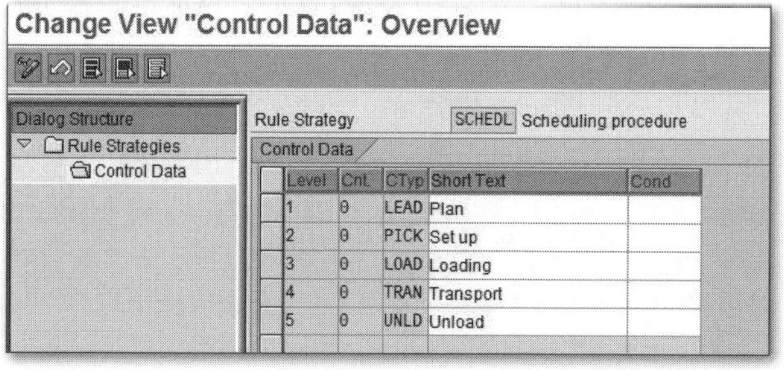

Figure 5.9 Rule Strategy

The next step is rule determination. As shown in Figure 5.10, access Transaction /SAPCND/AU11 to input your master data for characteristics combination PLANT/ SHIP.POINT under the CONDITION TYPE "TRAN." Click the KEY COMBINATION button for the shipping point and plant combination. Input the transportation lead time for the combination in hours.

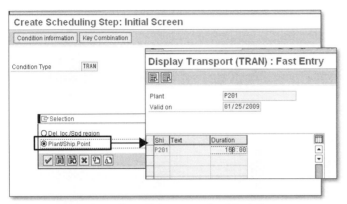

Figure 5.10 Condition Type Maintenance for Scheduling

Test your work by using simulation Transaction /SAPAPO/SCHED_TEST (shown in Figure 5.11). This simulation is important to validate that the customization is correct and that the master data maintained for the defined condition type is picked correctly from the condition table. Figure 5.11 shows that the maintained transportation lead time is displayed correctly for the shipping point and plant combination for condition type TRAN.

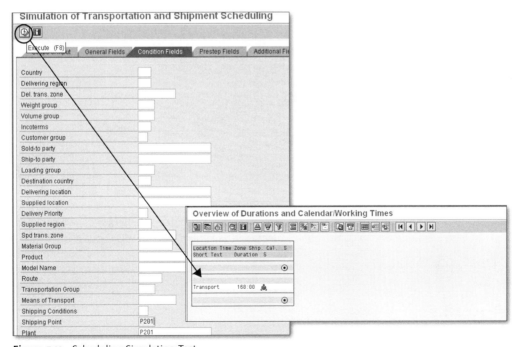

Figure 5.11 Scheduling Simulation Test

If the simulation fails, follow the configuration steps in the next subsection from the beginning, or validate the rule determination table.

5.1.3   Condition Technique Scenario Testing

The condition technique method can now be tested with the SAP ERP and SAP SCM integration. Create a new sales order in SAP ERP using Transaction VA01. Technically during the creation and saving of the sales order, the shipment scheduling is read, and calculated dates are populated in the SALES ORDERS – SHIPPING tab. For our example, we can see these lead-time dates in the DELIVERY DATE, MATERIAL AVAIL.DATE, and the SHIPPING POINT fields (see Figure 5.12) in the sales order. The difference between the delivery date and MAD takes into account the TRAN lead-time that is maintained.

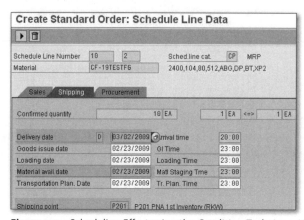

Figure 5.12   Scheduling Effect using the Condition Technique Method

---

Note

Make sure the consistency between the SAP APO Supply Network Planning (SNP) result and the Global ATP check is correct by matching the transportation lane lead time (maintained via Transaction /SAPAPO/SCC_TL1) and the condition technique transportation maintenance as explained earlier in Figure 5.10 (via Transaction /SAPCND/AU11). Any inconsistencies in this information may result in supply plans being shown in different planning buckets when the SNP plan is published to SAP ERP.

The condition technique method customization and master data maintenance provides great business value in accurately scheduling the sales orders for correct MAD and delivery date commitments. Use this method if your supply chain is simple, and the average lead time across the business activities for transportation and warehouse is consistent. For complex supply chains that have shipping and warehouse constraints, we recommend the configurable process scheduling method, which we explain next.

5.2 Transportation and Shipment Scheduling using the Configurable Process Scheduling (CPS) Method

The configurable process scheduling (CPS) method is used for business scenarios where you need to perform calendar, time zone, or location determination while performing scheduling functions. Different supply-chain constraints can be modeled using this method. A good example is a company's business requirement to ship goods when the time zones between the sourcing plant and the customer are different, and goods need to arrive in specific time windows. Another business requirement might be to ship specific materials only from specific locations. These complex activities are not supported in the basic condition technique method. Additional activities (e.g., quality inspection) can be designed in the CPS schema to map the transportation and logistics activities of the company. The relationship between these activities is modeled in the CPS schema.

CPS is a cross-application function that you can use to schedule several freely definable business processes according to your own rules. Using CPS, business users can configure dates such as the MAD (activity MBDAT) and goods issue date (activity WADAT). By using time stream calendars, you can configure cut-off times for shipping the goods to customers in the defined time windows.

CPS uses process alias, which is the name of the business process (e.g., SCHEDL_SDD for sales-order processing). Within the process alias, many dates are required for the planning process where goods receipt and goods issue dates are derived. Different process alias techniques are defined to model different business scenarios. These scenarios include sales distribution for different route determination or third-party order processing.

Let's say we have a scenario where the paper manufacturing company ships goods to one cluster of customers every working day, while for another cluster of customers there is a weekly replenishment. This is achieved in CPS by using sales-order scheduling with a shipping calendar constraint. The process alias refers to the scheduling schema where different transportation constraints can be defined per business requirements. Each of the business scenarios can have different scheduling activities defined per business requirements and the process alias definition. There are two ways of finding the process alias: either by assigning it to an item category or by condition technique. The assignment to the item category is done via the configuration explained in Section 5.2.2. Note that assignment of the item category to the process alias is ignored if the system has previously found a process alias using the condition technique.

For our example, let's assume we have set CPS so that the system calculates the following derived date types according to the business activities and conditions:

- **Unloading date (ELDAT):** The unloading date is greater than or equal to the delivery date.

- **Delivery date (LFDAT):** The delivery date is greater than or equal to the goods issue date.

- **Goods issue date (WADAT):** The goods issue date is greater than or equal to the loading date.

- **Loading date (LDDAT):** The loading date is greater than or equal to MAD (MBDAT).

- **Transportation planning date (TDDAT):** The loading date is greater than or equal to the transportation planning date.

Keep reading to understand how you can configure CPS in your own system.

5.2.1 Configurable Process Scheduling (CPS) Configuration

The configuration objects in chronological order for CPS are shown as a flow chart in Figure 5.13, which we will explain in the following configuration steps.

Your first step is to make sure that transportation scheduling is active for the sales document type in SAP ERP. The menu path to the activation screen is IMG • SALES AND DISTRIBUTION • BASIC FUNCTIONS • DELIVERY SCHEDULING AND TRANSPORTATION SCHEDULING • DEFINE SCHEDULING BY SALES DOCUMENT TYPE (see Figure 5.14). In the screen, make sure that the TRANSPSCHD checkbox is marked for the sales order item categories in scope.

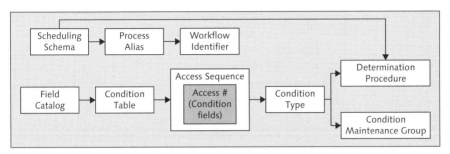

Figure 5.13 Configuration Objects for CPS Setup in Global ATP

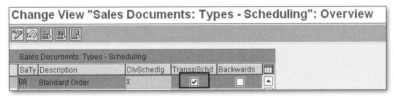

Figure 5.14 Sales Document Relevancy for Transportation Scheduling

Next, define a scheduling schema. A scheduling schema or procedure (e.g., SCHEDL_ SDD) is used within a process definition, which includes the business activities for the dates that need to be calculated. The procedure is used to control the behavior of a sales order or stock transport order (STO) when it is scheduled. There is no need to define a new Z schema, as standard SAP SCM schemas are good enough. SCHEDL_SDD has the following activities: transportation planning lead time (LEAD), goods loading (LOAD), goods picking (PICK), source determination lead time (SLEAD), transportation (TRAN), and unloading goods at destination (UNLD), which are more comprehensive than the condition technique. This allows the business users to define the warehouse and transportation activities in more detail.

To define a scheduling schema, follow the menu path IMG • SCM BASIS • CONFIGU- RABLE PROCESS SCHEDULING • SCHEDULING SCHEMA • DEFINE SCHEMA. The resulting screen in Figure 5.15 shows the determination types. Depending on the business requirement you will need to customize LOCATION, DURATION, CALENDAR, TIME ZONE scheduling schemas with various business process activities.

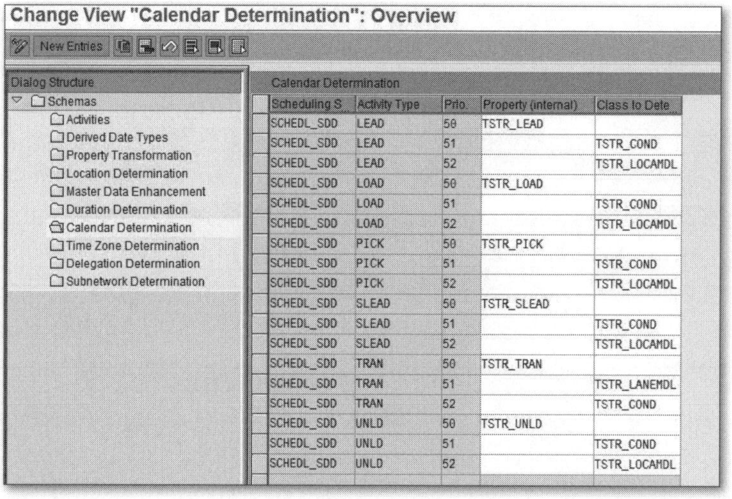

Change View "Calendar Determination": Overview					
New Entries					
Dialog Structure	**Calendar Determination**				
▽ ☐ Schemas	Scheduling S	Activity Type	Prio.	Property (internal)	Class to Dete
☐ Activities	SCHEDL_SDD	LEAD	50	TSTR_LEAD	
☐ Derived Date Types	SCHEDL_SDD	LEAD	51		TSTR_COND
☐ Property Transformation	SCHEDL_SDD	LEAD	52		TSTR_LOCAMDL
☐ Location Determination	SCHEDL_SDD	LOAD	50	TSTR_LOAD	
☐ Master Data Enhancement	SCHEDL_SDD	LOAD	51		TSTR_COND
☐ Duration Determination	SCHEDL_SDD	LOAD	52		TSTR_LOCAMDL
☐ Calendar Determination	SCHEDL_SDD	PICK	50	TSTR_PICK	
☐ Time Zone Determination	SCHEDL_SDD	PICK	51		TSTR_COND
☐ Delegation Determination	SCHEDL_SDD	PICK	52		TSTR_LOCAMDL
☐ Subnetwork Determination	SCHEDL_SDD	SLEAD	50	TSTR_SLEAD	
	SCHEDL_SDD	SLEAD	51		TSTR_COND
	SCHEDL_SDD	SLEAD	52		TSTR_LOCAMDL
	SCHEDL_SDD	TRAN	50	TSTR_TRAN	
	SCHEDL_SDD	TRAN	51		TSTR_LANEMDL
	SCHEDL_SDD	TRAN	52		TSTR_COND
	SCHEDL_SDD	UNLD	50	TSTR_UNLD	
	SCHEDL_SDD	UNLD	51		TSTR_COND
	SCHEDL_SDD	UNLD	52		TSTR_LOCAMDL

Figure 5.15 Scheduling Schemas Determination Types

Maintain the priority of the determining class to determine CALENDAR/DURATION/ TIME ZONE. These are SAP SCM standard classes and can be changed according to your business requirement. In each class, the sequence of priority is displayed from where the source master data needs to be determined for scheduling calculation.

Example

If paper goods need to be shipped on specific weekdays, you can define the shipping calendar either on the SAP APO transportation lane or the calendar master data. This allows the business users to maintain the master data in transportation lanes or directly in the calendar.

We can see in Figure 5.15 that for CALENDAR DETERMINATION, the first priority goes to condition records (if maintained) and then to location master data for all paper manufacturing business activities except the transportation activity, which looks at the transportation lane master data first.

Now you need to make sure that the name of the scheduling schema matches that of the process alias. The process alias is mapped to the workflow identifier. The path to view the SAP SCM standard process alias or maintain the new process alias is IMG • SCM BASIS • CONFIGURABLE PROCESS SCHEDULING • PROCESS DEFINITION • DEFINE PROCESS ALIAS.

Next, you need to define the configurations similar to the condition technique method. The link between the process alias and this set of configuration is made via the determination procedure as shown earlier in Figure 5.13.

In the condition table, you can influence MAD and also define the transit time. MAD can be moved by using the activity LEAD, and transit time can be determined by using the activity TRAN. Follow the path IMG • ADVANCED PLANNING AND OPTIMIZATION • GLOBAL AVAILABLE-TO-PROMISE • TRANSPORTATION AND SHIPMENT SCHEDULING • SCHEDULING USING CONFIGURABLE PROCESS SCHEDULING • DEFINE CONDITION TABLE. In the resulting screen, select APPLICATION SCH and USAGE DU (Usage DU stands for "duration").

Create condition table CUS88 with the field PLANT and the field DELIVERY PRIORITY for lead-time definition. Create a separate condition table named CUS681 with a field named TRANSPORTATION GROUP for transit time modeling (as shown in Figure 5.16). Defining the condition table offers the flexibility to business users to maintain the various supply chain lead times on the defined field characteristics combination.

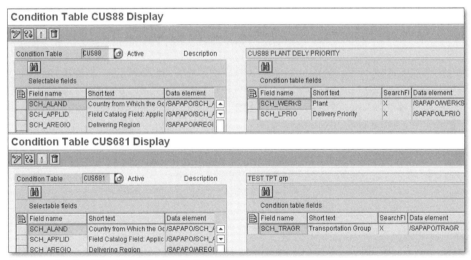

Figure 5.16 Condition Table Customization

Define two access sequence entries (shown in Figure 5.17), and assign the condition table. To do this, follow the menu path IMG • ADVANCED PLANNING AND OPTIMIZATION • GLOBAL AVAILABLE-TO-PROMISE • TRANSPORTATION AND SHIPMENT

SCHEDULING • SCHEDULING USING CONFIGURABLE PROCESS SCHEDULING • DEFINE ACCESS SEQUENCE.

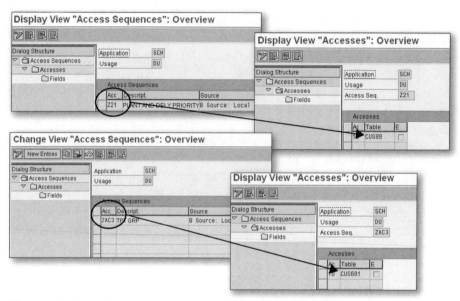

Figure 5.17   Access Sequence

Now follow the path IMG • ADVANCED PLANNING AND OPTIMIZATION • GLOBAL AVAILABLE-TO-PROMISE • TRANSPORTATION AND SHIPMENT SCHEDULING • SCHEDULING USING CONFIGURABLE PROCESS SCHEDULING • DEFINE CONDITION TYPE. Here you will include both the access sequences in one condition type (this is shown in Figure 5.18) by inserting two line entries. Including both the access sequences will help you cumulate the two business activities scheduling lead times.

Change View "Condition Types": Overview

Application SCH
Usage DU

Condition Types

Co	Description	Acc	To	from
ZLD	LEAD-PLANT /DELY PRI	Z21	The date 12/31/9999 is propc	Current date
ZTPT	TPT GROUP	ZAC3	The date 12/31/9999 is propc	Current date

Figure 5.18   Condition Types

Define the determination procedures ZTPTGR and ZLEAD (see Figure 5.19) by following the path IMG • ADVANCED PLANNING AND OPTIMIZATION • GLOBAL AVAILABLE-TO-PROMISE • TRANSPORTATION AND SHIPMENT SCHEDULING • SCHEDULING USING CONFIGURABLE PROCESS SCHEDULING • DEFINE DETERMINATION PROCEDURE.

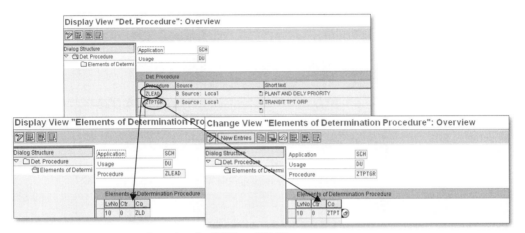

Figure 5.19 Determination Procedure for LEAD and TRAN

Next you need to define the condition maintenance group (see Figure 5.20) via the path IMG • ADVANCED PLANNING AND OPTIMIZATION • GLOBAL AVAILABLE-TO-PROMISE • TRANSPORTATION AND SHIPMENT SCHEDULING • SCHEDULING USING CONFIGURABLE PROCESS SCHEDULING • DEFINE CONDITION MAINTENANCE GROUP.

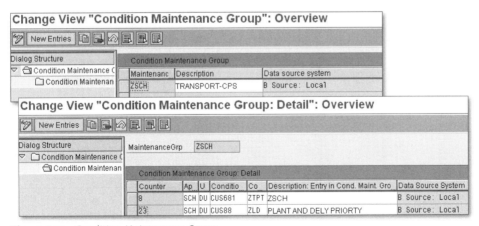

Figure 5.20 Condition Maintenance Group

Assign the scheduling schema and activity to a determination procedure (Figure 5.21) in path IMG • Advanced Planning and Optimization • Global Available-to-Promise • Transportation and Shipment Scheduling • Scheduling Using Configurable Process Scheduling • Assign Schema and Activity to a Determination Procedure.

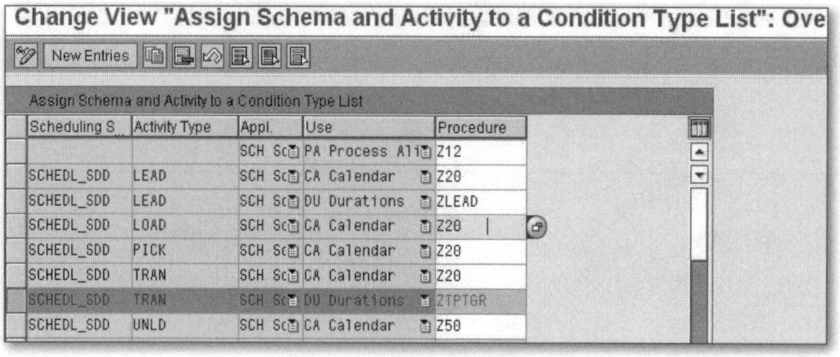

Figure 5.21 Assign a Schema and an Activity to a Determination Procedure

Now we have completed the baseline configuration for the CPS. The next section explains a couple of additional configurations that need to be performed to make the solution suit the specific business requirements of our paper company.

5.2.2 Additional Configuration Steps

The additional configuration involves more master data settings for maintaining the calendar and defining the sales order type applicable for the CPS. One of the additional business requirements is to define the calendar when the customer would like to receive the goods.

Time Stream Calendars

We can define the time stream calendars to influence how each business activity needs to occur. The CA Calendar usage in the Use column shown in Figure 5.21 earlier is mapped to time stream calendars. We can use time stream along with the factory calendar to change the working time of the paper manufacturer's delivering location or the working time of the customer's receiving location (customer – ship to).

Time stream calendars can also be used to cause the business activities to occur on a specific day of the week. For example, we can define the start day of the week when the transportation activity TRAN can commence. If we want post goods issue (PGI) to happen on particular days, we can control this using time stream calendars and assigning these calendars to appropriate fields. An example of a time stream calendar is shown in Figure 5.22 for defining the calendar consisting of only one weekday—Friday. This in turn can be linked with customers who only want consolidated shipments on Fridays. The time stream calendar can be maintained by accessing Transaction /SAPAPO/CALENDAR.

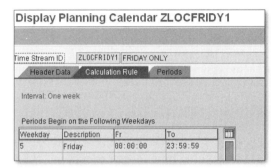

Figure 5.22 Time Stream Calendar

Assignment of an Item Category to the Process Alias

This configuration can be used if CPS needs to be executed by certain item categories or in specific order types. In the example of a STO, there is no item category available, so the system finds a process alias using a condition technique.

Maintain the item category in scope and the process alias using the path IMG • ADVANCED PLANNING AND OPTIMIZATION • GLOBAL AVAILABLE-TO-PROMISE • TRANSPORTATION AND SHIPMENT SCHEDULING • SCHEDULING USING CONFIGURABLE PROCESS SCHEDULING • DETERMINE ASSIGNMENT OF ITEM CATEGORY TO PROCESS ALIAS. This configuration (shown in Figure 5.23) helps to limit the item categories or order types in scope.

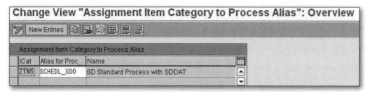

Figure 5.23 Assignment of an Item Category to the Process Alias

CPS Enhancements User Exits

Often you may need additional custom development specific to an industry or business process that is not covered in SAP ERP standard software. Development in CPS can be done in two of the SCM user exits (accessed via Transaction SE37):

▶ **EXIT_/SAPAPO/SAPLVCRM_001:** Scheduling: Inbound interface

▶ **EXIT_/SAPAPO/SAPLVCRM_001:** Shipment scheduling: Data determination

5.2.3 Configurable Process Scheduling (CPS) Scenario Testing

Now you need to maintain the condition record (Transaction /SAPCND/GCM) in the form of master data to influence the scheduling function. In this master data, we connect the various condition types with the factory calendar and the time stream calendar to define the working days of the business activities. The example in Figure 5.24 shows different calendars that are assigned to a combination of PLANT and SHIP-TO PARTY.

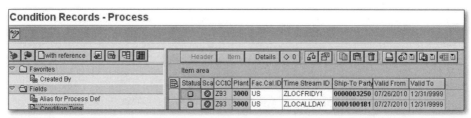

Figure 5.24 Condition Record Master Data Maintenance

Condition type Z93 is assigned to procedure Z93. Procedure Z93 is assigned to activity TRAN and usage duration. The business example shows that for a specific customer (SHIP-TO PARTY "3250"), we can only ship goods on Friday, whereas for a different customer (SHIP-TO PARTY "100181"), we can ship the goods on any weekdays.

After the sales order is created and saved, you can view the CPS log (accessed via Transaction /SCMB/SCHED_DEL). You can see from the screenshot in Figure 5.24 that customer 3250 will always have a PGI date of Friday, and customer 100181 can be shipped to on any weekdays. During the sales order creation for SHIP-TO PARTY customer 3250, the condition record is found using a condition technique (shown in Figure 5.25). This is reflected in the TRAN activity type where the start date (STRAN) and end date (ETRAN) are based on the calendar definition.

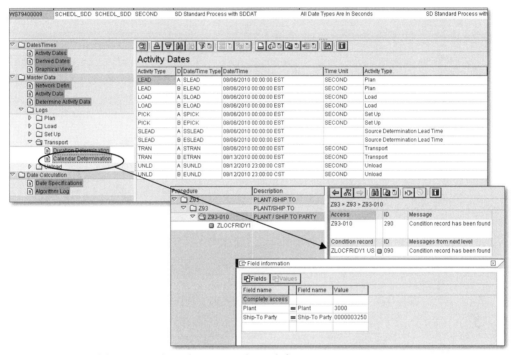

Figure 5.25 Scheduling Log and Condition Record Match for Customer 3250

The result in SAP ERP shows the PGI (the date the goods are shipped to the customer from the warehouse) date on Friday, based on the requested delivery date from the warehouse of 08/06/10 (Figure 5.26). After the sales order is saved, the scheduling result is seen in the SALES ORDER – SHIPPING tab (accessed via Transaction VA03) where the goods issue and delivery dates are published per the scheduling method.

Next, you create a sales order for a customer for which the goods can be shipped on any weekday, as shown in Figure 5.27.

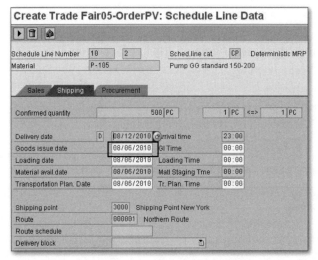

Figure 5.26 Sales Order Scheduling on Friday Shipment Condition

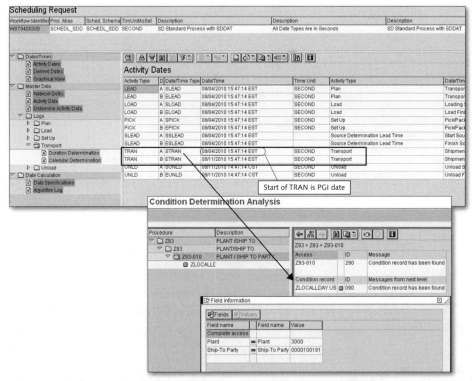

Figure 5.27 Scheduling Log and Condition Record Match for Customer 100181

The results in the system show the PGI date based on scheduling, which is based on the requested delivery date from the warehouse of 08/04/10 (see Figure 5.28). Based on the scheduling and the calendar definition, the goods issue date is posted on 08/04/2011 per the requested delivery date from the warehouse.

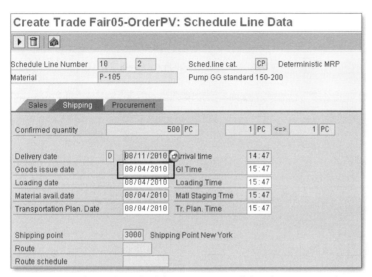

Figure 5.28 Sales Order Scheduling on Any Weekday Shipment Condition

CPS offers flexibility to business users to model their order-execution business activities in a detailed way to accurately reflect business operations. Using this method, the business can gain confidence in accurately determining the delivery date commitments for customers. This in turn increases customer satisfaction via reliable order-delivery performance.

5.3   Summary

Transportation and shipment scheduling plays an important role in the confirmation of customers' order dates. The scheduling function identifies when the material needs to be available at the source location, but also takes into account various logistics and transportation constraints in the supply chain. Global ATP condition technique and CPS functionality gives both the width and breadth for the businesses to expand these supply-chain constraints on business activities to get accurate fulfillment dates.

The next chapter shows how you can correct the supply-chain disparity on demand and supply balance using rules-based ATP. Rules-based ATP serves as an important capability for companies to implement global ATP for inventory optimization, location consolidation, and increased customer-service levels.

The global rules-based ATP solution allows companies in a branched supply chain network to take full advantage of multiple shipping assets to ship goods from alternative sites. It also permits certain products to be substituted to fulfill customer demand.

6 Designing Your Supply Chain ATP with Rules-Based ATP

This chapter introduces the rules-based ATP concept and explains business scenarios that show the global ATP product or location substitution, multi-item single delivery (MISL) locations, and consolidation location with stock transport order (STO) options, which will help you understand how to manage business requirements during the order-fulfillment process.

For example, a computer manufacturer may search for inventory across the network during its sales order ATP check using location substitution or may provide product substitution on its range of products to the customer. The rules-based ATP with consolidation location feature can also be modeled in an export business where a computer manufacturer may want to consolidate its shipment before sending to the overseas customers. The computer manufacturer may also want to use the MISL feature for its full deliveries to be shipped from a single location due to transportation costs.

This chapter explains these business scenarios and also provides direction on how to customize your system and implement master data settings to model these situations in global ATP.

6.1 Overview of Rules-Based ATP

The rules-based ATP check falls under the advanced method in global ATP and is combined with basic methods (e.g., product availability check) during the ATP check. This method supports various business rules and can be defined based on a company's geographical locations, customer groups, products, or product groups. For example, a computer manufacturer might serve a specific customer from specific warehouses in its network. Unlike the ATP check, which is restricted for checks on a single location (plant), the rules-based ATP feature allows the computer manufacturer to search its entire defined warehouse in sequence for inventory before giving any requirements to the manufacturing location.

Technically, rules-based ATP is supported in sales orders (SAP ERP or SAP CRM), inquires, quotations, scheduling agreements, and STO document types. Where applicable, rules-based ATP (location or product substitution) creates an additional schedule line in sales orders with different item categories to distinguish confirmation based on the rules-based ATP check method.

Let's look at our first business case study, in which the computer manufacturer wants to perform product or location substitution during its customer sales order ATP check.

6.2   Business Case Study I: Product and/or Location Substitution

In our first business case study, we look at the computer manufacturing company using the rules-based ATP method. The company's product is manufactured in multiple sites and is distributed for sales from multiple warehouse locations. During the sales order processing, if the computer product is not available from one warehouse, the company manufacturer wants to ship the products from different locations based on business rules.

The computer manufacturer can introduce a new product to replace an older computer model with a newer one as part of rules-based ATP product substitution. Rules-based ATP is also useful during primary product shortage; the ordered computer can be replaced with same kind of products acceptable to customer. The manufacturer can set business rules to replace a lower-quality product with a higher-quality product. If a product is not available at an alternate location, then production can be triggered at the primary location. Figure 6.1 illustrates rules-based ATP dimensions for product, location substitution, and alternate procurement methods.

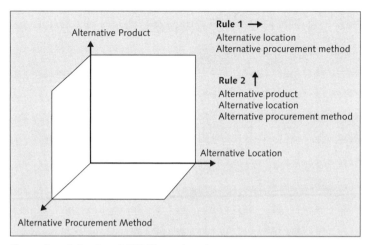

Figure 6.1 Rules-Based ATP Dimensions Axes

Let's look at the basic configuration steps needed to model the product and/or location substitution in global ATP.

6.3   Basic Configuration

The check instructions, condition technique, and integrated rules maintenance are all technical steps that are required to trigger the rules. The check against availability, product allocation, and forecast are all basic methods of availability check. If we combine any two basic methods, this combination becomes an *advanced method*.

Business Example

During the sales seasons, the computer manufacturer may want to reserve a large inventory of high-demand products by quota allocation/reservation of stocks for its customers or distributors in advance.

Define check instructions via IMG • Advanced Planning and Optimization • Global Available-to-Promise • General Settings • Maintain Check Instructions. As shown in Figure 6.2, the first check is the product availability check. You can combine this check with the product allocation check (as a second check) to make it an advanced method.

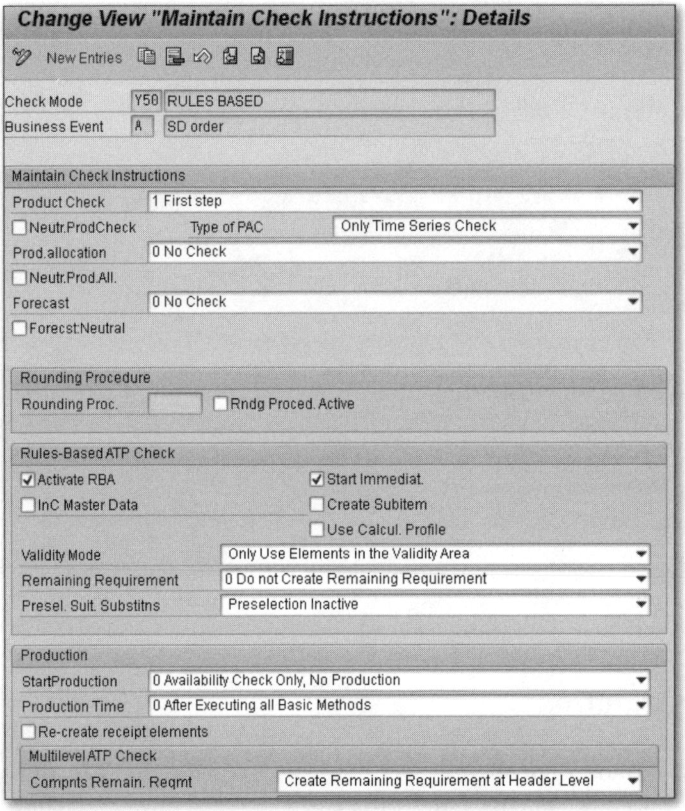

Figure 6.2 Maintain Check Instructions for Rules-Based ATP

The Maintain Check Instructions screen provides a combination of the CHECK MODE (ATP group in SAP ERP) and BUSINESS EVENT boxes (checking rule in SAP ERP). The screen also includes options that control whether product allocation should be executed or not, and if production should be triggered after the availability check or third-party order processing. You can also determine whether or not the ATP check will be rules-based. As shown in Figure 6.2, the ACTIVATE RBA flag sets the ATP as rules-based. The START IMMEDIAT. flag determines whether the system performs a rules-based ATP check for the original (generating) requirement without using rules at first, or if it uses rules immediately. The system performs a rules-based check immediately, and the original requirement is checked afterwards, if necessary, in accordance with the settings in the substitution rules.

In the SAP ERP system, you have to maintain a business transaction and assign it to an order type. Choose the option CUSTOMIZING FOR SALES AND DISTRIBUTION via

BASIC FUNCTIONS • AVAILABILITY CHECK AND TRANSFER OF REQUIREMENTS • AVAILABILITY CHECK • RULES-BASED AVAILABILITY CHECK • DEFINE BUSINESS TRANSACTION AND ASSIGN BUSINESS TRANSACTION TO SALES ORDER TYPE.

6.3.1 Condition Technique

Business rules for product or location substitution are determined using the condition technique. The condition technique provides flexibility to a business to configure complex and constantly changing rules by creating specific business case example to generic condition records. Let's look at how you can customize a condition technique for the computer manufacturer who wants to perform location substitution for one of its key products. Rules will be assigned to the sold to, ship to, and product combination, as shown in Table 6.1. This location substitution can be based on product availability or validity dates.

Sold To	Ship To	Product	Rule for Location Substitution
1200	1210	P100	Location 1 to Location 2
1400	1410	P100	Location 1
1500	1510	P100	Location 1

Table 6.1 Business Scenario of a Rule

The condition technique customization includes the following sequence of technical set up steps, which are further explained in the following subsections:

▸ Define the condition table.

▸ Define the access sequence.

▸ Assign the condition table to the access sequence.

▸ Define the condition type.

▸ Assign the condition access sequence to the condition type.

▸ Define the rule strategy.

▸ Define the rule strategy sequence.

▸ Assign the rule strategy.

▸ Create the condition records.

6.3.2 Define the Condition Table

In the condition table, select the field characteristics to maintain the rules. For our computer manufacturing scenario, we will maintain the ship-to (customer) and product combination to perform the location substitution. Follow the path in IMG • ADVANCED PLANNING AND OPTIMIZATION • GLOBAL AVAILABLE-TO-PROMISE • RULES-BASED AVAILABILITY CHECK • DEFINE CONDITION TABLE. Select the field characteristics of the ship-to party and customer (shown in Figure 6.3 Define the Condition Table) for condition record maintenance.

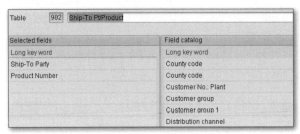

Figure 6.3   Define the Condition Table

6.3.3 Define the Access Sequence

Next, define the access sequence by following the path IMG • ADVANCED PLANNING AND OPTIMIZATION • GLOBAL AVAILABLE-TO-PROMISE • RULES-BASED AVAILABILITY CHECK • MAINTAIN ACCESS SEQUENCE. Assign the condition table to an access sequence by double-clicking the ACCESSES folder (see Figure 6.4).

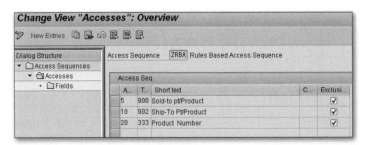

Figure 6.4   Define the Access Sequence

To create an access sequence, proceed as follows:

1. Choose NEW ENTRIES, and enter an alphanumeric key (maximum four digits) and a name.

2. Select the entry, and choose ACCESSES.

3. Choose NEW ENTRIES.

4. In the field SEQUENCE NUMBER, define the sequence of the access within the access sequence. Enter a sequence number, even if you are only defining one access.

6.3.4 Define the Condition Type

Now you can define the condition type and assign the access sequence to the condition type (see Figure 6.5).

Figure 6.5 Define the Condition Type and Assign the Access Sequence

The configuration path is IMG • ADVANCED PLANNING AND OPTIMIZATION • GLOBAL AVAILABLE-TO-PROMISE • RULES-BASED AVAILABILITY CHECK • MAINTAIN CONDITION TYPE. On the resulting screen, follow these steps to create a condition type:

1. Define an alphanumeric value (maximum four digits), and specify a name.

2. Assign an access sequence to the condition type by choosing an access sequence.

6.3.5 Define the Rule Strategy and Assign the Condition Type

Next, define the rule strategy, and assign the condition type to the rules strategy. The configuration path to do this is IMG • ADVANCED PLANNING AND OPTIMIZATION • GLOBAL AVAILABLE-TO-PROMISE • RULES-BASED AVAILABILITY CHECK • MAINTAIN RULE STRATEGY. To create a rule strategy (shown in Figure 6.6), proceed as follows:

1. Choose NEW ENTRIES, and enter a value.

2. Determine the rule strategy type (INCLUSIVE or EXCLUSIVE).

3. Enter a name for the rule strategy in the STRATEGY column.

Figure 6.6 Define the Rule Strategy

4. Assign the condition type to the rule strategy by double-clicking the CONTROL DATA folder (shown in Figure 6.7).

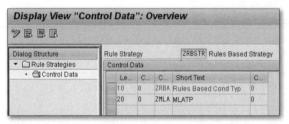

Figure 6.7 Assign the Condition Types to the Rule Strategy

6.3.6 Define the New Rule Strategy Sequence

You can define the rule strategy sequence to determine which rule strategies the system evaluates together and the sequence in which the system evaluates these rule strategies. The configuration path is IMG • ADVANCED PLANNING AND OPTI-MIZATION • GLOBAL AVAILABLE-TO-PROMISE • RULES-BASED AVAILABILITY CHECK • MAINTAIN RULE STRATEGY SEQUENCE.

To create a rule strategy sequence, proceed as follows:

1. Create a rule strategy sequence (e.g., "ZSEQ").

2. Assign rule strategies to the rule strategy sequence under CONTROL. Determine the sequence in which the system is to evaluate the inclusive rule strategies by allocating rule strategy numbers (see Figure 6.8).

Figure 6.8 Define the Rule Strategy Sequence

Next, you need to assign a rule strategy with a combination of TECHNICAL SCE-NARIO, ACTION TYPE, and BUSINESS TRANSACTION function options (as shown in Figure 6.9).

T	B...	A	R...	Strategy	Handling of CP	
	ZOR	A	ZSEQ		0 Substitute	▼
AA			ZSEQ		0 Substitute	▼
AA	ZOR	A	ZSEQ		0 Substitute	▼
AA	ZOR	B	ZSEQ		0 Substitute	▼
AA	ZOR	C	ZSEQ		0 Substitute	▼
AA	ZORA			ZRBSTR	0 Substitute	▼
BB	ZOR	A		ZRBSTR	0 Substitute	▼
BB	ZOR	B		ZRBSTR	0 Substitute	▼
BB	ZOR	C		ZRBSTR	0 Substitute	▼
EE	ZOR	A		ZRBSTR	0 Substitute	▼
EE	ZOR	B		ZRBSTR	0 Substitute	▼
EE	ZOR	C		ZRBSTR	0 Substitute	▼

Assign Rule Strategy or Rule Strategy Sequence

Figure 6.9 Assign a Strategy or Strategy Sequence to the Technical Scenario, Business Event, and Action Type

Technical Scenario

The TECHNICAL SCENARIO option represents the business transaction we perform for the computer manufacturer. Examples of the technical scenario are AA (online sales order), BB (batch processing), EE (backorder processing), and DD (EDI processing). These values are hardcoded in the SAP system.

Action Type

The ACTION TYPE option corresponds to any change, update, or deletion of the sales orders based on computer business requirements. Possible manipulation techniques include creating, changing, and copying transaction data (e.g., "A" for create a sales order, "B" for change a sales order, and "C" for copy a sales order).

Business Transaction

The BUSINESS TRANSACTION option for the computer manufacturer corresponds to the business context in which a rules-based ATP check should be carried out. The business transaction is created in SD and assigned to an order type.

Now that we've finished the configuration steps, the next step is to maintain rules in the master data.

6.4 Basic Master Data: Rule Maintenance

Master data for rules-based ATP primarily consists of basic master data, as described in Chapter 4, together with rule maintenance. In this section, we will only focus on the integrated rule maintenance that you can access via Transaction /SAPAPO/ RBA04. Integrated rule maintenance has many components (rule, rule type, location or product determination procedure, rule control, calculation profile, and activity type), which we will explain in the following subsections.

To perform location substitution for our computer manufacturing scenario, we first need to identify the rule type required for the business case. The different kinds of rule types are listed in Table 6.1.

Rule Type	Rule Description
Inclusive	The substitute products and locations defined in an inclusive rule are incorporated into the substitution list.
Exclusive	The substitute products and locations defined in an exclusive rule are excluded from the substitution list.
MISL	The locations for MISL are listed in the rule category. The system transfers the determined locations to the rules-based ATP check of the individual items. The system checks whether one of the locations from this substitution list can supply the complete requirement of a requirements grouping.
Alternative	The substitute locations defined in an alternative rule are incorporated into the substitution list as alternatives for excluded locations.

Table 6.2 Different Types of Rule Types Available in Global ATP

For our business scenario, we will use the inclusive rule type whereby the products can be sourced from either locations. Next, we need to define the location determination procedure. The location determination procedure has a list of locations for substitution. If a product is not available at a location, the system proposes a second location that you have maintained in the location determination procedure. You can define the location determination procedure in the following types:

▸ Substitution chain (only serial structures allowed; e.g., Loc1→Loc2→Loc3)

▸ Network (no restrictions defined; e.g., Loc1→Loc2, Loc2→Loc3)

▸ Fan-shaped structure (only single-level branching allowed; e.g., Loc1→Loc2, Loc1→Loc3)

▸ List (serial structure, single values possible) for SAP CRM

▸ Alternative (only single-level branching allowed)

Similarly, you can define a product determination procedure in the rule for lists of products to be substituted. For our computer manufacturer scenario, we will use the substitution chain listing all the ATP check locations in serial order. Figure 6.10 displays the integrated rule maintenance transaction with the location determination procedure assigned.

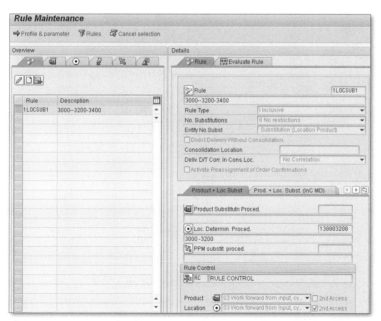

Figure 6.10 Integrated Rule Maintenance

Let's look at other components within integrated rule maintenance.

6.4.1 Rule Control

Rule-control strategies (product and location strategy) control check processing in a single list. The product strategy control checks processing in a product substitution list. The location strategy control checks processing is in a location determination list. Figure 6.11 illustrates the strategies that are used in the rule control.

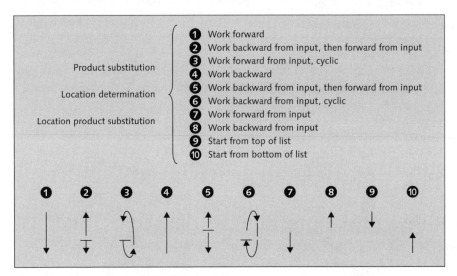

Figure 6.11 Access Strategies for Rule Control

The qualified product or the qualified location is used to restrict the substitution list. Figure 6.12 shows the rule control maintenance in the master data. For our computer manufacturer scenario, we use the *work forward from input, cyclic* ❸ case.

Define the combination rule sequence of products and locations on which the ATP check will be performed in the following two combinations:

▶ COMBINE QUALIFIED LOCATION WITH ALL PRODUCTS: All products from the product substitution list are combined with the locations from the restricted location substitution list.

▶ COMBINE QUALIFIED PRODUCT WITH ALL LOCATIONS: All locations from the location substitution list are combined with the products from the restricted product substitution list.

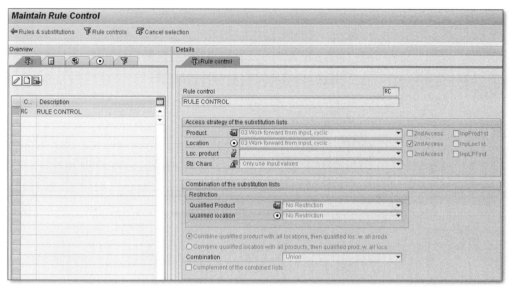

Figure 6.12 Rule Control with Access Strategy Maintenance

If you flag the second access, the system executes the rule even if the delivering plant from SAP ERP is not specified in the rules of location determination procedure. The same procedure applies to the material as well—if the material is not included in the product determination procedure, then this rule is executed anyway.

6.4.2 Calculation Profile

The calculation profile determines the number of days by which the confirmed material availability date (MAD) is permitted to differ from the determined MAD for a delayed confirmation to be permissible. You can use the calculation profile to define the package size; for example, if you want the ATP check to confirm only in regards to a full pallet.

6.4.3 Activity Type

In an activity, you maintain a number of actions that are carried out if a determination is executed. The activity type is maintained through rule control. The activities list consists of the following:

▶ MEANS OF TRANSP.: Transportation mode for shipping the goods.

▶ BUSINESS EVENT: Specify the business transactions (for example, sales order or delivery) for which ATP needs to be performed.

▶ CHECK MODE: Determines the scope of ATP check.

▶ STARTPRODUCTION: Linked with a make-to-order (MTO) scenario to trigger production on ATP shortages.

▶ STOCK TRANSFER: Check mark this option to automatically create stock transport requisitions (STRs) from the source location during the global ATP check.

Figure 6.13 shows the business example for the computer manufacturer to source the product from the third-party suppliers if not available in its warehouses. This is a type of external procurement in which a purchase order (PO) is issued to a vendor with the instruction to supply the ordered materials to a third party.

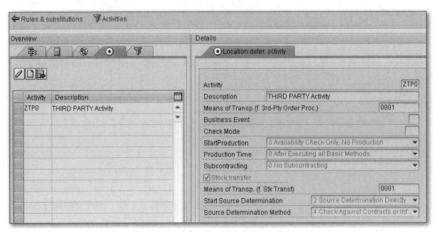

Figure 6.13 Activity Type Maintained for the Third-Party Processing

6.4.4 Maintaining Condition Records

A condition record serves as the master data in establishing the link between the rule and the product number. You can maintain the condition records for rules (see Figure 6.14) via Transaction /SAPCND/AO11, or menu path ADVANCED PLANNING AND OPTIMIZATION • MASTER DATA • RULE MAINTENANCE • /SAPCND/AO11 – CREATE RULE DETERMINATION. Here, you can assign the rule to the key field, which is the product number for our business scenario.

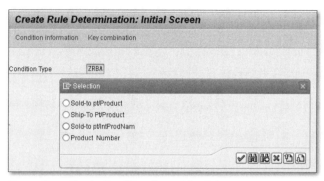

Figure 6.14 Create Condition Record for Rule

The access sequence is defined in a condition record, so if a record exists for SHIP-TO PT/PRODUCT combination, it will take precedence over the rule for PRODUCT NUMBER (see Figure 6.15). Per the condition technique, the access sequence has an EXCLUSIVE indicator for access 10. Due to this indicator, the system does not search for additional records after the first successful access to a record for a condition type in an access sequence.

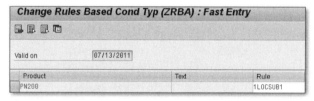

Figure 6.15 Create Condition Record for Key Fields

Now that we've discussed the customization rules for the rules-based ATP check, let's now look at the key steps for performing the business transactions.

6.5   Scenario Testing for Location Substitution

The computer manufacturer business users can evaluate the location substitution rules in the simulation mode to validate that the rules defined are correct. The simulation is performed via Transaction /SAPAPO/AC04, or ADVANCED PLANNING AND OPTIMIZATION • GLOBAL ATP • REPORTING • /SAPAPO/AC04 – ATP SIMULATION.

Using simulation in the SAP SCM system will verify that rules are configured correctly and the fields required to execute a rule exist. This transaction validates not only the rule customization, but also the master data in the form of the condition record and integrated rule maintenance.

> **Note**
>
> Alphanumeric material does not require leading zeros in the fields of the characteristics, but numeric material *does* require leading zeros.

Figure 6.16 shows an example of location substitution, where computer product PN200 has a requirement of 1,000 pieces. At the primary location, 0 pieces are available, so the alternative location 3000 is substituted by 3200.

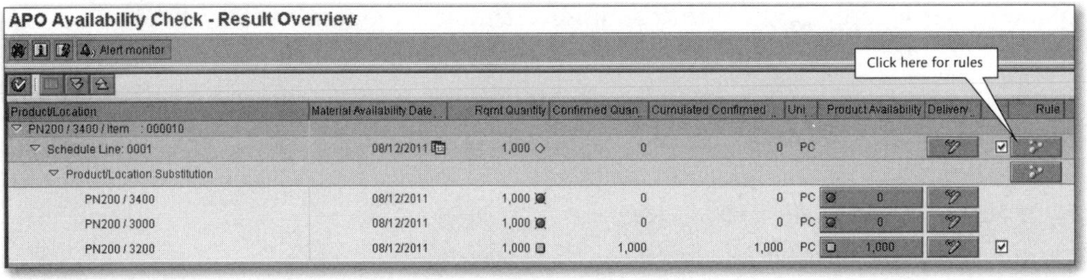

Figure 6.16 Product Availability Check Using Rules-Based Planning

Note in the screen that besides the quantity display, there is also visual representation in the form of colored traffic lights; the red traffic light icon represents zero confirmation, the yellow traffic light represents partial confirmation, and the green traffic light shows full confirmation. Additionally, the business users can access the rules that were triggered by our configuration steps in the prior section from the APO AVAILABILITY CHECK: RESULT OVERVIEW screen shown in Figure 6.16; for example, if you click LOC. DETERMIN. PROCED. shown in Figure 6.17, you can see the locations included in the procedure.

You can also view the computer product characteristics of the field catalog from the AVAILABILITY CHECK screen by clicking the "i" blue icon (see Figure 6.18). The information presented in this screen is very useful to determine what sales orders detail is being passed from SAP ERP to SAP APO for rules-based ATP.

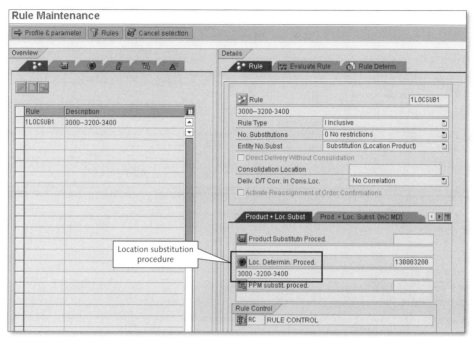

Figure 6.17 Understanding Location Substitution

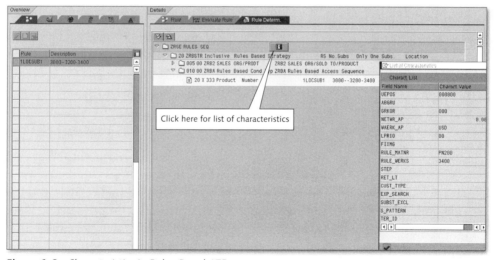

Figure 6.18 Characteristics in Rules-Based ATP

The condition record field value can be viewed again from the AVAILABILITY CHECK screen as well by clicking the "i" blue icon (see Figure 6.19).

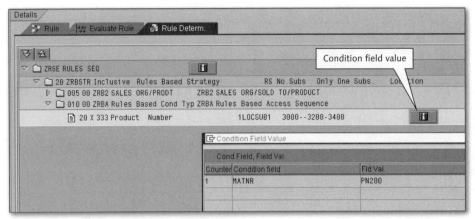

Figure 6.19 Condition Field Value in Rules-Based ATP

Let's see some additional business scenarios other than regular sales orders that can use rules-based ATP, such as consolidation locations, STOs, and scheduling agreements, in the following sections.

6.6 Business Case Study II: Consolidation Location

Our second business case study focuses on the export business for the computer manufacturer. The company combines its export sales orders into a single shipment while shipping the goods overseas. For this business scenario, global ATP provides the *consolidation location* functionality, which matches business requirement to consolidate products from different locations and further consolidate the products into a single delivery.

Figure 6.20 shows a business scenario in which the customers raise export sales orders on the consolidation location (plant 3000) where the ATP check fails. Using the earlier configured location substitution rules, it searches inventory at a warehouse location (plant 3200). If fulfilled, the source location creates STRs to fulfill the sales orders. If the ATP check fails in 3200, the manufacturing location (plant 3400) is given the requirement, which may trigger production. The manufacturing location creates the STR to the consolidation location with full confirmation of the computer product ordered.

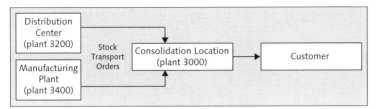

Figure 6.20 Consolidation Location Business Scenario

During the ATP check, the system creates an ATP tree structure in the background that stores the details of the simulated STRs. The sales orders are confirmed based on these STRs. To convert an ATP structure to an STR, you must have one of the following options configured in your system:

▶ PP/DS horizon maintained in the product master.

▶ PP/DS horizon maintained in the planning version (Transaction /SAPAPO/MVM – Model and Version Management).

▶ Customized global settings of PP/DS (Transaction /SAPAPO/RRPCUST1). The menu path is IMG • ADVANCED PLANNING AND OPTIMIZATION • SUPPLY CHAIN PLANNING • PRODUCTION PLANNING AND DETAILED SCHEDULING (PP/DS) • GLOBAL SETTINGS • MAINTAIN GLOBAL PARAMETERS AND DEFAULTS. The user can maintain the horizon in days for which the system should convert the confirmed ATP tree structures into STRs. The maintenance is done in the PLANNING tab under the field SCHED. HORIZON FOR ATP TREE STRUCTURES (see Figure 6.21).

The number of days specified in SCHEDULING HORIZON FOR ATP STRUCTURES is used to immediately convert the ATP tree structure into a procurement proposal (e.g., STR). The duration of the scheduling horizon is defined in calendar days. If none of these conditions are met when the sales order is saved, the system saves the ATP tree structure. You can convert the ATP tree structure with requirement dates outside the scheduling horizon (PP/DS horizon) using the following two options:

▶ Transaction /SAPAPO/RRP_ATP2PPDS (Conversion of ATP Tree Structures) is used to maintain the offset to the scheduling horizon.

▶ Transaction /SAPAPO/ATP2PPDS (Conversion of ATP Tree Structure in Background) is used to convert the ATP tree structure into an STR in the background.

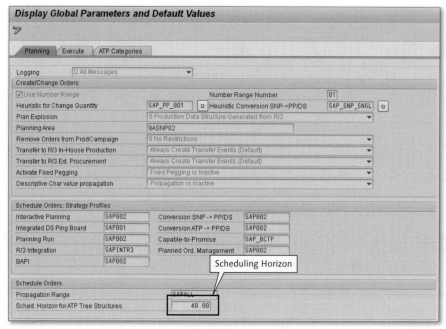

Figure 6.21 Scheduling Horizon for ATP Tree Structure

Next, let's look at an example of a consolidated scenario, which was illustrated earlier. Plant 3000 is a consolidated location. In the case of a product shortage at plant 3000, an STO is created from plant 3400 to 3000, although the delivering plant in the sales order remains plant 3000 (see Figure 6.22). (Note the delivering plant at line item.)

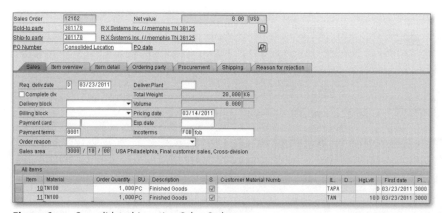

Figure 6.22 Consolidated Location Sales Order

The delivery proposal shown in Figure 6.23 shows partial confirmation from the primary plant (200 units), and a balance from the alternate plant (800 units), against the total demand of 1,000 units.

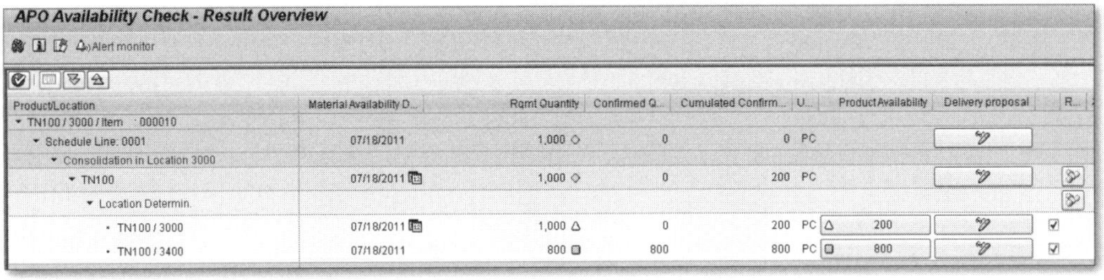

Figure 6.23 Consolidated Location Delivery Proposal

You can see the STR created at consolidated location 3000 in the SAP APO product view, which you access via Transaction /SAPAPO/RRP3.

The transportation lane master data is required between the source and destination location for the STR creation.

The RULE (11CONSLOC) required to activate the consolidated location is shown in Figure 6.24. Make sure that the DIRECT DELIVERY WITHOUT CONSOLIDATION flag is not checked, or location consolidation will not occur.

You can use the DELIV. D/T CORR. IN CONS. LOC. (delivery date and time correlation the consolidation location) field to deliver all products that have been transferred to a consolidation location to a customer on one specific date. The system can perform the delivery date/time correlation in one of two ways:

▶ **Simple correlation**
The system determines a common unloading date for all products in the consolidation location. This common unloading date can lead to dates that have already been confirmed in the source locations being changed. When it performs a simple correlation, the system does not check whether the new dates/times in the source locations are still valid.

▶ **Correlation with second check step**
The system performs the delivery date/time correlation in the same ways as for a simple correlation. In addition, the system checks if the new dates/times in the source locations are valid.

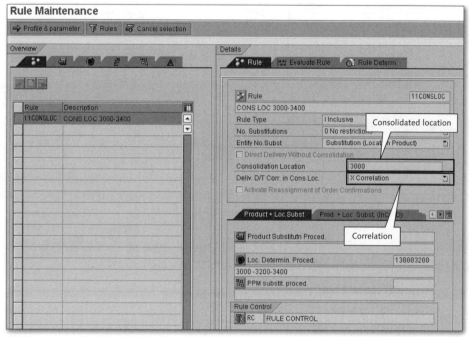

Figure 6.24 Rule for Consolidated Location

6.7   Business Case Study III: Stock Transport Orders

Our third business case study focuses on replenishment orders between the computer manufacturer warehouse locations. The computer manufacturer performs weekly replenishment of final computer products from its central warehouses to its regional warehouses. The STOs are created to move the stock between plants in a company. For example, the computer manufacturer may want to substitute a computer product with another model of the computer product in the STO in case of non-availability at the supplying plant. The STO can also use rules-based material substitution. Whenever alternate material is proposed due to non-availability of the primary product, the system creates an additional line item with a sub-item. You'll find the customization steps needed to model this business scenario in global ATP in the following subsections.

6.7.1   Configuration in SAP ERP

The following two steps are needed as configuration steps in SAP ERP:

▶ Define and assign the requirement profile (profile at requirements level for SAP APO) to a purchasing document (STO) type. The same requirement profile will be assigned to the strategy in SAP SCM. The configuration path is IMG • MATE-RIALS MANAGEMENT • PURCHASING • PURCHASE ORDER • SET UP STOCK TRANSPORT ORDER • DEFINE REQUIREMENT PROFILE.

▶ After you have defined the requirement profile, assign the requirement profile to a delivery type and checking rule (e.g., Z001). The configuration path to do this is IMG • MATERIALS MANAGEMENT • PURCHASING • PURCHASE ORDER • SET UP STOCK TRANSPORT ORDER • ASSIGN DELIVERY TYPE AND CHECKING RULE. Figure 6.25 shows the screen for a specific purchase order (UB) and supplying plant (3000) combination, the assignment of delivery type (NL), requirement profile (RP), and checking rule (Z001) for ATP check on the replenishment order for inter-plant transfers.

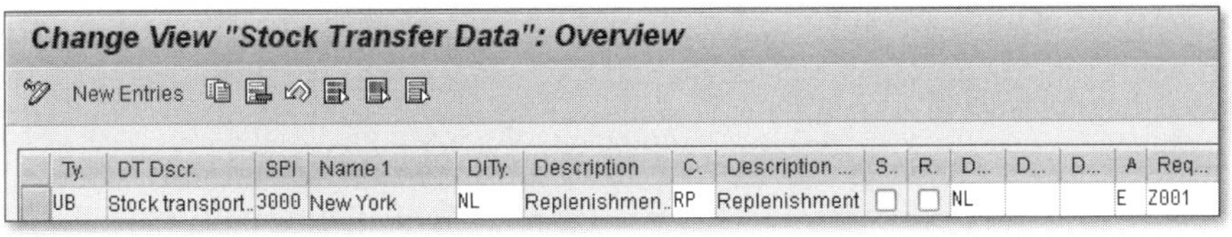

Change View "Stock Transfer Data": Overview

Ty.	DT Dscr.	SPl	Name 1	DlTy.	Description	C.	Description ...	S.	R.	D...	D...	D...	A	Req...
UB	Stock transport.	3000	New York	NL	Replenishmen..RP	RP	Replenishment	☐	☐	NL			E	Z001

Figure 6.25 Assign Requirement Profile to STO Type in SAP ERP

6.7.2 Configuration in SAP APO

Next, maintain the requirement profile in SAP APO. The menu path to do this is IMG • ADVANCED PLANNING AND OPTIMIZATION • GLOBAL AVAILABLE-TO-PROMISE (GLOBAL ATP) • GENERAL SETTINGS • REQUIREMENTS PROFILE • MAINTAIN REQUIRE-MENTS PROFILE. Assign CATEGORY "BI" (from the drop-down list), BUSINESS EVENT "RP" (checking rule in SAP ERP), and TECH. SCENARIO "AA" to the requirement profile Z001.

Maintain the rule strategy sequence via the path IMG • ADVANCED PLANNING AND OPTIMIZATION • GLOBAL AVAILABLE-TO-PROMISE (GLOBAL ATP) • RULES-BASED AVAIL-ABILITY CHECK • ASSIGN RULE STRATEGY OR RULE STRATEGY SEQUENCE.

Assign rule strategy sequence to TECH. SCENARIO "AA," and make sure that you keep BUSINESS TRANSACTION and ACTION TYPE blank so that they are applicable for all the sales order changes, updates, or deleted business transactions.

> **Note**
>
> For stock transfers in SAP ERP, the value for the ACTION TYPE remains the initial default value. The remaining configuration related to the condition technique remains the same.

> **Business Case**
>
> There is a shortage of the computer product PN200, so PN200 is substituted by a different comparable model (PN100) that the customer will accept. This creates additional sub-items in an STO. These sub-items behave just like sub-items of sales orders; that is, the availability check can be triggered again on a saved STO.

The availability check in the delivery proposal of the STO explains how rules are determined using the condition technique (see Figure 6.26).

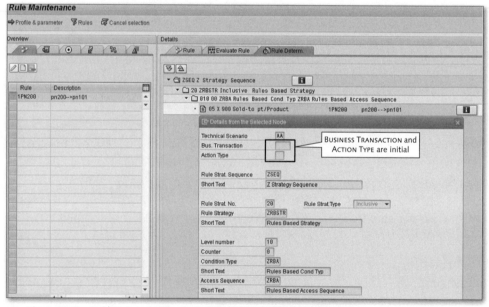

Figure 6.26 Rule Determination in the Stock Transport Order Scenario

The condition technique is used in this case to determine the rule. You can maintain condition records by a combination of sold-to and product via Transaction /SAPCND/AO11. In the STO setup in SAP ERP, you can assign the customer number to the shipping data of the receiving plant. The same customer is the sold to in this case, as visible in Table T001W and field KUNNR.

6.8   Business Case Study IV: Sales Scheduling Agreement

Our last business case study for the computer manufacturer looks at the sales scheduling agreement. The sales scheduling agreement is accessed via Transaction VA31. The document contains the details of the delivery schedule, and the deliveries are made to the customer per the schedule entered in the document.

Rules can be triggered for the sales scheduling agreement (type DS) based on defined business rules. The configuration for rules-based product or location substitution is similar to what happens with sales orders. In SAP ERP, the business transaction is assigned to the scheduling agreement. In SAP APO, the condition technique and other configurations explained earlier invoke rules-based product or location substitution. Figure 6.27 shows sub-items in a scheduling agreement due to product substitution.

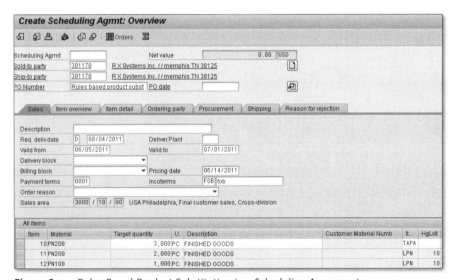

Figure 6.27 Rules-Based Product Substitution in a Scheduling Agreement

6.9 Enhancements

During implementation of global ATP, the computer manufacturer realizes that to meet business requirements that are not supported in SAP ERP standard programs, additional enhancements are required in the form of custom developments. The enhancements can be implemented either in the SAP ERP or global ATP systems as explained in the following subsections.

6.9.1 Enhancements in the SAP ERP Field Catalog for Rules-Based ATP

You can use enhancements in SAP ERP to create additional field characteristics for the condition records applicable for the rules-based ATP checks. For example, in the sales order approval process, the ATP check should trigger product substitution only after the approval of the sales order line item.

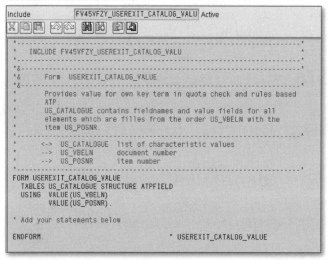

Figure 6.28 Enhancing Field Catalog for Z Fields in the User Exit

For this requirement, use the user exit INCLUDE FV45VFZY_USEREXIT_CATA-LOG_VALU (see Figure 6.28) to create custom fields for a field catalog; the Z fields can be added by appending US_CATALOG during runtime. We will define a custom field ZAPPROVAL and business scenario to create a condition record by

ZAPPROVAL. If a user approves a line item on the sales order, only then should the rule for product substitution be triggered. This field will be passed in the user exit FV45VFZY_USEREXIT_CATALOG_VALU as ZAPPROVAL.

> **Note**
>
> SAP OSS Notes 376773, 385039, 993452, and 174969 provide very detailed information about adding Z fields in SAP ERP and in SAP APO.

6.9.2 Enhancement in SAP APO for Global ATP

The enhancement possibility in SAP APO for global ATP can be similar to the process of adding custom fields for the condition records. The enhancement can also be extended toward master data for mass upload during the implementation phase. You can enhance structure /SAPAPO/KOMGOZ for the Z field that is required by the computer manufacturer to define business rules for the substitution. The custom Z field is added in user exit INCLUDE FV45VFZY_USEREXIT_CATALOG_VALU during the rules-based ATP check of computer manufacturer sales order.

For our second example scenario, the business add-in (BAdI) for creating master data for rules in integrated rules maintenance is /SAPAPO/RBA_RBAS, which you can use to automate the process of rules creation (as discussed in Section 6.4) from a flat file, Excel sheet, or the SAP ERP system interface. This is primarily required with the data migration or data conversion activities during the implementation or major organizational structural changes during the post implementation phase. The system calls the active BAdI within integrated rule maintenance when you save changes to master data to automatically create rules. In a rules-based ATP check, the rule evaluation can be influenced by this enhancement. You can activate this enhancement if the evaluation controls implemented do not satisfy the business requirements. The influence exerted can lead to two different points in time in the rule evaluation:

▶ **Time 1: Before determination of the rules**

  ▶ Before the rules are determined, the parameters, which are used to select the rules, can be changed (function module EXIT_/SAPAPO/SAPLATPR_001).

  ▶ During a rule evaluation, this point in time can be reached several times. Note that for the same entries, the same modifications will be carried out.

▶ **Time 2: After evaluation of the rules**

- ▶ After evaluation of the rules, the result of rule evaluation can be post-processed (function module EXIT_/SAPAPO/SAPLATPR_002).

- ▶ This point in time is always reached if the evaluation of the rules has delivered substitutions for the requested location product for which an availability check can be carried out; that is, the point in time can be passed through several times per requirement.

These user exits can be used to influence the results from a rule. For example, a user might maintain a list of products in the product substitution procedure, and the business requirement is to exclude certain products with the ABC indicator as C.

6.10 Summary

As you learned in this chapter, rules-based ATP allows for location or product substitution, which is done per business logic. Rules-based ATP can be freely combined with any other ATP techniques wherever required or used independently. The check method is primarily used to promise availability of products whose inventories are spread across multiple locations. This method is also used for confirming availability to customers wherever product substitutes exist and are acceptable.

This chapter explained four different business scenarios for a computer manufacturer using rules-based ATP checks. The first business scenario was the location and/or product substitution for optimizing inventory across a network before giving the requirements to the manufacturing plant. The second case study looked at the export business for consolidation of computer products for export sales. The third scenario looked at inter-location replenishment using STOs. The last scenario studied the sales scheduling agreement. These scenarios used different rules-based ATP techniques to model the business requirements of both the sales and replenishment process.

The chapter explained the basic configuration and master data requirement to make all these business scenarios work with the rules-based ATP functionality and closed by explaining a few different enhancement possibilities in SAP ERP and global ATP in terms of the rules-based ATP check.

The next chapter studies how companies can use the product allocation functionality to allocate products across its distribution chains based on business rules.

Product allocation is the tool used by businesses to manage demand against constrained supply. You can manage ATP based on business rules, rather than a first come, first serve basis.

7 Managing Your Supply Chain ATP with Product Allocation

In today's competitive order-processing environment, companies are challenged to deliver the requested quantity of a product to the customer at the requested time. Unpredictable problems, such as breakdowns in production or increased demand, can lead to critical situations in order processing that must be brought under control before they develop further. Product allocations provide control and enable your company to avoid these critical situations in demand and procurement.

In this chapter, we'll follow a real-world example of a computer PC manufacturing company to explain the global ATP product allocation concept and how you can customize it in the system. The product allocation uses the SAP APO demand planning (DP) concept, integrated with global ATP to offer flexibility to businesses to allocate stocks on customer orders.

7.1 Overview of Product Allocation in Global ATP

Product allocation represents total allocation quantity, which can't be more than the incoming customer orders for a material in a specific time period. It can also be termed as a quota for allocation of inventory, based on business rules. The product allocation can support the following business scenarios:

▶ **Allocation of quantity during peak period**
During inventory shortage, the PC manufacturer prioritizes the allocation of inventory to its key customers yielding high profit margins.

▶ **Products with a volume promotion**
During a sales and marketing promotion, the PC manufacturer performs quantity allocation to its distributor for equal distribution of its products.

▶ **Products in short stock supply**
Due to raw material or manufacturing constraints, the PC manufacturer allocates inventory based on business profit margin.

▶ **Products prior to a price increase**
Sales increase of computer items in the promotion periods before the product returns back to its retail price.

▶ **Seasonal products**
The PC manufacturer distributes its products across all channels with proper allocation.

Depending on your company's sales and operation planning process cycle, you may decide to allocate products for specific customers or regions on a weekly or monthly bucket. The restriction criteria are flexible to your company's needs. If you use product allocation when a product is in short supply, you can avoid allocating the entire available quantity to the first customer, which would either delay the confirmation of subsequent sales orders or make confirmation impossible.

Figure 7.1 illustrates what happens when product allocation is performed in global ATP:

❶ During the sales order creation process, the ATP check is triggered. The product allocation falls under the advanced check method with the combination of the basic product availability check. The confirmed quantity from the basic check method performed against stock and receipts can be further checked against the product allocation defined quantity.

❷ The ATP quantity is checked further with the product allocation group in global ATP. The product allocation group splits the sales order quantity based on the specific customer or region.

❸ The incoming sales order quantity becomes the input to the demand allocation planning. The quota allocation is maintained in DP for a characteristics combination, which aggregates and disaggregates the incoming order quantity and passes the allocation quantity back to global ATP. The confirmations in the sales orders are based on what the allocations are for the criteria that you preset in allocation planning.

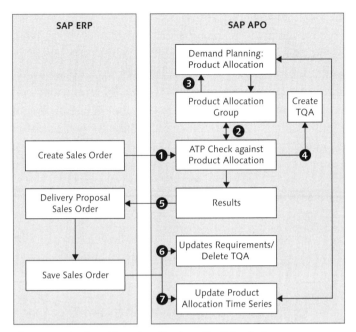

Figure 7.1 Product Allocation Check on the Sales Order

❹ A temporary quantity assignment (TQA) is created on the result allocated quantity before passing back to SAP ERP.

❺ The result is seen as a delivery proposal for the sales order before the order is saved in SAP ERP.

❻ After the sales order is confirmed, the TQA is deleted, and the confirmation is updated in the sales order.

❼ Also during the sales order save, the product allocation order quantity is saved in the SAP APO time series, which again is synchronous with demand allocation planning.

Now that we've discussed the product allocation concept, let's look at a business case study focused on using the functionality.

7.2 Business Case Study: Product Allocation

The PC manufacturing company operates in many countries and has three sales organizations defined. The company wants to allocate its computer products based on each sales organization and customer group. The sales organization can have more than one customer group based on its market distribution channel (e.g., retail or wholesaler). Based on its operational sales plan, the PC manufacturer wants to allocate its product distribution per the schema displayed in Figure 7.2, which shows the hypothetical schema of customers' consumption by sales order and other characteristics. Businesses can provide allocation in different channels, and the same product can be allocated to different sales organizations as well as within the same sales organization to different customer groups.

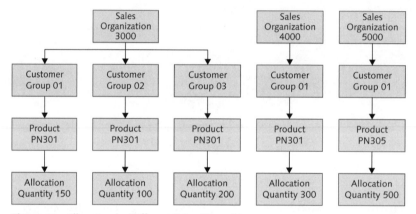

Figure 7.2   Allocation by Different Sales Hierarchies

Table 7.1 illustrates that customer groups 01 and 02 have allocations of 150 units and 100 units of computer products, respectively, while the other customer groups (e.g., 03 or 04) in sales organization 3000 have an allocation of 200 units. Other customer groups in different sales organizations have product allocations of 300 units (# used as a wild card represents all the possible values for the field characteristics). Other customer groups in different sales organization for a different product (PN305) have allocations of 500 units.

Product Allocation Object	Product	Sales Organization	Customer Group	Product Allocation Quantity
ZPAOBJ3	################	####	##	500
ZPAOBJ3	PN301	####	##	300

Table 7.1   Quantity Allocation Based on Sales Organization and Customer Group Combination

Product Allocation Object	Product	Sales Organization	Customer Group	Product Allocation Quantity
ZPAOBJ3	PN301	3000	##	200
ZPAOBJ3	PN301	3000	01	150
ZPAOBJ3	PN301	3000	02	100

Table 7.1 Quantity Allocation Based on Sales Organization and Customer Group Combination (Cont.)

Now that we've reviewed the business case study, let's look at the customization steps you need to model this scenario using the global ATP product allocation functionality.

7.3 Basic Configuration of Product Allocation in SAP APO

Customization of product allocation can be broadly divided into two areas: demand planning (DP) and allocation group.

SAP APO DP configuration consists primarily of designing the planning books for the PC manufacturer business users to enter the allocation quota based on a characteristics combination. It consists of the configuration objects planning object structure, planning area, and planning book.

Global ATP allocation group configuration consists of configuring allocation groups and allocation procedures for confirming the sales orders during the ATP check. This consists of the following configuration objects:

▶ Field catalog for characteristics
▶ Product allocation object
▶ Product allocation group
▶ Consumption period
▶ Product allocation procedure
▶ Connection to planning area
▶ Product allocation settings

Let's first look at the three DP configuration objects in the following subsection.

7.3.1   Creating a New Planning Object Structure

You assign a characteristics combination in the planning object structure. The characteristics are the objects taken from the product and customer hierarchy, which businesses use for planning purposes. Characteristics can be the sales organization, customer group, sales district, or product used for selecting data records.

Using Transaction /SAPAPO/MSDP_ADMIN, you can create a planning object structure named ZPRDALL to assign the required characteristics for the computer manufacturing scenario. Assign the product allocation group, product, sales organization, and sold-to customer to the master planning object structure by transferring the relevant characteristics from the right column to the left column, as shown in Figure 7.3.

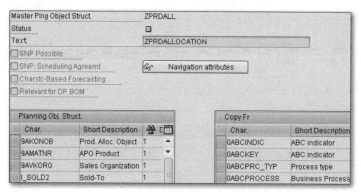

Figure 7.3   Creating a New Planning Object Structure

Similarly, you can create a second planning object structure ZATP3 with the characteristics product allocation object, product, sales organization, and customer group.

7.3.2   Creating a New Planning Area

Next, you need to create the planning area to define the basic planning parameters used by the PC manufacturer. The basic parameters can be the planning base unit of measure used for planning, currency used for financial calculation, storage bucket profile (historical and future horizon the planning data is stored in SAP liveCache) for historical and future data analysis, and key figures. The key figures are the reporting elements for a specific characteristic, and the values entered are stored in the SAP liveCache as a time-series object. The planning area is created using Transaction

/SAPAPO/MSDP_ADMIN. You link the planning area with the planning object structure created earlier and inherit characteristics in this way.

As shown in Figure 7.4, maintain the two key figures in the KEY FIGS tab (accessed via Transaction /SAPAPO/MSDP_ADMIN). The first key figure is the incoming sale orders that the PC manufacturer needs to allocate quantity. The second key figure is the allocation quantity that the PC manufacturer can confirm with the customers after the allocation quota calculation.

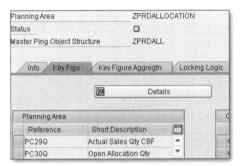

Figure 7.4 Planning Area with Key Figure Assignment

> **Note**
>
> Always run Report /SAPAPO/TS_PAREA_INITIALIZE to initialize the new planning area for creating new planning time-series objects. In the report selection, input information regarding the planning area and the planning time horizons.

7.3.3 Define a New Planning Book

The PC manufacturer business users use a *planning book* to define the percentage or quantity allocation for the characteristics combination. Depending on this allocation percentage or quantity, the business users can view the allocated quantity confirmation for the customer. The planning book serves as a business decision support tool for the users to adjust the allocation plan before the release to SAP ERP.

The planning book is linked with the planning area created earlier and inherits the characteristics and key figures in this manner. The assignment is done in Transaction /SAPAPO/SDP8B by following the menu path EDIT • ASSIGN PLANNING AREA. The business user can visualize the allocation as described in Table 7.1 (shown earlier) in the planning book for a characteristics combination set. The planning book is created using Transaction /SAPAPO/SDP8B and can include multiple data views. The data view defines which key figures are visible to the business planners for which characteristics combination. It also defines the time horizon for which the data view is applicable, as shown in Figure 7.5 (52 weeks).

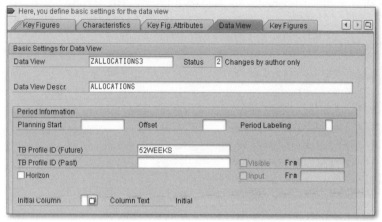

Figure 7.5 Planning Book Definition

SAP provides a planning book wizard that takes you through the steps to create the custom planning book. You can select the key figures and move from the Planning Area to Planning Book by clicking on the ADDITION icon.

This completes the basic configuration for SAP APO DP. The remaining subsections focus on the allocation group.

7.3.4 Maintain Field Catalog for Characteristics

Global ATP provides standard characteristics from product and customer hierarchies for allocation, which are used to define allocations in the field catalog. For our PC manufacturer, the characteristics selected are customer group, sold-to customer, sales organization, and product to be used for product allocation. The characteristics are selected based on how the company markets its product to customers. For our business scenario, the PC manufacturer distributes its products to different customer groups based on region and sales volume (e.g., retail or wholesale). The configuration path to choose these characteristics is IMG SPRO • ADVANCED PLANNING AND OPTIMIZATION • GLOBAL AVAILABLE-TO-PROMISE (GLOBAL ATP) • BASED AVAILABILITY CHECK • PRODUCT ALLOCATION • MAINTAIN FIELD CATALOG.

The PC manufacturer wants additional fields available from the product hierarchy as selection criteria for which we may need additional custom Z fields. This will require a small enhancement on the SAP APO side by including the additional new fields in the structure /SAPAPO/KOMGOZ. Also, the custom fields need to be included in the SAP ERP user exit INCLUDE FV45VFZY_USEREXIT_CATALOG_VALU.

> **Note**
>
> If you are combining rules-based products or location substitutions with product allocation, then the field RULE_WERKS should be used instead of WERKS in the product allocation group. For product allocation for product substitution, you can use field RULE_MATNR instead of MATNR in the product allocation group for the requested product.

7.3.5 Maintain the Product Allocation Object

The product allocation object is used to allocate products based on the defined characteristics combination. The product allocation object can be represented by customer group, sold-to party, or product for our PC manufacturer. Depending on the business scenario, the business user can define the allocation percentage or quantity assignment on the characteristics combination.

The configuration path for defining the product allocation object is IMG ADVANCED PLANNING AND OPTIMIZATION • GLOBAL AVAILABLE-TO-PROMISE (GLOBAL ATP) • PRODUCT ALLOCATION • MAINTAIN PRODUCT ALLOCATION OBJECT. You can define the new product allocation object by following these steps:

1. Click NEW ENTRIES.

2. Specify the product allocation object by entering an OBJECT key (maximum 18 characters) and an OBJECT DESCRIPTION.

3. Choose SAVE.

7.3.6 Maintain the Product Allocation Group

A product allocation group lists a group of characteristics against which the business can define the allocation quantity. These characteristics come from the field catalog. The configuration path to maintain a product allocation group is IMG • ADVANCED PLANNING AND OPTIMIZATION • GLOBAL AVAILABLE-TO-PROMISE (GLOBAL ATP) • PRODUCT ALLOCATION • MAINTAIN PRODUCT ALLOCATION GROUP. The configuration is important because it links the global ATP and DP area. To create a product allocation group as shown in Figure 7.6, follow these steps:

1. Choose New Entries.

2. Enter a product allocation group in Prod. Alloc. Grp.

3. Using the input help ([F4]), choose the communication structure in Comm. structure. You can choose from the following check dates (for our scenario, choose MAD):

   ▶ Delivery date

   ▶ Material availability date (MAD)

   ▶ Goods issue date

4. Using the input help ([F4]), choose the time buckets profile in the Time bkts prfl field.

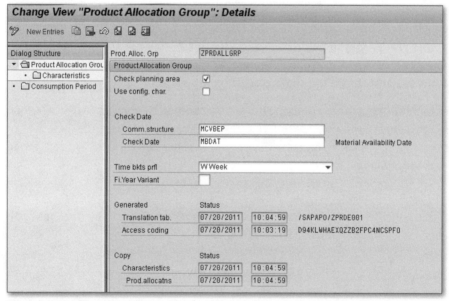

Figure 7.6 Product Allocation Group

5. The fiscal year is determined in the Fi. Year Variant field. Using the fiscal year variant, you define the following:

- ▸ How many posting periods exist in a fiscal year

- ▸ How many special periods you need

- ▸ How the system should determine the posting periods when posting

6. Press F3. A message appears, indicating that you need to check object validities when changing the period category. You may ignore this message when creating a period category.

7. Press Enter.

> **Note**
>
> When you save your entries in this step, a message appears indicating that errors have occurred when generating internal objects. This message appears because you still have not maintained any characteristics for the product allocation group. The product allocation object must always be the first characteristic. Press Enter.

8. Choose CHARACTERISTICS. You get the message that no entries exist. You can ignore this message when creating characteristics.

9. Choose NEW ENTRIES.

10. Using the input help (F4), choose the characteristics and their sequence. Note that the product allocation object must always be the first characteristic.

11. Choose CONSUMPTION PERIOD.

12. Choose NEW ENTRIES. Using the input help (F4), choose the product allocation group, and define the consumption periods.

13. Save your entries.

As shown in the Figure 7.6, if you set the CHECK PLANNING AREA switch, the product allocations are read directly from the planning area maintained by the business users during the sales order processing of the PC products and ATP check.

There are pros and cons regarding maintenance with this check switch. The advantage is that the business users can see the product allocation result immediately on the orders because the additional step of transfers of product allocation time series from DP to product allocation is not required. The cons are more on the system performance side, as the planning area will be locked during the check period, and the system will not allow any business users to edit the product allocation in the planning book. The planning and checking will be done simultaneously. If this switch is not used, the product allocations are read from the product allocation group.

For our PC business scenario, we have configured different planning areas for data storage so the ATP check and the planning do not conflict with each other. There are two methods to connect to planning areas:

▶ **Asynchronous connection:** Copying data from and to planning areas separately so the planning and availability check occurs without locking.

▶ **Synchronous connection:** Direct access to the planning area, which requires no batch job update.

Next, assign the characteristics to the product allocation group via configuration path IMG • Advanced Planning and Optimization • Global Available-to-Promise (Global ATP) • Product Allocation • Maintain Product Allocation Group, and double-click the Characteristics folder.

You also need to define the Consumption Period. The Consumption Period (shown in Figure 7.7) is used for the consumption of the allocation quantity of PC products by the incoming customer orders.

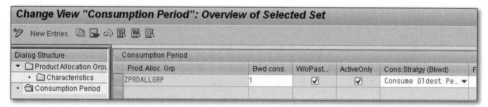

Figure 7.7 Consumption Period Maintenance

There are two primary consumption techniques defined:

▶ **Backward consumption** (Bwd cons.)
Specifies the number of days before the product allocation date that the incoming sales order can be used to calculate the product allocation quantity for consumption. The unused product allocation quantity is cumulated before the current product allocation check date.

▶ **Forward consumption** (FWD CONS.)
Specifies the number of days after the product allocation date that the incoming sales order can be used to calculate the product allocation quantity for consumption.

The period type (day, week, month, and posting period) is defined in the settings for the product allocation group. If you have set the w/O Past Periods indicator, product allocations from past periods (before today) are not used—even if they are in the consumption period.

7.3.7 Maintain the Product Allocation Procedure

The product allocation procedure determines how PC products are allocated. You must enter product allocation procedure in the SAP APO product location master record via Transaction /SAPAPO/MAT1. The configuration path is IMG • ADVANCED PLANNING AND OPTIMIZATION • GLOBAL AVAILABLE-TO-PROMISE (GLOBAL ATP) • PRODUCT ALLOCATION • MAINTAIN PRODUCT ALLOCATION PROCEDURE.

To create a new product allocation procedure, proceed as follows:

1. Choose NEW ENTRIES.
2. Enter an alphanumerical key (maximum 18 characters) in PROD. ALLOC. PROCE-DURE and an accompanying name for the procedure in PROCEDURE NAME.

Next, determine the step sequence by following these steps:

1. Choose the STEP SEQUENCE folder, and then click NEW ENTRIES.
2. If you want the system to check product allocations in two or more steps, enter the corresponding number and a name in the STEP field. Note that the step counter may not be zero.
3. Using the input help ([F4]), choose the desired PRODUCT ALLOCATION GROUP, and assign it to the product allocation procedures.
4. Specify for which combinations you want to use the *masking indicator*, using character "#". You can choose the masking indicator using the input help ([F4]). The search for collective product allocations is thereby activated.

To determine the control for product allocations, proceed as follows:

1. Choose the CONTROL folder, and then click NEW ENTRIES.
2. Assign the product allocations objects to procedures by choosing the object using the input help ([F4]).
3. Specify a validity period for each object.
4. Determine which assignments should be active.
5. Using the product allocations factor, you can display how the product allocation quantity is consumed by the requested quantity of a sales order (e.g., if the factor in a product allocation period has been set to 2, and a sales order with 100

pieces is created, a product allocation quantity of 200 pieces is than consumed by the sales order).

6. Save your entries. Your screen should now look like Figure 7.8.

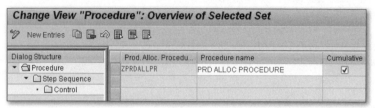

Figure 7.8 Product Allocation Procedure

Cumulated Check (Using ATP Logic)

The PC manufacturer may get sales orders in different time buckets and want to use the cumulated allocation quantity for future sales orders. Using the standard ATP checking logic, the incoming sales quantity is consumed against the remaining product allocation quantities still available. This check helps the business keep control of its inventory. Unused product allocation quantities from past periods are included in the calculation of the available product allocation quantity for the current period.

Configuration for Characteristics Combinations for Collective Product Allocations

As shown earlier in Table 7.1, you may have a business scenario where there is no restriction on the product, sales organization, or customer group characteristics value. In this scenario, you can use a *wild card*, or *masking* character, to define the characteristics value combination (CVC) for a generic combination, if you do not want to maintain and plan CVC for every combination. This helps business in mass maintenance of the data using the wild card entry to represent a group of master data under that specific business rule.

A product allocation group, which determines the criteria for selecting the product allocation time series, is assigned to the product allocation step in the sequence of product allocation procedures (shown in Figure 7.9).

Once customized, the allocation procedure can be maintained in the SAP APO product location. You can assign the product allocation procedure and sequence on the ATP tab of the product master.

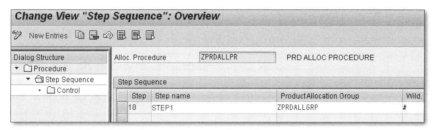

Figure 7.9 Wild Card (#) Maintenance in Product Allocation

7.3.8 Maintain the Sequence of the Product Allocation Procedure

If the quantity in a product allocation procedure cannot be fully confirmed in the check, product allocations are carried out for the remaining quantity in the next product allocation procedure in the sequence. The first product allocation procedure used is the product allocation procedure from the product master record. All other procedures are derived from the sequence of product allocation procedures (shown in Figure 7.10). If the product allocation procedure from the product master record reappears in the list, the system ignores it.

The configuration path to maintain the sequence of the product allocation procedure is IMG • Advanced Planning and Optimization • Global Available-to-Promise (Global ATP) • Product Allocation •Maintain Sequence of Product Allocation Procedure.

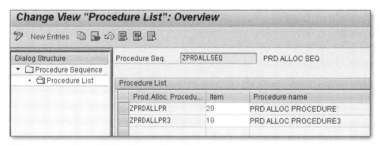

Figure 7.10 Maintain Product Allocation Sequence

7.3.9 Maintain the Connection to the Planning Area

The PC manufacturer wants to view the allocation quantity for its incoming customer orders. This customization establishes the link between DP and the product allocation group. Now you need to assign the product allocation group to the planning area so that you can transfer the time series. In this step, you can use various time buckets such as a weekly, monthly, or daily bucket. Another option is to use a fiscal year variant based on company's financial reporting structure. The fiscal year variant contains number of posting periods in the fiscal year and the number of special periods. The planning version 000 represents the active version, which is integrated in SAP ERP.

The configuration path is IMG • ADVANCED PLANNING AND OPTIMIZATION • GLOBAL AVAILABLE-TO-PROMISE (GLOBAL ATP) • PRODUCT ALLOCATION • MAINTAIN CONNECTION TO PLANNING.

Next you need to map the characteristics and key figures for DP and the allocation group. You map the characteristics of the allocation group with the defined characteristics in SAP APO DP. You assign the four characteristics identified: sales organization, customer group, sold-to party, and product to production allocation group. Assign all characteristics of a product allocation group (CHARACT.) to an INFOOBJECT, as shown in Figure 7.11, which can be later used as selection criteria for inputting the allocation quantities in the SAP APO planning book.

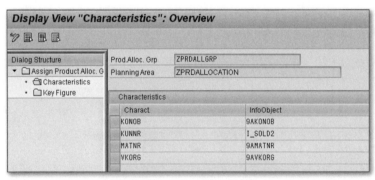

Figure 7.11 Mapping the Characteristics with InfoObjects

You also need to map the key figures to the DP InfoObjects, which are required in product allocation. This will ensure that the data consistency is working between DP and the allocation group. Figure 7.12 shows the key figures between the allocation group and DP.

▸ "AMENGE" is the incoming orders quantity.

▸ "KCQTY" is the product allocation quantity.

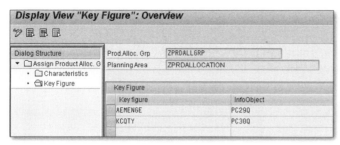

Figure 7.12 Mapping Key Figures with InfoObjects

7.3.10 Check the Product Allocation Settings

The configuration path to check the product allocation settings is IMG • Advanced Planning and Optimization • Global Available-to-Promise (Global ATP) • Product Allocation • Check the Product Allocation Settings. From here, you can check the product allocation settings after you define the CVC using Transaction /SAPAPO/MC62. If characteristics mapped to an InfoObject are different in text length, then you get warning message. The user may rectify the technical length or ignore the warning message to proceed further.

Then you use Transaction /SAPAPO/ATPCQ_GENER to generate the objects for the product allocation group. The object's translation table, access coding, search help, and display screen are generated automatically according to the settings made in the product allocation group.

Now that you have completed the basic configuration for both DP and the allocation group, let's look at the master data maintenance for the product allocation.

7.4 Basic Master Data for Product Allocation

Working with the primary master data consists of maintaining the characteristics combination of PC products for which you want to scope the product allocation method. The characteristics need to be created for both DP and the product allocation group, which we will discuss in the following subsections.

7.4.1 Characteristics Combination for Demand Planning

First, you need a CVC for the planning object structure, which is a combination of characteristics against which you want to do the allocation planning. You can perform allocation planning only for those characteristics (customer group, sales organization, product, sold-to) for which you have created CVCs. The CVCs are created and deleted using Transaction /SAPAPO/MC62. The maintenance screen for CVC is shown in Figure 7.13.

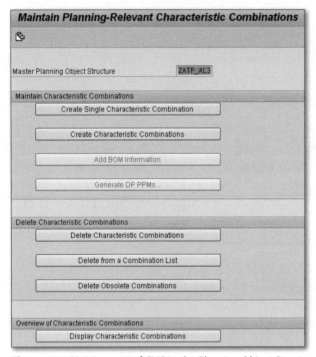

Figure 7.13 Maintenance of CVC in the Planning Object Structure

To create a CVC, you can upload CVC information from an Excel spreadsheet or CSV file. PC business users can maintain various combinations offline, and these combinations can be uploaded easily using Transaction /SAPAPO/MC62. To create CVCs, click the CREATE CHARACTERISTIC COMBINATION icon to open the CREATE CHARACTERISTIC COMBINATIONS screen shown in Figure 7.14.

We can create new CVC from an InfoCube using Transaction /SAPAPO/MC62 or using program /SAPAPO/TS_PLOB_MAINTAIN (see Figure 7.15). We can execute this program in the background batch job.

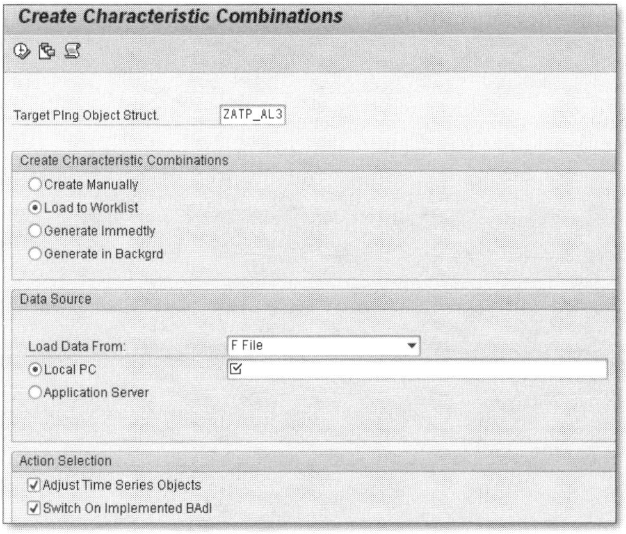

Figure 7.14 Loading CVCs from a Flat File in the Planning Object Structure

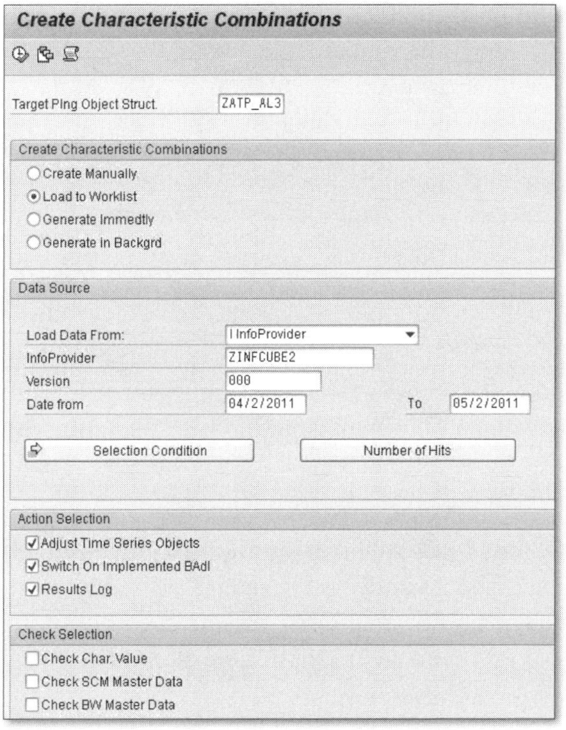

Figure 7.15 Creation of CVC from InfoCube

7.4.2 Characteristics Combination for the Product Allocation Group

Similar to the DP characteristics combination master data, you need to create characteristics of collective product allocations using Transaction /SAPAPO/ATPQ_COLLECT for global ATP master data, as shown in Figure 7.16.

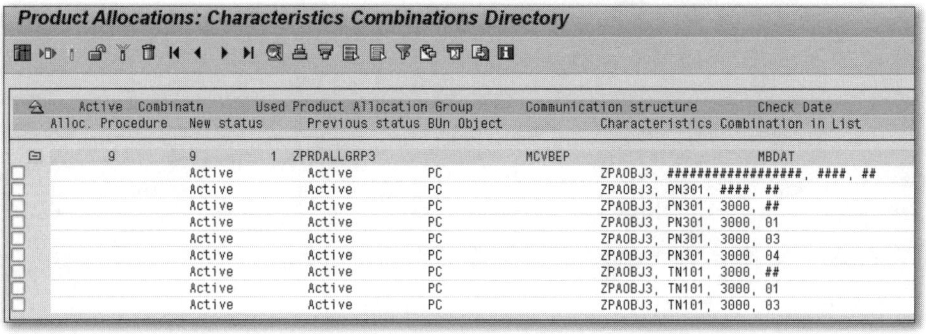
Product Allocations: Characteristics Combinations Directory

Active / Alloc. Procedure	Combinatn / New status	Used / Previous status	Product Allocation Group / BUn	Communication structure / Object / Characteristics Combination in List	Check Date
9	9	1	ZPRDALLGRP3	MCVBEP	MBDAT
	Active	Active	PC	ZPAOBJ3, #################, ####, ##	
	Active	Active	PC	ZPAOBJ3, PN301, ####, ##	
	Active	Active	PC	ZPAOBJ3, PN301, 3000, ##	
	Active	Active	PC	ZPAOBJ3, PN301, 3000, 01	
	Active	Active	PC	ZPAOBJ3, PN301, 3000, 03	
	Active	Active	PC	ZPAOBJ3, PN301, 3000, 04	
	Active	Active	PC	ZPAOBJ3, TN101, 3000, ##	
	Active	Active	PC	ZPAOBJ3, TN101, 3000, 01	
	Active	Active	PC	ZPAOBJ3, TN101, 3000, 03	

Figure 7.16 CVC Creation for Collective Product Allocation

> **Note**
>
> You can create a new wild card using Transaction RSKC, which can be different from other standard delivered wild cards such as _, @, -, *, +, and #. These wild cards help in representing a large pool set of master data in scope. Using wildcard we can avoid maintenance of individual characteristics combination.

You can also use Transaction /SAPAPO/ATPQ_PAREA_K to copy the CVC from the DP area to the global ATP product allocation group.

After you have created the characteristics combination, the allocations can be maintained directly in the DP book. Access the planning book using Transaction /SAPAPO/SDP94, and define the allocation by CVC, for example, product and sold-to party. The planning book offers the flexibility of downloading and uploading the offline allocation values, as shown in Figure 7.17.

The data from the planning book can be downloaded in CSV Excel format and uploaded in CSV Excel format. You can use additional key figures such as "remaining quantity" to calculate the balance of incoming order and allocation quantity. This can be achieved using an SAP APO macro in Transaction /SAPAPO/ADVM. The simple macro in this case will be the following:

"Remaining Quantity" = Allocation Quantity – Actual Sales Quantity

Figure 7.17 Maintenance of Allocation in the Planning Book

You can use also use macro alerts to highlight a custom alert situation in a product allocation business scenario when the incoming order quantity is greater than the allocated quantity or when the incoming order quantity becomes negative. This can happen due to inconsistencies in the allocation area. You can include database alert types to highlight a planning situation or inconsistent situation after the last macro run. The database alerts can be accessed via Transaction /SAPAPO/AMON1.

The other option is to upload data from the BW InfoCube using Transaction /SAPAPO/TSCUBE. You can load the InfoCube from a flat file.

The InfoCube is created using SAP Business Information Warehouse (SAP BW) Administrator Workbench. To load the data from a flat file into the InfoCube, the following prerequisite configuration must be done in the Administrator Workbench (Transaction RSA1):

▶ Create an InfoCube by adding relevant characteristics and key figures.

▶ Create an InfoSource.

▶ Assign the source system to the InfoSource.

▶ Create update rules.

▶ Create and schedule an InfoPackage.

To load and access the CVC for the product allocation planning area (shown in Figure 7.18), follow the steps:

1. For the source, enter the InfoCube and the version.

2. For the target, enter the planning area and the planning version.

3. Define the horizon for future planning dates.

Figure 7.18 Load Planning Area Version

4. Include restrictions for data selection (characteristics) if necessary.

5. Create assignments between the key figures in the InfoCube and those in the planning area.

6. Create assignments between the characteristics in the InfoCube and those in the planning area.

7. Set the LOG INDICATOR to generate and display a log.

8. Choose Execute ([F8]).

> **Note**
>
> Refer to these SAP Notes, which are related to the performance of the loading planning area:
>
> ▸ **Note 428102:** Performance: Loading Planning Area Version
> ▸ **Note 705068:** Performance: Loading Data from an InfoCube

After the maintenance of allocation in the DP book, use Transaction /SAPAPO/ATPQ_PAREA_R to copy allocation from the planning area. This way the SAP ERP sales order will find the product allocation quantity during the ATP check.

Now that we've covered the configuration for the product allocation, let's look at how the business scenario can be tested.

7.5   Key Steps in Scenario Testing

To simulate the PC manufacturer example for product allocation, use Transaction /SAPAPO/AC42 (Display Product Allocation Situation). While accessing this transaction, input the product allocation group and then click the CHARACTERISTIC COMBINATION PER PERIOD button located on top menu bar section. This will further require you to input the product allocation object. Then click the DISPLAY PRODUCT ALLOCATION button located on top menu bar section to view the results.

The product allocation result is further evaluated during the ATP check of the sales orders. The ATP check results provide you with a DELIVERY PROPOSAL screen from which you can further drill down to the PRODUCT ALLOCATION screen. By clicking the CHCKTYPE button (shown in Figure 7.19), you can identify whether the customer sales order confirmation is coming from the availability check or the product allocation.

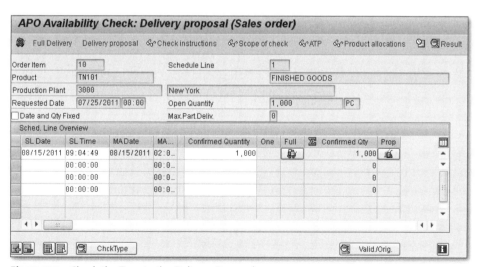

Figure 7.19   Check the Type in the Delivery Proposal

The confirmation of check type provides you with a result, as shown in Figure 7.20. The check type is for both product availability and product allocation. The result proves that the ATP check was done first for product availability, and then a further product allocation check was performed for the confirmed quantity.

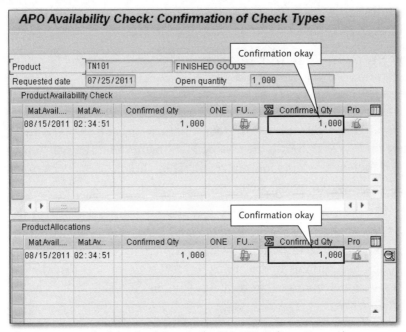

Figure 7.20 Result of the Check Type in the SAP APO Delivery Proposal

You can see further view results of product allocation by clicking the PRODUCT ALLOCATION icon. For our business scenario, we have defined two product allocation procedures. The first allocation procedure is performed for the characteristics of a product, sales organization, and customer group. The second allocation is for characteristics of a product, sales organization, and sold-to party.

Figure 7.21 displays the product allocation sequence of two product allocation procedures. The first procedure is ZPRDALLPR3, and the second procedure is ZPRDALLPR. The first allocation procedure gives a confirmation of 200 pieces, and the second allocation procedure gives a confirmation of 800 pieces.

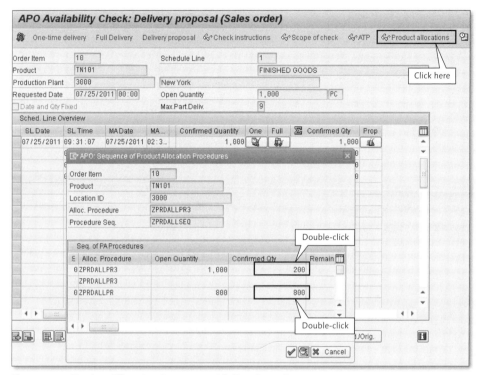

Figure 7.21 Product Allocation Sequence with Two Procedures

The allocation procedure ZPAOBJ3 contains master data in the form of a characteristics combination of product number, sales organization, customer group, and sold-to party. During the product availability check, when the characteristics of DP matches with CVC of the product allocation group, the product allocation time series is selected. The check is then performed against this time series.

The characteristics passed from sales orders in SAP ERP should match with the CVC that is specified in the product allocation group. You can view the characteristics in the SAP APO delivery proposal during the availability check, as shown in Figure 7.22. You can also view the forward and backward consumption result in the APO: PRODUCT ALLOCATION RESULT screen.

To display the product allocation assignment by each sales order of the PC products, use Transaction /SAPAPO/ATPQ_CHKCUST. Figure 7.23 displays the result for each sales order if you just input "product" as the selection criteria.

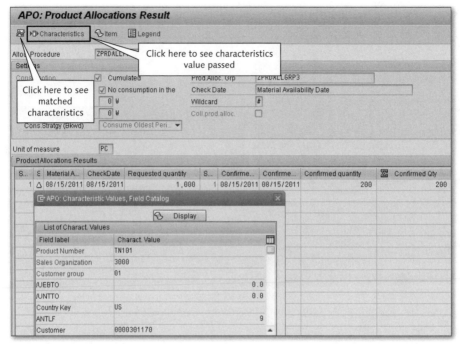

Figure 7.22 Characteristics Passed in the Field Catalog from SAP ERP

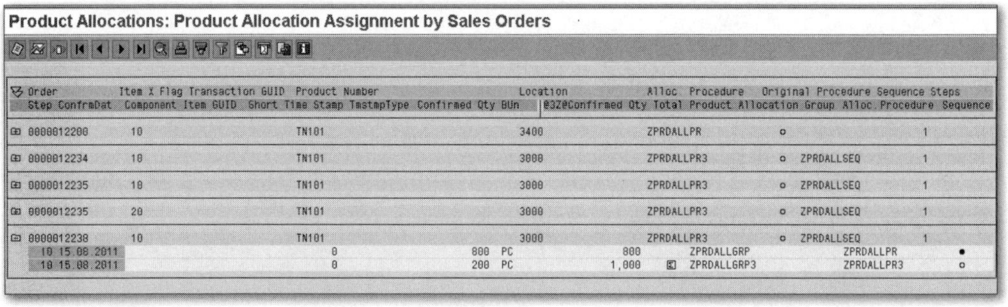

Figure 7.23 Product Allocation by Sales Order

After the product allocation check is completed, we recommend running Transaction /SAPAPO/ATPQ_PAREA_W to copy the result data back to the planning area from the product allocation group.

> **Note**
>
> Report /SAPAPO/RMQUOT_USAGE_ORDER gives a good overview of product allocation for each sales order. You can deactivate the product allocation by removing the product allocation procedure in the product master in SAP APO.

Next, let's look at the technical enhancement possibilities in product allocation.

7.6 Enhancement for Product Allocation

When the standard functionality of the product allocation does not completely match the business process, you need to perform enhancements to make changes to the standard SAP ERP behavior. The enhancements for product allocation can be done in either SAP ERP or SAP APO. This section shows example of enhancement that can be performed in SAP APO and SAP ERP to suit business requirements.

7.6.1 Enhancements in the SAP ERP Field Catalog for SAP APO Product Allocation

The sold-to party, or technical field KUNNR, is a 10-digit field in SAP ERP, but in SAP APO, the field /SAPAPO/KUNNR is a 20-digit field. When you create a sales order for a CVC with sold-to party as one of the fields, then it fails to match in this case due to the difference in the length of the fields. When allocation fails to find the specific CVC, the system maps to the next level of generic CVC or wild card characteristic value combination.

A user exit in the SAP ERP INCLUDE FV45VFZY_USEREXIT_CATALOG_VALU can be enhanced to match the field length in SAP APO. Figure 7.25 shows the ABAP Debugger screen of the user exit during the product allocation check to identify the field length for the sold-to party characteristics.

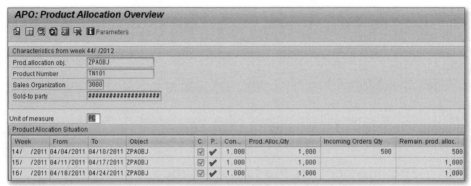

Figure 7.24 CVC Mapped before Changing the Field Length

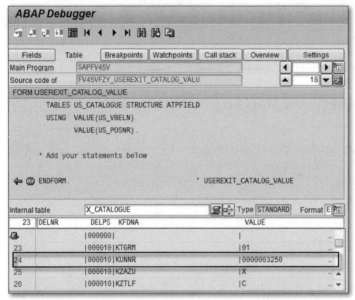

Figure 7.25 Changing the KUNNR Field Length in the User Exit

Perform the enhancement by changing the field length of KUNNR from 10 to 20 by adding leading zeros in front of it to match KUNNR with /SAPAPO/KUNNR. The result after the enhancement is shown in Figure 7.26.

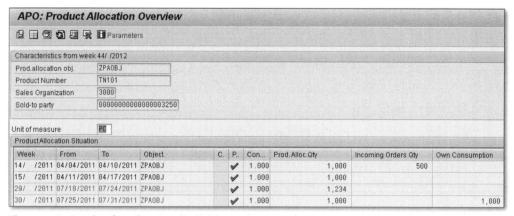

Figure 7.26 Results after Changing the Field Length in an Enhancement

7.6.2 Enhancements in SAP APO for Product Allocation

The enhancement on the SAP APO side is primarily for the creation of the custom Z fields to be used in the product allocation, which is not available in the standard SAP ERP fields. The user exits that can be used for product allocation in SAP APO are listed here:

▶ **EXIT_/SAPAPO/SAPLCIF_QUOT_001:** Inbound processing: allocations and their schedules.

▶ **EXIT_/SAPAPO/SAPLCIF_QUOT_002:** Inbound processing: customizing settings for product allocations.

The important tables for product allocations are:

▶ **/SAPAPO/SDQTVB:** SD Order: Product Allocation Assignment.

▶ **/SAPAPO/BOPQTVB:** ATP, BOP: Product Allocations Assignment.

▶ **/SAPAPO/OBREF:** Object Reference in SAP APO.

7.7 Summary

A company can use the product allocation functionality to control demand and supply situations. The ATP quantities are distributed according to allocated quantities, rather than on the basis of first come, first serve.

In this chapter, we showed you how a global PC manufacturer controls its quantity confirmation to the customer sales orders by using the product allocation functionality. The product allocation functionality is particularly important for the PC company during the business scenarios of allocation of quantity during peak period, product with volume promotion, products in short stock supply, or for seasonal products.

We also explained the customization steps that need to be performed in demand allocation planning and the allocation group. Product allocation enables a business to control which customer will receive which quantities. The demand planning book offers advanced features for calculating the product allocation quantities based on the product and customer characteristic combination per business rules. Product allocation is generally used with backorder processing to further redistribute the allocated quantities in a bucket. We will describe backorder processing (BOP) in detail in the following chapter.

The enhanced feature of backorder processing allows for the order reconfirmation based on business rules such as prioritization. This chapter shows how to configure the backorder processing functionality and also touches on the new event-driven quantity assignment feature.

8   Keeping Your Order Confirmation Firm with Global ATP Backorder Processing

Companies are constantly challenged to get their ATP results accurate, based on the latest demand and supply situation. To become profitable in business, companies need to build priorities on sales order allocation for customer sales orders. Backorder processing (BOP) serves as an important functionality within the order-promising business process to balance the business priorities with effective order fulfillment.

This chapter explains the following different business scenarios: Changing product availability dates/quantity, setting business priorities during supply shortages, making product allocation changes when BOP becomes critical, and setting system configurations for running BOP in the system efficiently.

We will explain the basic configuration and master data for BOP to solve these business challenges. The chapter also details event-driven quantity assignment in which the business transaction triggers to resolve the ATP situation instead of waiting for the next batch BOP run.

8.1   Overview of Backorder Processing (BOP) in Global ATP

BOP is an important step in sales order processing to reconfirm the customer orders based on latest inventory situations, and is performed either interactively or in a batch. The output of the BOP is the confirmed sales orders with confirmed delivery date and quantity based on the current supply situation. BOP aligns business objectives by prioritizing the sales order processing based on business priorities. BOP plays a pivotal role when the supply plan is capacity constrained, and a company wants to build a business rule to serve the sales orders it wants to fulfill first.

BOP can also be called a "re-ATP" check to correct any inconsistencies on earlier ATP checks. It also reprocesses the backlog sales orders that were not fulfilled due to supply chain reasons. BOP takes into account that the sales order schedule line doesn't have a confirmed quantity. BOP can avoid the allocation of inventory on first come, first serve sales orders, and its frequency must be planned closely to the order execution fulfillment cycle. BOP should never be seen as a technical task, because clear communication needs to occur between the order management and warehouse operations entities.

The BOP functionality is available in both SAP ERP and global ATP. Although the former has fixed criteria, BOP in global ATP offers more flexibility when filtering the sales documents in scope, sorting sales order documents based on business priorities, and scheduling the orders. Business priorities might be serving key customers or delivering specific sales order types (e.g., rush orders), or they might be based on the material availability date (MAD). Running BOP in the background generates a log report of confirmed and unconfirmed orders. The business users can confirm or reject the BOP result.

Within BOP, global ATP offers a functionality called *event-driven quantity assignment* (EDQA), which allows the system to react immediately to predetermined events influencing the stock availability (e.g., a goods receipt to confirm high-priority sales orders). EDQA uses an order due list (ODL) that contains the filtered and sorted unconfirmed sales orders. Using a workflow concept, EDQA triggers the workflow, which runs the BOP against the ODL.

BOP provides the following benefits:

▶ Increased reliability of ATP and improved customer satisfaction for targeted customers by appropriate prioritization based on business rules

▶ Optimized billings or revenue with efficient use of supply and faster inventory turns

▶ Improved stability in shipping and operations with fewer stockouts

▶ Greater flexibility to adapt quickly to changes in business rules and structures

▸ Improved customer service by focusing on real "shortage" alerts by planners and customer service

▸ Extended interfaces to legacy system possible with post-processing mode reserving ATP

8.1.1 Backorder Processing Comparison in SAP ERP and Global ATP

Both SAP ERP and global ATP have the BOP functionality, but there are some differences in the functionality between the two. Table 8.1 highlights the main differences between performing BOP in SAP ERP versus in global ATP.

Functionality	SAP ERP	Global ATP
Filter type helps identify the sales document type BOP needs to run (scope).	The selection criteria are limited to only MATERIAL and PLANT.	Wide selection criteria are available with the option of implementing user exits for more additions.
Sort profile helps define the business priorities (e.g., customer) on which the sales orders need to be processed during BOP.	Offers DOCUMENT CATEGORY, DELIVERY PRIORITY, DATE, DOCUMENT NUMBER, and DOCUMENT ITEM.	Offers similar selection criteria to SAP ERP with flexibility on ascending and descending or special sorting the fields. More selection fields with the option of user exits.
Order selection is based on confirmation status.	Only unconfirmed orders are selected during the BOP run.	Offers the flexibility of selecting orders based on different confirmation status combinations.
Results are compared between the two BOP runs.	Changes are committed to the database with no comparison.	Able to confirm new results with old prior to database commit.
Date options are available for BOP.	Date configuration: No option (MAD is used).	Date configuration: MAD or goods issue.
Correlation groups are defined for products that need to be packaged and shipped together.	This feature is not available in SAP ERP.	Checking the CORRELATION box ensures the correlation calculation is done when the BOP runs.
Multi-Item Single Delivery (MISL) helps to verify that all items in sales orders are available in a single location (complete delivery functionality).	This feature is not available in SAP ERP.	This feature is available in BOP and taken into account if the MISL check box is marked during the BOP runs.

Table 8.1 Backorder Processing Comparison between SAP ERP and Global ATP

Functionality	SAP ERP	Global ATP
REDISTRIBUTION flag releases the already confirmed and redistributes the quantities to the orders in scope.	NO REDISTRIBUTION flag—releases all orders assigned quantities, and then rechecks them if they didn't have a check before. Does not differentiate between confirmed quantity and requested quantity.	REDISTRIBUTION flag available for the product availability check, product allocation, forecast check methods, and also for enhanced confirmation logic (preserves the already committed quantity to orders). Possible to preserve the lesser quantity that has been agreed upon without giving more.

Table 8.1 Backorder Processing Comparison between SAP ERP and Global ATP (Cont.)

8.1.2 Business Case Study Example

There can be different supply chain scenarios where the ATP result needs to be reevaluated to reflect the current demand and supply situations. In the following subsections, we will present some example scenarios that BOP in global ATP will attempt to resolve and provide further correction.

Scenario 1: Changes in the Product Availability Dates or Quantity

This business scenario for the computer manufacturer may arise when an already confirmed sales order is risked by changes in either the already committed date or the quantity due to supply chain issues. BOP provides correction by rescheduling the delivery dates to future dates when the receipts are available. Based on this new delivery date, the order management team can inform the customers.

Scenario 2: Business Priority during Supply Shortage

This business scenario for the computer manufacturer may arise when there is a shortage of supply, and the order management team has to put priority on which sales orders to serve first. The computer business doesn't want to always follow the first come, first serve basis on the order-fulfillment cycle, but instead it wants to serve strategic customers first to generate higher profit margins. During the re-ATP, BOP first considers the business priorities and then processes the priority orders.

Scenario 3: Product Allocation Changes

The computer manufacturer's production allocation protocol allows the pre-allocation of the inventory based on the quota defined per product and customer combination. Any change in the supply chain situation might also require the supply allocation to be revisited and aligned with the business goals. BOP works with the allocation plan during the reprocessing of the orders and aligns the demand with the supply.

Scenario 4: Important Business Events Recorded on Transactional Data

BOP can also be triggered when some important business events are recorded in SAP ERP. Examples of these events include:

- Change to purchase order document
- Changes in sales documents (quantity, for example)
- Change in the stock data

BOP acknowledges these business process activities and corrects the ATP situation accordingly.

All four of the business scenarios presented can be resolved or corrected with the use of the BOP basic configuration of the filter type and sort profile. Whereas the filter type helps define the scope, the sort profile defines the business priorities for the ATP check.

Next, let's look at the configuration in global ATP to run BOP for the business scenarios we just described.

8.2   Basic Configuration for Backorder Processing

For global ATP BOP to work, the filter type and the sort profile must be configured. The filter type defines the scope of BOP, and the sort profile defines how BOP needs to be performed. We will discuss each of these configurations separately in this section.

8.2.1 Filter Type

The filter type is primarily used to define the order categories and the criteria (characteristics) by which the system selects the sales order documents for BOP. The configuration path to define the filter type shown in Figure 8.1 is IMG • ADVANCED PLANNING AND OPTIMIZATION • GLOBAL AVAILABLE-TO-PROMISE • BACKORDER PROCESSING • MAINTAIN FILTER TYPES.

Select the order categories for which BOP should run. BOP can be executed either for the sales documents (sales orders, deliveries) or purchasing document (purchase orders [POs], stock transport orders [STOs]) depending on the business requirements. Figure 8.1 shows the list of the order categories that can be defined in the filter type.

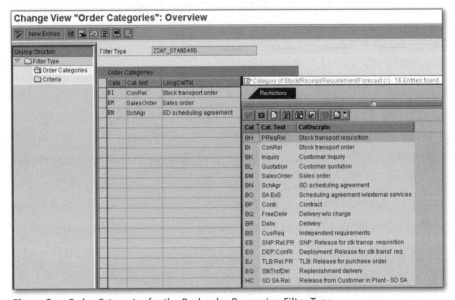

Figure 8.1 Order Categories for the Backorder Processing Filter Type

Next, double-click the CRITERIA folder to select the characteristics that you want for the sales orders for BOP. For example, you may use PRODUCT to define only items you want to run BOP, ITEM CATEGORIES to exclude the documents you do not want to run BOP, or PLANTS for which BOP needs to run. The flexibility of defining both the order categories and the criteria (characteristics) is one of the main advantages of using BOP.

8.2.2 Sort Profile

BOP searches for all open sales orders in the system and thereafter uses the sort profile to sort these sales orders by predefining business priority criteria in the configuration. For example, the computer manufacturer may opt to perform BOP based on the location, product, and MAD sequence. These criteria are identified based on the business rules and can be related with how the orders can be grouped for ATP check. You can remove the earlier confirmation on these sales orders and perform the ATP check again based on the sequence defined in the sort profile.

The sort profile can also serve a prioritization order in which sales orders are treated. It helps to define the sequence in which sales orders are ATP checked during a supply shortage. The configuration path to define the sort profile is IMG • ADVANCED PLANNING AND OPTIMIZATION • GLOBAL AVAILABLE-TO-PROMISE • BACKORDER PROCESSING • DEFINE SORT PROFILE.

You need to maintain the following entries in the sort profile:

▶ FIELDNAME
Maintain the fields according to which criteria you want to sort. The available entries are displayed, including the user exit option.

▶ FIELD LABEL
Description of the field name.

▶ SEQUENCE
Signifies the priority for the field name according to which the sales orders are sequenced. For example, you can sort all the sales orders according to the location first, then the MAD, then the delivery priority, and finally the product priority.

▶ CHANGE SORT
This field identifies whether the sorting needs to be done either by ascending or descending or special sorting values.

▶ SORT
Here, you have the options of "Ascending," "Descending," or "Special sorting." Special sorting is used to define specific values according to which the sales orders need to be sequenced. For example, you can maintain special sorting with customer numbers based on their priority (shown in Figure 8.2).

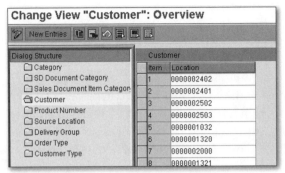

Figure 8.2 Special Sorting in the Sort Profile

Now that you've seen the basic configuration for BOP, let's look at how the configuration of the filter type and sort profile can be set up as master data for performing BOP in the next section.

8.3 Basic Master Data for Backorder Processing

The master data for BOP primarily consists of maintaining location master data and creating different variants for filter type and sort profile per the business scenarios. For interactive BOP, you need to create a BOP worklist as well. These master data, in the form of a filter type variant, allow you to run BOP both in interactive and background mode. The filter variant contains the filter type and sort profile configuration performed earlier.

▶ **Location master (Transaction /SAPAPO/LOC3)**
Maintain the business event for BOP. Location delivery priority (DELIV. PRIORITY field) can also be maintained in this view (see Figure 8.3).

▶ **BOP (Transaction /SAPAPO/BOP)**
This transaction consists of defining various parameters:

  ▶ WORKLIST tab: Brings together the FILTER TYPE and SORT PROFILE defined earlier in the configuration (Figure 8.4). Also define the CORRELATION and MULTI-ITEM SINGLE DELIVERY LOCATION (MISL) scenario if applicable.

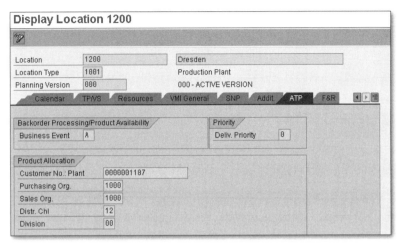

Figure 8.3 Location Master for ATP

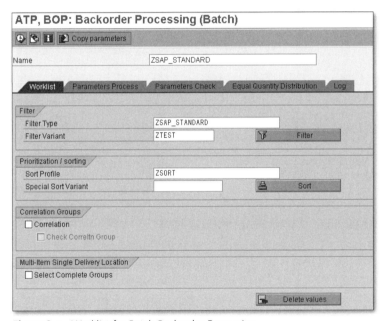

Figure 8.4 Worklist for Batch Backorder Processing

▶ FILTER VARIANT field: Defines the scope of BOP by including the attributes in the scope of BOP (see Figure 8.5).

The filter variant also defines the confirmation status, which displays the options for considering and filtering the orders that the system should consider as part of the BOP run (e.g., consider orders that have MAD in the past).

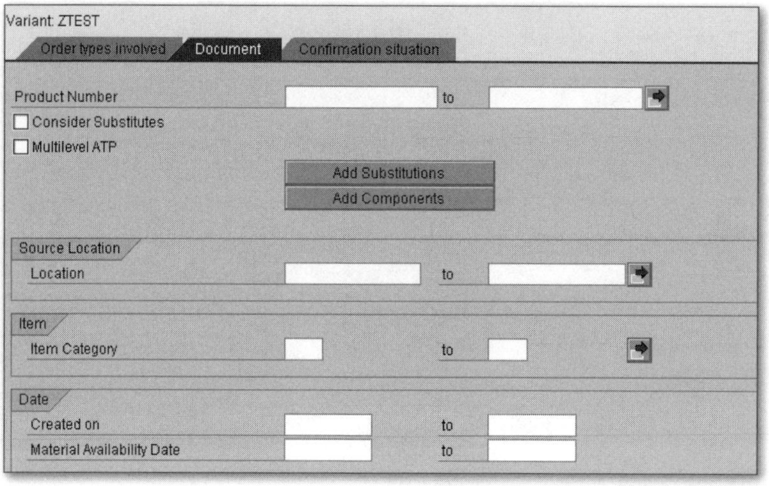

Figure 8.5 Filter Variant

▶ PARAMETERS PROCESS tab: Defines the parameters that influence the result of BOP. The NEW DISTRIBUTION FOR section determines whether to redistribute the existing confirmed quantities before the BOP run. Un-checking the options means the system will retain the original confirmation quantity and will not release all the earlier sales order confirmations. All the three basic ATP check methods are available to support the first three scenarios discussed earlier. In the CUSTOMIZING section, you can instruct BOP to read the allocation procedures and check modes from the product master during the BOP run. The EXECUTION MODE section enables the business user to save BOP as a simulation (SIMULATION), update SAP ERP sales orders directly (UPDATE CHANGES), or store the result (WITH POSTPROCESSING) in the buffer and update them interactively.

▶ PARAMETERS CHECK tab: Helps to select the orders for which the system should cancel confirmation. Define the additional FILTER TYPE and FILTER VARIANT to exclude the orders from the BOP run. You can also run BOP based on the MATERIAL AVAILABILITY DATE (MAD) or GOODS ISSUE DATE.

Now that we've covered the master data for BOP, let's apply the configuration and master data settings to the business scenarios defined earlier.

8.4 Key Steps in Scenario Testing

The first two business scenarios are explained in this section with the BOP testing results. In the first business scenario, due to manufacturing capacity issues or critical raw material availability, there is a delay in production. Due to this delay, all the sales orders already committed earlier based on planned production need to now be rescheduled. BOP takes the input from the supply planning the latest inventory and manufacturing date and reschedules to a future date.

Figure 8.6 shows the planned orders and sales orders pegged together to fulfill the order at 23/05, but now, due to the production issue, the new planned orders date is scheduled to 15/06.

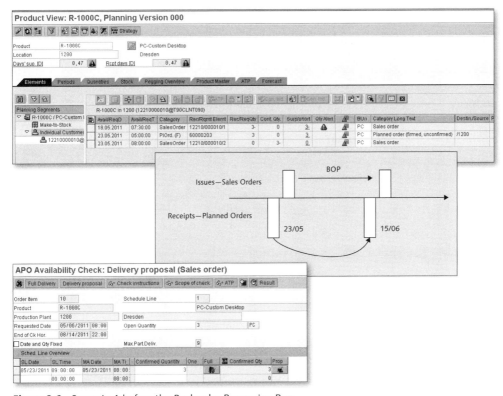

Figure 8.6 Scenario 1 before the Backorder Processing Run

Running BOP, either interactively or in a batch, corrects this latest situation and schedules the confirmation date to the future date of 15/06 as shown in Figure 8.7.

After running BOP, the sales order is updated in both SAP APO (shown in Product View – Transaction /SAPAPO/RRP3) and sales orders display (Transaction VA03) with the new delivery dates.

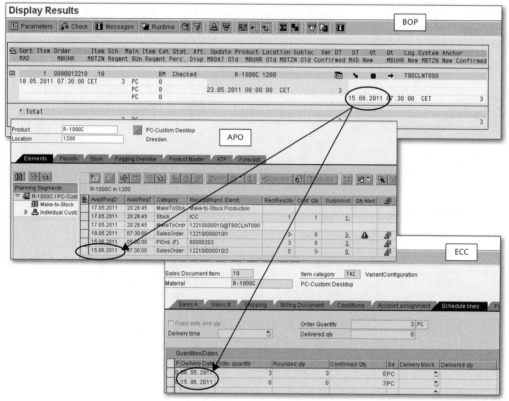

Figure 8.7 Scenario 1 after the Backorder Processing Run

The second business scenario focuses on setting customer priority during supply shortage situations. In this scenario, you have two customer orders of the same quantity, but there is just enough production stock to fulfill one of the customer orders (see Figure 8.8). The customer priority is set in the special sorting configuration in the sort profile. The business situation may arise when the lower priority sales order arrives first for order processing and only available stock is allocated to this order (based on a first come, first serve rule). After some time, the second sales order arrives, which has a higher business priority and needs to be allocated stock. BOP aims to correct this business situation (via deallocation and reallocation of stock) and reassign the planned stock to the order having the higher customer priority in the special sorting definition.

Figure 8.8 shows the two sales orders with the stock allocated to the lower priority sales order initially before the BOP run. The sort profile contains the list of the customers from higher to lower priority.

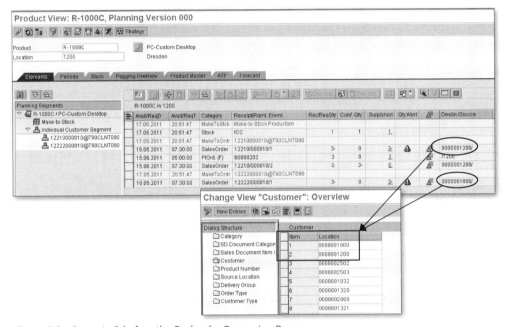

Figure 8.8 Scenario 2 before the Backorder Processing Run

During the BOP run, the sequence of the sales orders is based on the customer priority. Based on the BOP PARAMETERS PROCESS settings, the planned stock is released from the first sales order and then assigned to the customer's order that has higher priority. This scenario is common during rush orders where the reassignment of the supply needs to align with the business objectives. Figure 8.9 displays the correct assignment of the planned stock to the higher priority sales orders.

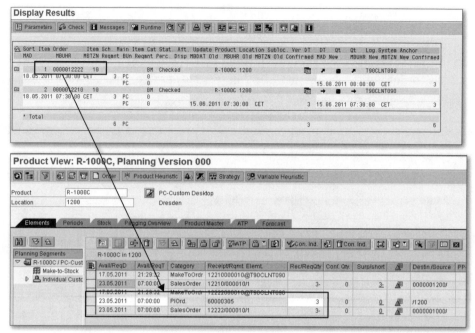

Figure 8.9 Scenario after the Backorder Processing Run

Table 8.2 details some of the key transactions related to BOP. These transactions can be used not only for performing the interactive and background processing of the transaction, but also for simulation comparisons, results analysis, and BOP results maintenance.

Transactions	Transaction Description
/SAPAPO/BOPIN	Interactive BOP
/SAPAPO/BOP	Batch BOP
/SAPAPO/BOP_WORKLIST	BOP Worklist
/SAPAPO/BOP_COMPARE	BOP Comparison
/SAPAPO/BOP_MONITOR	BOP Monitor
/SAPAPO/BOP_RUNTIME	BOP Runtimes
/SAPAPO/BOP_RESULT	BOP Result

Table 8.2 Key Transactions for Backorder Processing

Transactions	Transaction Description
/SAPAPO/BOP_DELETE	Delete BOP
/SAPAPO/BOP_UPDATE	Update BOP

Table 8.2 Key Transactions for Backorder Processing (Cont.)

BOP for the computer manufacturer can be performed in different modes. The selection of each mode will vary based on the business process maturity on understanding of BOP results. The modes can also be applied depending on the customer group or product group to reflect the specific business requirements.

Some business users may want to analyze the BOP result before publishing it to SAP ERP, while another group of users may want the system to directly update SAP ERP and correct the ATP situation. The modes are primarily used for the ATP situation correction and depend on the business operations linked with order fulfillment as to how often the BOP job needs to be performed in the daily cycle. For all our business scenarios, the computer manufacturer may decide to run a daily background batch job for one group of products, while for the other, with a faster inventory cycle, the company may run multiple batches or an interactive BOP job over the course of the daily shipping cycle. The available modes for running BOP can be selected by the radio button under Execution mode on the PARAMETERS PROCESS tab in Transaction /SAPAPO/BOP and are listed here:

▶ **Direct update of batch BOP (Transaction /SAPAPO/BOP)**
BOP runs and immediately updates the results to the database without an intermediate step. In this scenario, the business users want to directly publish the result due to the volume transaction and focus on the exception management to identify where the BOP ATP corrections didn't happen.

▶ **Batch BOP with post processing (Transaction /SAPAPO/BOP)**
BOP runs, saves the results to a buffer, and protects the assigned quantities with temporary quantity assignments. The results can be updated or rejected. If rejected, the temporary quantity assignments are deleted. In this scenario, the users analyze the results before publication to the SAP ERP system. BOP is scheduled to run in the background, and the business users can select the run to view, analyze, and publish the result.

191

▶ **Batch simulation (Transaction /SAPAPO/BOP_COMPARE or /SAPAPO/BOP)**
BOP can be run in simulation. No temporary quantity assignments are written to SAP liveCache. No orders are updated in SAP ERP. The results can be viewed in a log, but cannot be updated interactively. The result can be saved in the buffer or deleted. In this scenario, the business simulates multiple BOPs and compares the results before publishing to the SAP ERP system.

▶ **Interactive (Transaction /SAPAPO/BOPIN)**
Interactive provides online decision making. In this scenario, the business user performs BOP interactively and analyzes the results manually before the SAP ERP publication.

Now let's look at how the fourth scenario is resolved using the event-driven quantity assignment (EDQA) functionality. The functionality combines global ATP and SAP Business Workflow to resolve any pending ATP situation based on specific business operation activities.

8.5   Overview of Event-Driven Quantity Assignment (EDQA)

EDQA is a feature within BOP that allows the system to react immediately, based on the business events that are affecting the stock availability situation. This functionality reacts to the fourth scenario explained earlier when an important business transaction is recorded. Instead of waiting for the next BOP batch run, EDQA resolves the ATP check inconsistencies with a list of defined activities.

Some of the business events that can be modeled in EDQA are the goods receipt of inventory, changes in purchasing or sales documents, or changes in the sales order confirmation. For example, the computer manufacturer may have a sales order for an important customer that was acknowledged but is waiting for the arrival of inventory. After the inventory arrives in the warehouse and the goods receipt is performed, the business user wants to correct the sales order confirmation situation and allocate the stock to the sales order via EDQA instead of waiting for the next BOP run, which is scheduled in the daily background job. Figure 8.10 illustrates the business events for which the system can automatically trigger the activities in EDQA.

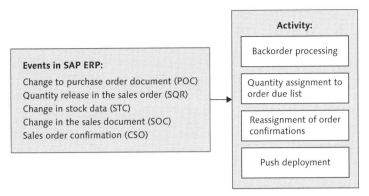

Figure 8.10 Event-Driven Quantity Assignment in Global ATP

EDQA works on the order due list (ODL), which identifies how the system filters and sorts the sales order based on business priority. The activities performed in the EDQA are:

▶ **BOP**
Performs the re-ATP check on the sales order document in scope based on the latest supply situation. EDQA triggers an ODL-based BOP via an SAP Business Workflow event. The high-priority customer orders are taken into account automatically from the ODL.

▶ **Quantity assignment to ODL**
Filters and sorts sales orders to be processed for the re-ATP check based on business rules and urgency. This activity corrects all ATP inconsistencies that may occur between two BOP runs. The ODL filters and sorts the customer orders that have high business priorities.

▶ **Reassignment of order confirmations**
EQDA triggers confirmation via ODL, which contains the list of high- and low-priority confirmed or unconfirmed sales orders. This activity will deallocate stock (removes confirmation) from low-priority sales orders and allocate stock to high-priority sales orders based on the business goals. The business may view this deallocation and allocation of sales orders in a customized report.

▶ **Push deployment**
Deployment deals with the distribution of the goods in the supply network. The deployment takes the input from the ODL and proposes an STO for today's execution. After the goods receipt is performed at the plant, the inventory can be pushed to the warehouses, which is important for the fast-moving consumer

goods industry. This process is important for the replenishment business process so the users can monitor the stock availability for sales commitments to customers and know when the goods can be shipped to fulfill sales orders.

Basic Configuration for EDQA

The customization for EDQA primarily consists of ODL, process category, and workflow management. Figure 8.11 shows the configuration objects that are all needed to make EDQA work.

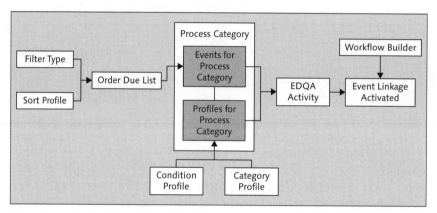

Figure 8.11 Configuration Objects for EDQA

The ODL processing is similar to BOP, where the sales order priorities can be adjusted interactively. Similar to BOP, the ODL consists of the filter type and the sort profile. While defining the ODL FILTER TYPE and SORT PROFILE (shown in Figure 8.12), the fields of ODL should not be confused with BOP, as both field catalogs show different field characteristics with different technical names. As shown in the figure, both the filter type and sort profile have two tabs for selecting the field characteristics: BACKORDER PROCESSING (BOP) and ORDER DUE LIST (ODL). For EDQA customization, use the latter fields from ODL.

The configuration of ODL for setting up filter type and sort profile can be done in path IMG • ADVANCED PLANNING AND OPTIMIZATION • GLOBAL AVAILABLE-TO-PROMISE • EVENT DRIVEN QUANTITY ASSIGNMENT • MAINTAIN FILTER TYPE/DEFINE SORT PROFILE.

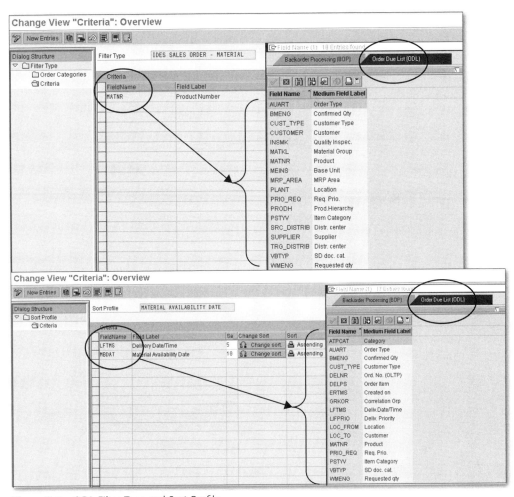

Figure 8.12 ODL Filter Type and Sort Profile

The ODL is defined in path IMG • ADVANCED PLANNING AND OPTIMIZATION • GLOBAL AVAILABLE-TO-PROMISE • EVENT DRIVEN QUANTITY ASSIGNMENT • QUANTITY ASSIGNMENT TO ORDER DUE LIST • CONFIGURE ORDER DUE LIST.

Input the FILTER TYPE and SORT PROFILE in the ODL configuration, and then click SAVE. After you save your work, click the GENERATE and ACTIVATE buttons on the ODL profile, as shown in Figure 8.13.

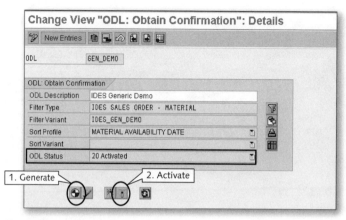

Figure 8.13 Order Due List

Next, you need to define the process category. As shown in Figure 8.14, define the EVENT for the PROCESS CAT., which is "EDQA Quantity". Input the ORDER DUE LIST created in the earlier configuration step, as well as the BOP VARIANT. The BUSINESS EVENT is "A" for sales orders. In the PROCESS FLOW field, select the IT ITERATIVE process to run to find the result with a maximum processing time (TIMEOUT) of 5 minutes.

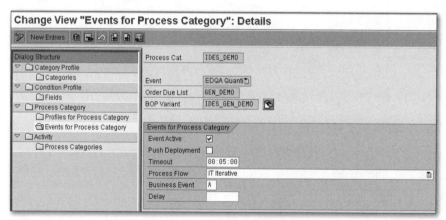

Figure 8.14 Process Category

The Process Category (Transaction /SAPAPO/EDQA_PD) also contains the CONDI-TION PROFILE and CATEGORY PROFILE (optional) folders. The CONDITION PROFILE can be used to define the fields used as selection criteria for the process category (an example of a condition profile is material). The CATEGORY PROFILE is used to change the ATP categories. As shown in Figure 8.15, link your customized process category (which you created earlier) with the event activity to trigger the overall EDQA process.

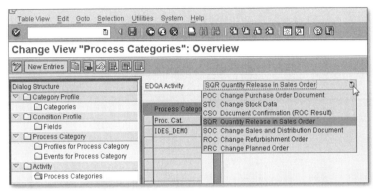

Figure 8.15 Activity Assignment to the Process Category

The last configuration revolves around the workflow management for the event trigger. A technical prerequisite for EDQA to work is that the event linkage is activated in Transaction /SAPAPO/EDQA_EC.

The SAP Business Workflow template can be used to model the workflow with business events. Use Workflow Builder (Transaction SWDA) to build the steps and link with the events in the SAP Business Workflow template (Transaction PFTC). The example in Figure 8.16 shows the standard EDQA template, listing the process activity and the condition that will initiate the process. You can leverage on this template and implement it in your EDQA process.

Now you need to activate the event linkage by checking LINKAGE ACTIVATED in Transaction SWETYPV as shown in Figure 8.17, which will launch the workflow. The event linkage opens up the communication link between global ATP and the SAP ERP system for workflow. The configuration includes the workflow template defined in an earlier step and the function module, which will trigger the EDQA process in the global ATP system.

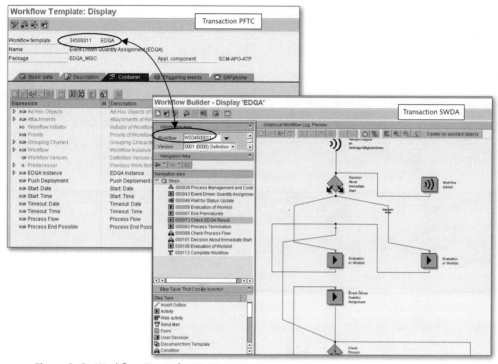

Figure 8.16 Workflow Events for EDQA

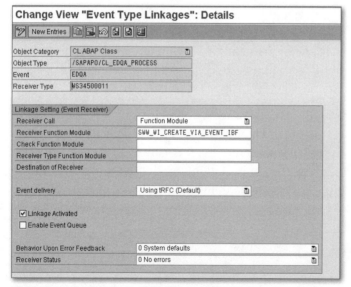

Figure 8.17 Event Linkage Activation

Now that we've completed the configuration steps for setting up the EDQA process in global ATP, let's move on to the testing steps for validating the EDQA process.

There are four main testing steps for EDQA:

1. ODL contains a backlog item (Transaction /SAPAPO/ODL). The business users receive this report either by background job or by interactively running the ODL report.

2. Perform goods receipt in SAP ERP (Transaction MIGO) or use Transaction MB1C for new inventory. The business users perform this transaction in SAP ERP.

3. EDQA shows the events performed (Transaction /SAPAPO/EDQA). The workflow log shows the tasks triggered by EDQA to adjust the sales order ATP (see Figure 8.18). All the technical steps occur in the background.

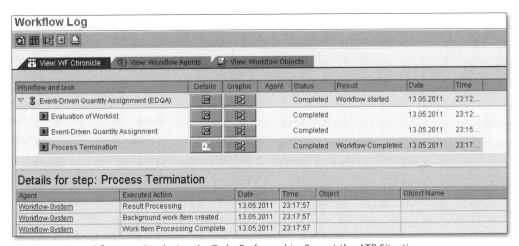

Figure 8.18 Workflow Log Displaying the Tasks Performed to Correct the ATP Situation

4. Review the BOP result in Transaction /SAPAPO/BOP_RESULT. This is a technical step and not intended for the business user, but meant for more technical analysis as an explanation log. Execute the transaction and provide the BOP name by selecting the F4 key. The BOP result is displayed from the SAP APO database.

Another feature that is available in BOP is the comparison between the current and earlier confirmations performed (as shown in Figure 8.19). To do this, execute the current BOP in simulation mode. The result is compared with the first confirmation or the first confirmation date. This allows the business users to view the various results and confirm the best suitable BOP result per their business goals. Once confirmed, BOP can be published to SAP ERP for the sales orders delivery date updates.

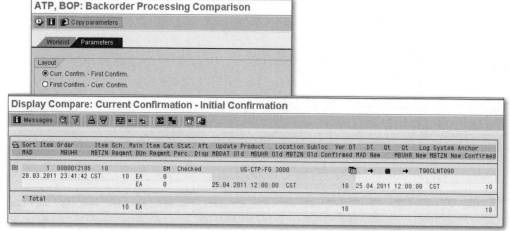

Figure 8.19 Backorder Processing Comparison

Next, let's look at the enhancement options for BOP. Enhancements enable the business to modify the existing standard functionality to suit their business requirements.

8.6   Enhancements in Backorder Processing

Enhancements are required to suit specific business requirements that are not supported by standard BOP functionality. User exits or enhancement spots can be implemented to influence the behavior of the functionality. For example, our computer manufacturer might add a few specific custom fields from the SAP ERP customer and product hierarchy for filtering or sorting for the BOP process. Because these hierarchy fields are not available in the standard field catalog in global ATP, an enhancement is necessary to append the structure /SAPAPO/KOMGU.

Table 8.3 displays the user exits available in BOP.

User Exit	Description
EXIT_/SAPAPO/SAPLBOP_000	BOP Initialization
EXIT_/SAPAPO/SAPLBOP_040	Scope of Check for BOP
EXIT_/SAPAPO/SAPLBOP_051	Results Transfer of BOP
EXIT_/SAPAPO/SAPLBOP_052	Results Transfer of BOP
EXIT_/SAPAPO/SAPLBOP_060	BOP Update
EXIT_/SAPAPO/SAPLBOP_069	BOP Update SL_DOC
EXIT_/SAPAPO/SAPLBOP_FILT_010	BOP: Filtering
EXIT_/SAPAPO/SAPLBOP_SORT_020	BOP: Sorting

Table 8.3 Backorder Processing User Exits

The BOP result may be extracted either by a user exit listed in Table 8.3 or with development effort by combining various internal SAP ERP tables. Use the user exit EXIT_/SAPAPO/SAPLBOP_052 to pull the BOP results. The results will be displayed under the two parameters CT_BOPREQ and CT_BOPCNF. If the SAP ERP tables are used for generating the report, use the combination of Tables /SAPAPO/BOPHEAD, /SAPAPO/BOPRESLT, and /SAPAPO/POSMAPN.

8.7 Summary

This chapter demonstrated the importance of BOP in correcting ATP inconsistencies and building business priorities in the reallocation of stock to customer orders. Although available in both SAP ERP and global ATP, the comparison table clearly shows the advantages of the latter method. The chapter also looked at event-driven quantity assignment (EDQA), which triggers BOP in the background without waiting for the nightly BOP run to correct the ATP situation.

The next chapter focuses on capable-to-promise (CTP), which integrates the ATP process directly with the manufacturing process. As part of the ATP check, a production can be triggered with finite resource planning. This functionality integrates with the SAP APO production planning and detailed scheduling (PP/DS) functionality and looks simultaneously at production capacity and product availability.

The capable-to-promise functionality integrates production and the ATP check functionality. This chapter shows how to use this functionality to create sales orders that can trigger production based on the finite scheduling of production resources.

9 Streamlining Your Manufacturing Planning with Capable-to-Promise

Real-time integration between the manufacturing shop floor and the order-promising business process is fast becoming a necessity for industries using characteristics-based planning, which range from automotive, mills (metal, paper), and construction to high-tech industries. The motivation in these industries requires the customer order ATP check to trigger the manufacturing process. This is where the capable-to-promise (CTP) functionality in global ATP adds business value.

The sales order commitment is best met not only by replenishment lead time, but also by directly interacting with the manufacturing capacity and scheduling production orders to best identify the material availability date (MAD) for shipping goods to a customer. In this chapter, we will study the advanced ATP check in the form of CTP, which delivers these capabilities.

This chapter explains how the CTP process can be configured in the SAP APO global ATP functionality and production planning and detailed scheduling (PP/DS) systems to link the sales order process directly with manufacturing planning. The chapter also provides an overview of the master data required to model the business scenario in the SAP Supply Chain Management (SAP SCM) system.

9.1 Overview of the Capable-to-Promise Process

Capable-to-promise (CTP) is a function in global ATP that integrates with the SAP APO PP/DS module. CTP calls PP/DS during the ATP check when the requested product is completely not available, in order to produce or procure the remaining quantity. A feasible availability date is determined in PP/DS from the result of scheduling the simulated planned orders (taking capacities and the product availability into account), and allowing the customer order management team to estimate a feasible order delivery date. CTP is supported by the following elements that need to be customized along with master data modeling:

▶ Characteristic-dependent forecasting (industries such as steel, paper, and chemical where order taking and planning is done at the characteristics level)

▶ Lot sizes

▶ Finite scheduling of resources

▶ Block planning, the pre-assignment of resource capacities for products with specific attributes, with the purpose of using the manufacturing capacities more balanced on a monthly bucket time period

CTP can be called (while accessing Transaction /SAPAPO/AC03) from the check instruction (configuration) or location determination activity when rules-based ATP is used, as explained in Chapter 6, Section 6.4. Figure 9.1 illustrates the CTP process flow.

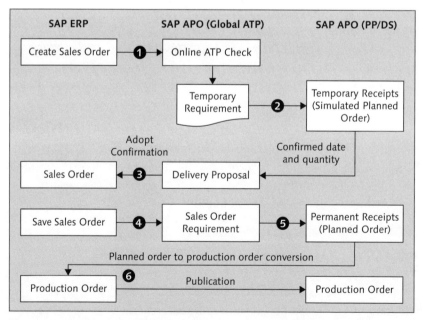

Figure 9.1 Capable-to-Promise Process Flow

Let's go over this illustration in detail for a typical mill industry (e.g., paper mill) scenario. A sales representative receives a call from a customer who requests the availability of a product per his specifications (e.g., size, width, length). The sales representative performs a simulation ATP check first (using Transaction /SAPAPO/ AC04), providing the suitable delivery date option. The customer confirms this date with the sales representative, who now creates the sales orders directly in SAP ERP to reserve the manufacturing capacity. After the sales order is saved, the production plan is created automatically to reserve the manufacturing capacity. The manufacturing department pulls the daily report to view this confirmed sales order and production plan for execution. The technical backend steps are as follows:

❶ Create a sales order in SAP ERP as a requirement element. Global ATP product availability is called online in real time for the ATP check on the requirement. Based on the CHECK INSTRUCTION customizing setting, the product availability is first checked. If there is enough inventory or receipt elements, no proposal is given to manufacturing. (If there is a receipt shortage, the production is triggered at a sourcing plant.)

❷ The requested product is checked for the requested date and quantity. If the request is only partially confirmed, the temporary requirement is passed to PP/DS, which creates simulated temporary receipts.

❸ The simulated planned orders created performs source determination, plan explosion, lot size calculation, and scheduling during the planned order creation. The system creates temporary requirements at the same time. The temporary requirements are assigned to the same ATP category as the checked requirement. If you are checking a sales order in a CTP check, the system displays the temporary requirement with the ATP category BM (Sales Order).

The temporary requirement is then assigned to the temporary planned order. This assignment cannot be changed. This ensures that a temporary quantity is assigned. The temporary planned order is protected from a planning run that is triggered by concurrent transactions. The system deletes the temporary requirement after the sales order is saved, and then the sales order is transferred to SAP APO.

❹ The confirmed date and quantity are displayed in the global ATP delivery proposal. After confirmation is adopted, the sales order processing screen is returned to the sales order creation screen.

❺ Upon saving the sales orders, the sales order requirement is generated in global ATP. Permanent planned orders are created from the temporary planned orders. Note that if you leave the sales order processing transaction without first saving the sales order, the temporary planned orders are deleted.

❻ The planned orders conversion is set in PP/DS, which in turn creates a production order in SAP ERP for execution. The production order is published to PP/DS and replaces the planned order. The production order is executed in the shop floor, and inventory is goods receipted for the sales order fulfillment.

9.2   Business Case Study Example

The CTP feature is commonly used in industries that have complex product structures with many characteristics. For example, a paper manufacturer deals with different characteristics (depending on grade, size, and length, etc.) and may use CTP because customer sales orders vary. CTP integrates global ATP and PP/DS to simultaneously provide information on both the production capacity and product availability. The paper manufacturer faces unique business challenges in matching demand and supply with the business objective of maximizing the yield and revenue.

Figure 9.2 illustrates how the paper manufacturer's customer sales order is matched to the overall manufacturing process. To reduce the paper cutting machine changeover time, the concept of PP/DS *block planning* is introduced. The blocks are defined as resource-availability periods for product characteristics (grade, width, length). A match between operation characteristics and resource characteristics is checked during scheduling (characteristics are treated as constraints). The blocks are adjustable based on the resource capacity utilization. The result of this program is that orders with similar characteristics are grouped together, allowing optimization of the bottleneck manufacturing resource. Scheduling the bottleneck resource to produce similar products reduces the resource changeover time during the production run. This reduction overall increases the efficiency of the resource utilization and component consumptions.

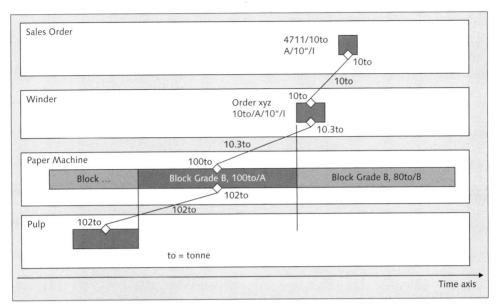

Figure 9.2 Paper Industry with Manufacturing Block Schedules Example

The integrated process flow for this business scenario (see Figure 9.3) can be viewed from the order-fulfillment planning to execution phase with the following four stages:

1. The first stage consists of taking the sales orders in SAP ERP and triggering the global ATP CTP check. This step, performed by the order-management team, is initiated by inputting the sales orders in SAP ERP, which performs the global ATP check on the requested data and time. Global ATP performs the ATP check and proposes delivery. The unconfirmed quantity is passed to SAP APO PP/DS for creation of the planned orders, and the feasible confirmed date is given back to SAP ERP regarding MAD or customer delivery date.

   This scenario is primarily created with no supply situation, and the creation/ scheduling of planned orders is based on the characteristics block resource capacity slots generated by PP/DS algorithm heuristics. CTP is able to react dynamically to customer orders based on the latest supply situations.

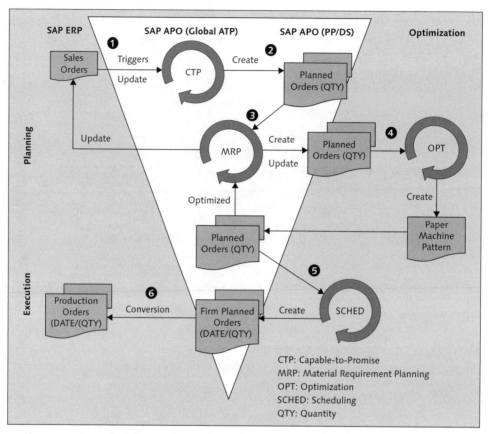

Figure 9.3 Integrated Process Flow with Real-Time CTP Commitment

2. The second stage is comprised of scheduling routine material requirement planning (MRP) runs to reflect the latest demand and supply situations that are caused by business operational issues. This step, performed by the supply planner, is primarily initiated via a regular daily supply planning (MRP) batch job. The supply plan run explodes the bill of materials (BOM) and creates requirements for the components either to be produced in-house or to be externally procured. These issues might arise due to customer order changes or cancellations. Alternatively, issues may be due to manufacturing capacity fluctuations caused by resource breakdown, maintenance, or additional shifts.

3. The third stage consists of running the paper industry optimization run (in this example, trim optimization) to best prepare the material grade, length, and width cut patterns. This step, which is performed by the master production planner,

is initiated by running the optimization either interactively or as a background job. The business may opt to run the optimization in the simulation version before merging with the active version, which is integrated with SAP ERP for execution. The planned orders are rescheduled based on this plan, which updates the sales order delivery dates.

4. The last stage consists of executing planned orders. This step, performed by the factory scheduler, is initiated when the production order needs to be released to the shop floor for execution. A detailed scheduling is performed with capacity leveling of the resource for a particular block and primarily is rescheduling orders to create a shop-floor manufacturing plan. The planned orders are converted to production orders for execution.

Now that you understand how the order management and manufacturing business process are integrated as an end-to-end process, let's move on to configure the CTP business scenario in global ATP to meet your business requirements.

9.3   Capable-to-Promise: Basic Configuration

The CTP configuration involves integrating the global ATP and PP/DS configuration objects. While the global ATP configuration objects are primarily used for the availability check and triggering production, the PP/DS configuration objects are used for modeling the factory constraints, creating planned production orders, and scheduling the planned orders per factory resource availability. In our business scenario, the paper machine resource is identified as a bottleneck resource because it is capacity-constrained by the paper roll size.

Completing the configuration in both global ATP and PP/DS ensures that you will have an integrated business solution to meet the business scenario. In the following subsections, we have outlined the basic configurations necessary in global ATP and PP/DS.

9.3.1   Global ATP – Check Mode

The Production Type in check mode controls how the system is to execute the product availability check:

- STANDARD (based on ATP time series)

- CHARACTERISTICS EVALUATION (based on characteristics)

- MULTILEVEL ATP CHECK (based on component availability)

- KIT CHECK (based on all items in kit availability)

The STANDARD option consists of generic settings used for CTP sales order and manufacturing integration scenarios. With this setting, the system executes the availability check based on the ATP time series. PP/DS is only called if receipt elements (planned orders or purchase requisitions) have to be generated during the check.

If characteristic value assignments were transferred to the availability check, these are taken into account during the ATP check. Characteristics-based ATP is a function of the basic method product availability check and is activated automatically if characteristic value assignments are transferred to the availability check, and the respective product is maintained for characteristics-based ATP. You can maintain the settings for characteristics-based ATP in customizing for SAP APO under GLOBAL ATP • PRODUCT AVAILABILITY CHECK • MAINTAIN CHARACTERISTICS VIEW.

9.3.2 Global ATP – Check Instruction

Check instructions help determine the sequence to check the product availability (product allocation and rules-based ATP) and trigger production based on a defined business rule. The settings shown in Figure 9.4 are maintained in Customizing for SAP APO under GLOBAL ATP • GENERAL SETTINGS • MAINTAIN CHECK INSTRUCTION. The combination of CHECK MODE and BUSINESS EVENT (sales orders or delivery) determines the check instruction in global ATP.

For CTP, you need to select the STARTPRODUCTION indicator with the "Availability Check First, Then Production" option that indicates the CTP should trigger production when there is a supply shortage. The following options are available in the PRODUCTION TIME dropdown menu to determine which point in the availability check and for what quantity the production should start:

- AFTER EXECUTING ALL BASIC METHODS
  The quantity requested for production is the initial requirements quantity minus the total quantity confirmed through the basic methods. The selection has no effect on the quantity produced and/or confirmed.

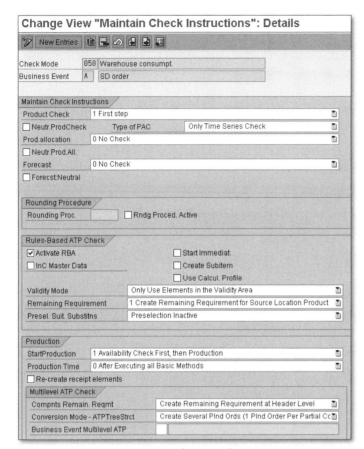

Figure 9.4 Check Instruction Configuration for CTP

▶ AFTER EXECUTING PRODUCT AVAILABILITY CHECK
The quantity requested for production is the requirements quantity transferred to the product availability check, minus the quantity that can be confirmed at the finished product stage. The selection has an effect on the quantity produced and/or confirmed.

9.3.3 Global ATP – Rules-Based CTP

In many manufacturing and distribution business models, you need to combine CTP with a rules-based ATP check to model product substitution before giving production requirement to the manufacturing plant. After performing the availability check across warehouses using the rules-based logic, the shortage supply requirement can be cascaded down to the manufacturing location for triggering the production schedule. Using Transaction /SAPAPO/RBA04 (see Figure 9.5), you can maintain the sequence list of warehouse and manufacturing locations for which the availability check should be performed. For the manufacturing location, maintain the activity (ACT) for the production trigger. The activity can be created earlier in the same transaction. Then navigate to the PROFILE & PARAMETER section and under the LOCATION DETERMINATION ACTIVITY tab to maintain the activity.

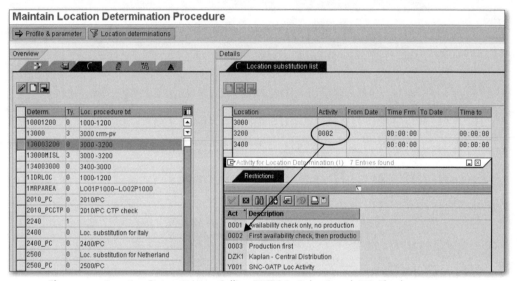

Figure 9.5 Location Determination Calling PP/DS in Rules-Based ATP Check

9.3.4 Production Planning and Detailed Scheduling: Production Planning Procedure

This configuration defines relevant events that can occur for the location product combination for each planning procedure. Here you will define the steps that PP/DS heuristics (heuristics are methods for matching supply and demand) will perform when either of the events occurs in the business process.

Follow the path IMG ADVANCED PLANNING AND OPTIMIZATION • SUPPLY CHAIN PLANNING • PRODUCTION PLANNING AND DETAILED SCHEDULING • MAINTAIN PLANNING PROCEDURES to view the available SAP ERP standard procedures. You can create your own custom planning procedure by copying the standard procedure and modifying the events accordingly. The most commonly used planning procedures are shown in boxes in Figure 9.6. These two different planning procedures are used based on business requirements.

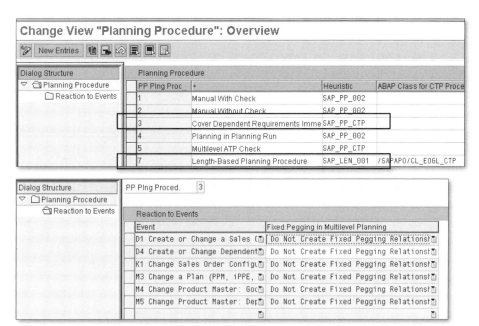

Figure 9.6 PP/DS Planning Procedure Commonly Used for CTP

Production Planning and Detailed Scheduling – Heuristics

A heuristics planning function executes planning for selected objects (products, resources, order, operations, etc.). SAP ERP provides a set of heuristics algorithms in the form of production planning (PP) heuristics and detailed scheduling (DS) heuristics. The PP heuristics create orders for a required date, but these dates may be influenced by the scheduling strategy selected. The DS heuristics are used for scheduling and sequencing orders, and no new orders are created.

Table 9.1 lists all the PP/DS heuristics that are commonly used in the CTP business scenario. Some of the heuristics are specifically modeled to suit the mill industry sector using CTP functionality.

PP/DS Heuristics	Heuristic Name	Heuristic Feature
SAP_CTP_DLG	Interactive CTP heuristic	Based on algorithm /SAPAPO/HEU_CTP_DIALOG, this heuristic is used for running interactive CTP for a single customer order. The planning consists of two steps: ▶ Deleting the existing planned orders to free capacity on the resource for the customer order ▶ Creating a new planned order to cover the customer requirement
SAP_LEN_001	Length-based heuristic	Designed for the mill industry, this heuristic can be used to plan materials on a length basis. Requirements and receipts can be assigned to characteristics that can be valuated individually. These characteristics and their characteristic requirements control the assignment of the receipts to the requirements.
SAP_PP_CTP	Planning shortage quantities for CTP	The heuristic based on the algorithm /SAPAPO/ HEU_PLAN_DEFICITS is intended for the CTP process. In standard customizing, the heuristic is assigned to planning procedure 3 (Cover Dependent Requirements), which is used in the CTP process for planning the end product and important components. The heuristic runs as a subsequent planning step after the sales order has been posted in SAP APO.
SAP_PP_002	Planning of standard lots	This is the most commonly used heuristic for MRP calculation based out of algorithm SAPAPO/HEU_PLAN_STANDARDLOTS to execute procurement planning to cover product requirements. The heuristic is based out of the lot-sizing method.
SAP_CDPBP_01	Reschedule blocks	This heuristic uses algorithm /SAPAPO/MC01_ HEU_BLOCKS_SCHED to reschedule scheduled activities on block-planned resources.

Table 9.1 Production Planning and Detailed Scheduling Heuristics Linked with CTP Business Scenarios

PP/DS Heuristics	Heuristic Name	Heuristic Feature
SAP_CDPBP_02	Adjust and reschedule block limits	This heuristic uses algorithm /SAPAPO/MC01_HEU_BLOCK_ADJUST to adjust the block limits of a resource, that have executed a block planning. It balances capacities between the blocks of a cycle. Blocks with overloads are extended, whereas blocks with free capacity are shortened.
SAP_CDPBP_03	Enhanced block maintenance	This heuristic uses algorithm /SAPAPO/BLRG_HEUR_BLK_MAINT to enable the creation and changing blocks that have been defined in a resource.

Table 9.1 Production Planning and Detailed Scheduling Heuristics Linked with CTP Business Scenarios (Cont.)

Production Planning and Detailed Scheduling – Strategy Profile

A scheduling strategy is a record of settings that controls the detailed scheduling of operations and orders in PP/DS. Using the detailed scheduling strategy, you can specify which rules and constraints the system uses to schedule and reschedule orders and operations, and which scheduling constraints (e.g., product and resource availability) it considers when doing this. For example, the following rules and constraints might be used:

▸ In which planning direction the system searches for a scheduling date

▸ Whether the system schedules activities finitely or infinitely on the resources

▸ How the system schedules the operations on the resources in the case of finite scheduling, for example, by inserting into or adding onto the existing schedule (scheduling mode)

▸ Whether the system considers the pegging relationships

▸ Whether the system considers the relationships between the activities of different operation

▸ Whether the system is also allowed to schedule activities in nonworking times

You define detailed scheduling strategies for PP/DS in a strategy profile that you access via the IMG path ADVANCED PLANNING AND OPTIMIZATION • SUPPLY CHAIN

PLANNING • PRODUCTION PLANNING AND DETAILED SCHEDULING • GLOBAL SETTINGS • MAINTAIN STRATEGY PROFILES.

You can define several scheduling strategies (that is, several records with different strategy settings) in the strategy profile. If scheduling or rescheduling in one setting is unsuccessful with a particular strategy, the system can use the next one, and so on. In the strategy profile, you define the following options:

▶ Which strategies in the strategy profile the system can use (you must mark the strategies as ACTIVE for this)

▶ The sequence in which the system can use active strategies (by numbering the strategies)

The active strategy with the smallest number has the highest priority during scheduling or rescheduling. If this strategy is not successful, the system uses the next active strategy with the next smallest number, and so on.

Production Planning and Detailed Scheduling – Block Planning

In industry sectors such as metal and paper, the manufacturing planning of orders and operations for various plants/resources/work centers is not solely based on available capacity and the sequence and priority of deadlines. More often, upstream planning at a plant is used to define which group of products with which characteristics/attributes are to be produced in a plant. In this situation, the business driver is the manufacturing resource setup to produce the group of products to justify the rational usage of capacities.

When customizing block planning, you begin by defining characteristics and classes. The characteristics and classes are transferred from SAP ERP via the Core Interface (CIF). The characteristics are displayed in Transaction CT04, whereas the classes can be accessed via Transaction CL02.

The block basis definition (see the screen in Figure 9.7, which is accessed via Transaction /SAPAPO/MC01_BBD), is the quantity of all characteristic requirements for the class on which the block is based. It enables the user to define several similar blocks of the same type at the same time. Several of these block basis definitions, together with a duration, form a reference cycle (explained further in Section 9.4).

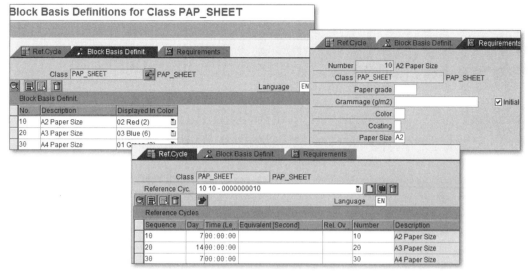

Figure 9.7 Block Definition for the Class

Now that we've discussed the configuration objects for global ATP and PP/DS, let's look at the master data requirement to make this integrated scenario work.

9.4 Basic Master Data Requirements

In this section, we'll maintain the master data for a paper mill industry where the manufacturing process has a resource constraint for machine making paper rolls. Each time there is change in paper size, the machine needs a set-up change, for which block planning is proposed. The block characteristics are the width, length, and size of the paper rolls. The master data needs to be maintained for both global ATP and PP/DS.

The basic master data for CTP involves a combination of master data in SAP ERP and SAP APO for product availability check and production. In this section, we provide the list of master data required for CTP.

9.4.1 Product Location (SAP APO Transaction /SAPAPO/MAT1)

The three tabs that are relevant to ATP are located in the product location master data. In the ATP tab (see Figure 9.8), the CHECK MODE, ATP GROUP, and CHECK HORIZON fields are transferred via CIF from SAP ERP material master MRP views, while the CHECKING HORIZON CALENDAR is directly maintained in SAP APO.

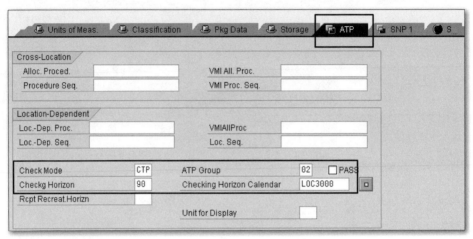

Figure 9.8 SAP APO Product Location—ATP Master Data Fields

If the actual quantity of paper sent to customers is slightly less than the requested quantity on the sales orders, we can use the *underdelivery* tolerance master data. This master data is maintained in the LOT SIZE tab (see Figure 9.9). In The PP/DS tab, maintain the PP PLNG PROCEDURE, PLAN EXPLOSION, and PP/DS HORIZON fields (Figure 9.9) for the planned order creation in the CTP process.

The planning procedure covers the automatic creation of the planned orders when the sales order requirement is given to the sourcing plant, while the plan explosion defines the BOM explosion using the production process model (PPM) or production data structure (PDS) master data. The PP/DS horizon identifies the manufacturing horizon within which the PP/DS planned orders can be created and scheduled. CTP processes support both the creation of in-house production or external procurement. The PROCUREMENT TYPE in the PROCUREMENT tab determines whether the CTP process will create a planned order or purchase requisition.

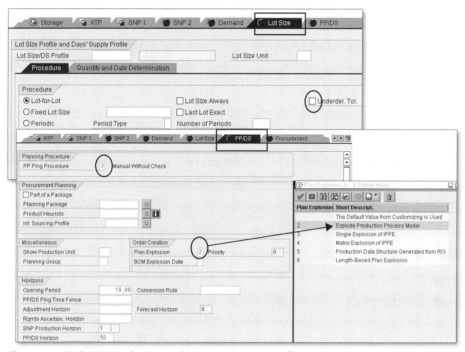

Figure 9.9 SAP APO Production and Lot Size Master Data for CTP

9.4.2 Work Center (SAP ERP Transaction CS03)

The work center transaction provides the means for tracking production and persons in the production process that have capacities assigned to them. The work center defines all the master data parameters that are required to calculate durations, capacity requirements, and costing.

9.4.3 Bill of Materials (SAP ERP Transaction CR03)

The BOM defines the planned material consumption for the components. The BOM contains the parent product and list of the raw materials that need to be assembled or processed to make the parent product.

9.4.4 Routing (SAP ERP Transaction CA23)

Routing defines the production rate (quantity per time unit) used to manufacture materials on the production line. The production quantities are scheduled according to the production rate and capacity requirements.

Each routing combination needs to have separate master data. Each routing master data defines the manufacturing operation/activity, work center, and control key. The operation/activity identifies the production activities that will be executed in a specific work center (resource). The CONTROL KEY field in operation in an important value that is used in scheduling the planned orders, determining capacity requirements for the resource assigned to the operation, costing, determining inspection characteristics for quality management, and reporting. Overall, the control key defines whether the manufacturing business process type is discrete, repetitive, or process manufacturing.

9.4.5 Production Version (SAP ERP Transaction C223)

The production version allocation combines the BOM and routing master data into predefined variants, which are required for launching production orders. The production version maintenance is done at material plant combination, which maintains the routing and BOM. The production version is further assigned to the material master.

9.4.6 Resource (SAP APO Transaction /SAPAPO/RES01)

This master data is created during the activation of the SAP ERP CIF integration model for the work center. SAP ERP master data requires proper maintenance of the work center capacity and work center formulas. In the SAP APO resource master, you can maintain day-to-day operational shifts, shift sequences, downtime, and the factory calendar accurately to better reflect ATP accuracy during order promising on sales orders.

Some additional master data in the form of *capacity reservation* can be used to reserve capacity for key customers. This master data can be maintained in the PP/DS bucket capacity (shown in Figure 9.10) by clicking the CAPACITY RESERVATION button and reserving resource capacity using the descriptive characteristics feature.

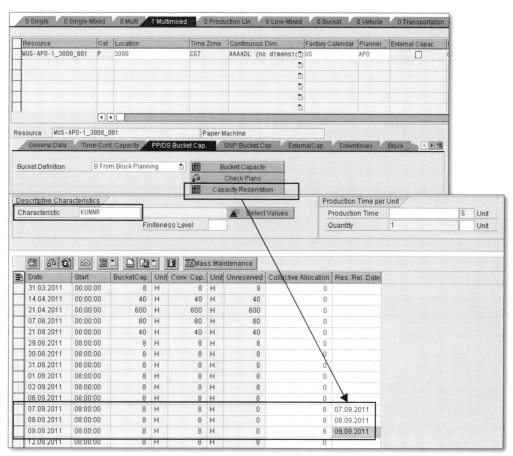

Figure 9.10 Capacity Reservation Feature in PP/DS Resource Master Data

Another master data appropriate to the CTP business scenario is the block planning schedules maintenance in the SAP APO resource master data. In the RESOURCE MASTER • BLOCK PLNG tab, input the CDP CLASS and BLOCK BASIS DEFINITION, which we defined earlier in Section 9.3.4. The block reference cycle intervals (see Figure 9.11) are maintained by inputting the date interval the different blocks would be scheduled. The blocks are planned to minimize the setup duration when the product configuration is changed (e.g., change of paper size). You can manually adjust the blocks per the resource capacity loads.

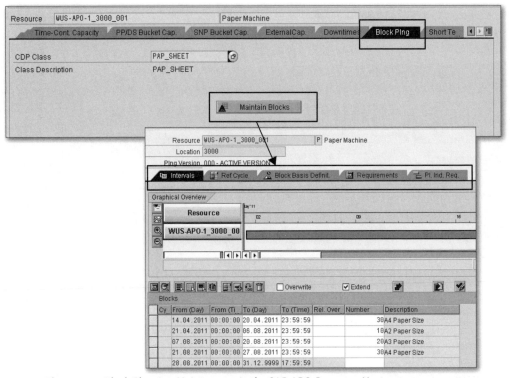

Figure 9.11 Block Planning Maintenance in the SAP APO Resource Master

9.4.7 Production Process Model (Transaction /SAPAPO/SCC03)

This master data is created during the activation of the SAP ERP CIF integration model for the production version. The SAP ERP production version combines routing and BOM master data. The PPM (see Figure 9.12) is used to calculate production time, production costs, material flow, and resource load in the plant.

As shown in the figure, the PPM structure has an OPERATIONS category to define production activities. For each operation, there are MODES (resource) and COMPONENTS that are assigned for the particular resource. The mode represents the throughput rate to produce the base quantity. The component represents the input and output components for the operation. The following information summarizes the PPM structure shown in the figure:

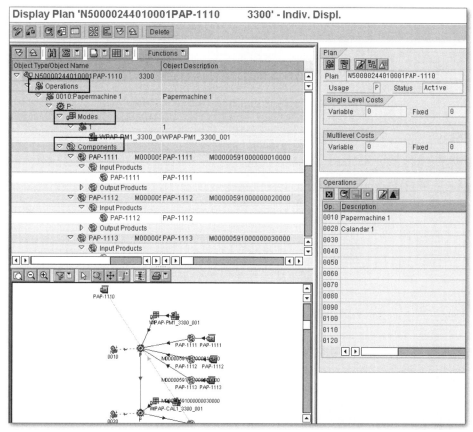

Figure 9.12 SAP APO PPM Structure

▶ Each PPM includes one or more operations, which are steps in the production process.

▶ Each operation includes one or more activities, the components consumed by the activity, and their sequence within the operation.

▶ The PPM has validity parameters by lot size and time intervals.

▶ The variable costs defined for a PPM include the costs of input material as well as the cost of production.

For modeling the bottleneck resource constraint using block planning, you need to maintain the characteristics value. As we mentioned, this is the paper size for our example, which is input as a characteristics value for the paper machine resource as shown in Figure 9.13.

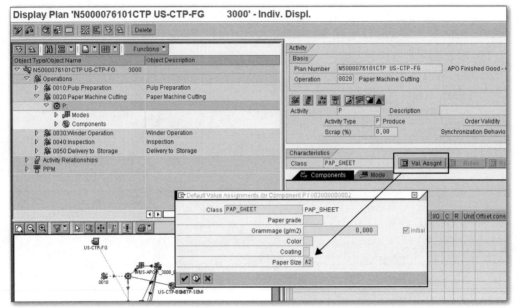

Figure 9.13 Maintenance of Characteristics in the Production Process Model for Block Planning

Assigning the characteristic values to the PPM is called *characteristic propagation*. This step ensures that orders created on a PPM can only be scheduled in a block with the same characteristic value. Characteristic values must be assigned to all activities of the PPM (required because it is the activity that is scheduled on a resource).

Now that we've completed the configuration and master data maintenance for global ATP and PP/DS, we can move on to business scenario testing.

9.5   Key Steps in Scenario Testing

In our first scenario, the manufacturing is modeled with a block-planning resource constraint so the sales orders fall under the production bucket based on product characteristics. This scenario relates to our mill industry (paper) example, where the paper machine is constrained with the characteristics values (size, length, or width). All requirements that are specific to the characteristics are bucketed in the resource blocks. In the short term, the blocks are adjusted accordingly to prepare the production schedule.

In the second scenario, the rules-based ATP and CTP integration is presented commonly for distribution and manufacturing companies (e.g., mill, high-tech, metal), whereby the stocks at the warehouses are checked before giving the net requirement to the manufacturing location for production during the ATP check.

9.5.1 Case 1: Block Planning Resource

During the sales order creation (see Figure 9.14), the user enters the product characteristics for a specific paper product, which triggers the CTP call in the global ATP system. During the sales order creation, the business users enter the requested paper configuration (grade, size, etc.) in the sales orders.

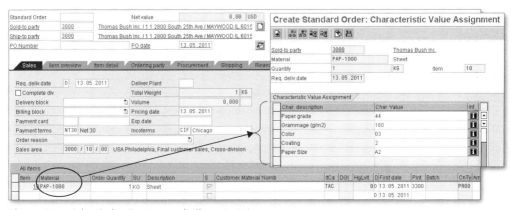

Figure 9.14 Sales Order Creation with Characteristics

Upon delivery of the proposal confirmation, the SAP APO PRODUCT VIEW screen (shown in Figure 9.15) displays the corresponding receipt elements (planned orders) and paper characteristics of the sales orders.

During the production planning run in the background, the planned orders of paper finished goods are further exploded to the lower-level paper component items. Receipts elements (planned orders and purchase requisitions) are created for the requirements. The SAP APO PP/DS planning board is accessed via Transaction /SAPAPO/CDPS0 and gives the schematic overview of the complete production schedule for different paper machines in the shop floor. The planning board displays the resource and product planned orders schedule and offers flexibility to business users to make any schedule adjustments, and allows business users to freeze the paper production plan for the shop floor to execute.

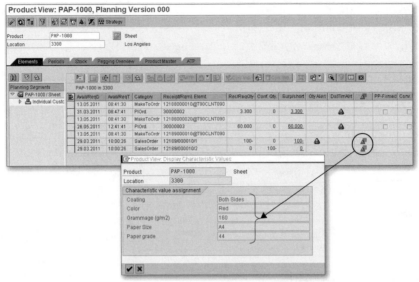

Figure 9.15 SAP APO Product View Screen Showing the Product Characteristics

For a sales orders created in SAP ERP with the requirement date of June 15th (shown in Figure 9.16), the CTP availability check proposes June 24th as the most feasible MAD. The result is yielded based on the scheduling of the paper material production lead time and manufacturing activities performed on the paper machine resource.

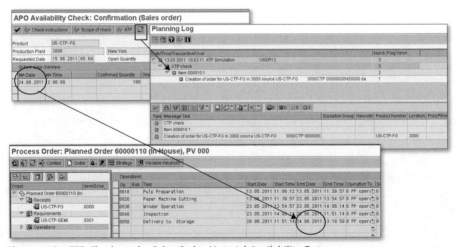

Figure 9.16 CTP Check on the Sales Order Material Availability Date

This scenario is also constrained with block planning for critical resources based on product characteristics. In our case, the paper size characteristic (A2, A3, A4 sizes) forms a basis that can be further expanded to grade, width, and length characteristics. The DETAILED SCHEDULING PLANNING BOARD screen shown in Figure 9.17 gives a schematic view of how the orders are scheduled based on blocks. The individual blocks define the size of the paper (A2, A3, or A4) according to which the requirements and planned orders are planned. Interactive heuristics are available to adjust the blocks and create a feasible manufacturing plan based on market demands.

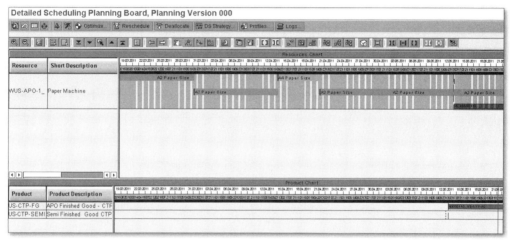

Figure 9.17 Block Planning Modeled for Critical Resource

9.5.2   Case 2: Location Determination Activity

In the second scenario, you use the location determination activity to trigger the rules-based scenario for CTP. The sales orders creation or update (shown in Figure 9.18) in SAP ERP triggers the rules-based ATP check of the primary location 3000. If the paper finished goods stocks are not available, the check looks at a second location 3200 in the rule and locates the inventory.

The sales order is confirmed based on the material availability in the secondary location.

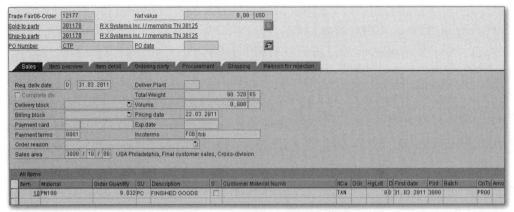

Figure 9.18 Sales Order Creation in SAP ERP for Rules-Based CTP

After the availability check is accepted, the sales order in SAP ERP is split into two schedule lines based on item categories: TAPA and TAN for the same material requirement (see Figure 9.19). As circled in the figure, the TAPA line contains the original request for a material on quantity and date, and TAN is the schedule line that appears after the ATP to fulfill this TAPA item category. The result using the rules-based ATP check shows that the original location will be substituted by a different location as maintained in the rule determination master data.

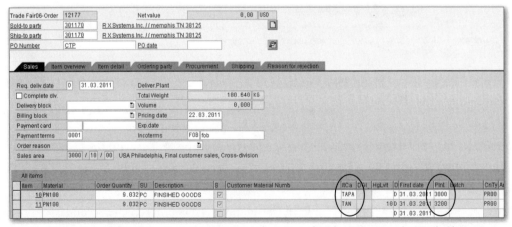

Figure 9.19 Sales Order Item Category Representation after the Rules-Based ATP Check

By accessing Transaction /SAPAPO/RRPLOG1, you have the option of looking at the application logs for the CTP checks (as shown in Figure 9.20) that are done using the PP/DS heuristics. This is a good representation regarding any master data or scheduling errors that are encountered during the PP/DS runs or CTP ATP. In this screen, select the CTP APPLICATION and the date range when the orders were processed.

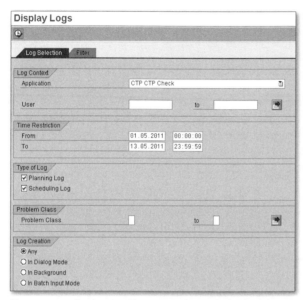

Figure 9.20 Production Planning and Detailed Scheduling CTP Logs

Now that we've completed our discussion of CTP as an advanced ATP check method with PP/DS integration, you should be comfortable with designing and modeling the manufacturing constraints with the order-fulfillment business process.

9.6 Summary

In this chapter, you followed a paper mill industry case study to understand how capable-to-promise in real time can identify supply chain bottlenecks in distribution (using rules-based ATP) and manufacturing constraints to give a feasible order fulfillment date and automatically trigger the manufacturing process with the creation of sales orders. By now, you should understand that the capability of CTP is best suited for industries that are using variant configuration or companies that are constrained with production capacity. Using PP/DS algorithms and the block planning concept, CTP not only creates planned orders, but also performs detailed scheduling on manufacturing resources to confirm customer sales orders. For a more detailed description of the properties and risks of CTP, refer to SAP Note 426563.

The next chapter introduces the multilevel availability check, which is the next level of manufacturing integration with order fulfillment. The chapter explains the basic configuration and master data setup that is required to model the multilevel availability checks in your supply chain, and introduces the concept of the ATP tree structure, which helps improve ATP performance.

Multilevel ATP checks are primarily focused on discrete and assembly-to-order manufacturing scenarios where products are configured for individual customers. This involves exploding BOMs and checking product availability of the components before committing to the customer.

10 Confirming Customer Orders with Multilevel ATP Component-Level Check

Many companies are now adopting the market demand pull-driven concept to reduce the inventory of finished goods and give flexibility to customers to design their end-product configuration. This allows customer to place their orders based on product characteristics (e.g., color) they want. The characteristics concept refers to a company giving its customers selection criteria (e.g., color of a car) to use when purchasing products.

The motivation for industries such as the high-tech, consumer electronics, engineering, and automotive to use the characteristics concept is that it minimizes the amount of effort it takes to create a high volume of master data, which provides supply chain transparency and possibly improves forecasting on components, as well as on configurable end products. The main driver for these industries is the availability of the critical raw materials that can be assembled for the finished product. To answer this concern, the multilevel ATP advanced check method is used to check the availability of these critical components during the order-promising process.

10.1 Overview of the Multilevel ATP Process

Multilevel ATP is generally used in high-tech and engineering industries where final assembly is only initiated when a customer sales order is entered in the SAP ERP system. While performing the SAP APO product availability check (Transaction /SAPAPO/AC03), similar to CTP, multilevel ATP can be called from the check instruction (configuration) or location determination activity when rules-based ATP is used. The key functionalities for multilevel ATP include the following:

- Availability promised based on manufacturing lead time and availability of components in the product bill of materials (BOM)
- Can handle multiple BOM levels (multilevel BOM explosion)
- ATP check at the component level
- Rules-based ATP at the component level and with stock transfer orders and product substitution
- Material allocations at the component level (unit-based capacity)
- Ability to exclude components from the check
- Receipts can be created at a later point in time with a planning run
- Capacity check on daily buckets (using allocation functionality)

In the multilevel ATP process, first the component availability check is done in the sales order, and the BOM is exploded during the ATP check. The sales order line item is confirmed only when the components are available. The ATP check triggers the creation of an ATP tree structure, and receipt elements are generated when the ATP tree structure is converted into a production planning and detailed scheduling (PP/DS) planned order. In a multilevel ATP business scenario, the production capacity is not bottlenecked if materials are not available, but the availability of the component (based on lead time) is the driving factor for the finished goods customer order confirmations.

Figure 10.1 illustrates the multilevel ATP process flow, and we detail each step in the following list.

1. Demand planning (DP) is done using characteristics-based forecasting (CBF) for finished goods. The forecast is then released to PP/DS for master schedule planning.

2. Production planning (PP) explodes the BOM for the components where the dependent demands are transferred to SAP APO Supply Network Planning (SNP) as a forecast (planned independent requirement). The forecast for the components becomes the basis for the production or procurement plan.

3. If a sales order is placed, the forecast of the component is consumed by the dependent demands of the components.

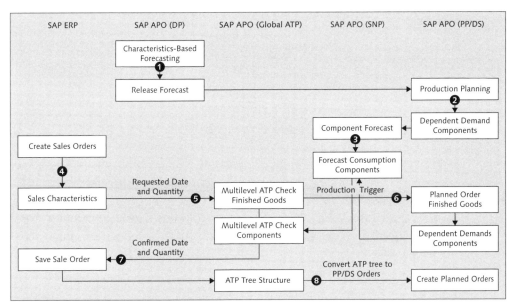

Figure 10.1 Multilevel ATP Process Flow

4. A sales order with characteristics (variant configuration) is created in SAP ERP, which triggers the multilevel ATP check. The multilevel ATP triggers the production plan for the finished goods with requested date and quantity. The PP/DS master data production process model (PPM) or production data structure (PDS) explodes the BOM, and a simulated planned order is created. The dependent demand for the components is passed back to multilevel ATP to check the availability for the components. The components can have separate *check instructions* and *check control*, which are defined to separate the *scope of check* between finished goods and components.

5. The sales order for the finished goods is confirmed per the component availability check result.

6. Upon the sales order being saved, no planned order is created, but an ATP tree is created in the background, which stores the detail of the simulated planned orders, based on which the sales order was confirmed (note that this differs from the CTP process). Based on the PP/DS horizon maintained in the customization or product master data, the ATP tree structure is converted to receipt planned orders. The planned order is created with the properties CHECKED AND FIRMED and the ATP category AL.

> **Note**
>
> Multilevel ATP does have a few limitations, which you can find information on in SAP Note 455421.

10.2 Business Case Study Example

The business scenario of the computer assembly industry best suits an example of multilevel ATP. The computer industry has a component-constrained supply chain, with the primary bottleneck being the availability of its key components (memory, disk drives, processors, etc.). The supply chain (illustrated in Figure 10.2) requires strong collaboration between the company (OEM), its third-party suppliers, and contract manufacturers.

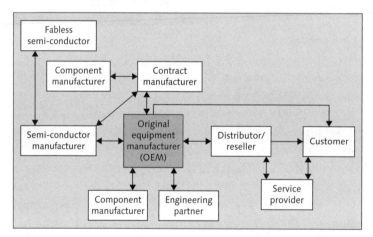

Figure 10.2 High-Tech Industry Supply Chain

The computer industry usually has two product structures for sales and distribution: *fixed configuration* and *open configuration*. The fixed configuration has unique serial codes, whereas the open configuration can be freely configured by the customer. The fixed configuration ordering lead time is lower, so the company can follow *made-to-order* policies, and usually retailers keep inventory up to an optimal level.

For open configuration, the customer or consumer has the flexibility to define the computer configuration and class under the *configure-to-order* policy. The serial code for the open configuration customer order is either defined newly in the final ordering business process or is based on the housing and system board base unit serial number. In summary, the made-to-order method can keep some inventory in the computer supply chain described earlier, but the configure-to-order method does not hold any inventory in the pipeline.

10.2.1 Fulfilling Business Logic and Rules

The dynamics of the computer assembly business supply chain and product structure requires an ATP functionality to scan all the best available options and propose the best feasible delivery date for customer orders. This ensures faster inventory turnaround.

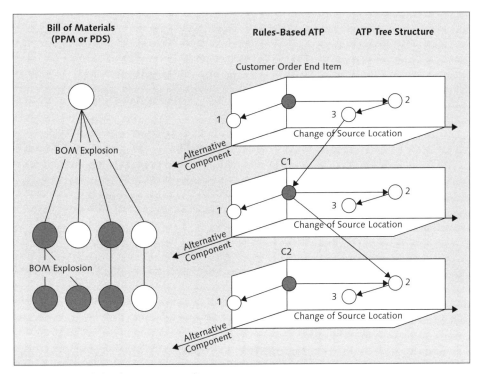

Figure 10.3 Multilevel ATP Functionality

The multilevel ATP functionality in combination with rules-based ATP fulfills the business logic/rules to a large extent. Multilevel ATP (see Figure 10.3) explodes the BOM for the customer end item and then checks the availability of each component before committing to the confirmed delivery date. The confirmation results are stored in the ATP tree structure to enable better performance and are converted to receipts elements at a later stage. The ATP tree structure is determined via the BOM and the substitutions at component level, in other words, via requirements at the component level or requirements on the issue side of stock transport requisitions (STRs).

10.2.2 Variant Configuration

Multilevel ATP also supports the *variant configuration* concept. The variant configuration has the following salient features:

▶ You do not need to create separate material master data for each variant combination.

▶ Super BOM and super routing master data is enough to represent all possible manufacturing variants and operations.

▶ You can react with more flexibility to customer demands.

▶ Collaboration (information exchange) increases among sales, engineering, and production functional areas.

For variant configuration support, a material with different product characteristics/options called a *configurable material* is created. These materials are created with material type KMAT or given the indicator CONFIGURABLE in the material master record (BASIC DATA VIEW 2).

Now that we've discussed the business scenario, let's move on to configure the basic requirements of the multilevel ATP check using the computer assembly industry to illustrate each step.

10.3 Basic Configuration of Multilevel ATP

The multilevel ATP configuration consists of customization steps in global ATP and PP/DS for an integrated solution. In the following subsections, we will walk through the basic configuration steps that you must follow in global ATP and PP/DS to set up multilevel ATP for the computer assembly industry scenario.

10.3.1 Global ATP: Check Mode

The production type you enter in the CHECK MODE field, as shown in Figure 10.4, controls how the system executes the product availability check. The check mode (with available options of CTP, multilevel ATP, kit check, and characteristics-based) will be input as material master data for the finished and component products. Similar check modes (accessed via Transaction /SAPAPO/ATPC06) need to be defined for the component for which further multilevel ATP needs to be performed.

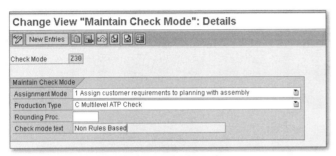

Figure 10.4 Check Mode for Finished Goods

10.3.2 Global ATP: Check Instruction

Next, configure your system's check instructions, which help determine the sequence to check the product availability (product allocation, rules-based ATP) and trigger multilevel ATP check, which is production-based per your company's defined business rules. In the following list, we provide the settings that are required for you to configure your system for multilevel ATP check instruction for both the finished goods and the components. These settings (accessed via Transaction /SAPAPO/ATPC07) are shown in Figure 10.5.

▶ COMPNTS REMAIN. REQMT
This field determines how the system should deal with a requirement quantity that is not confirmed during the second step of ATP checks on the component. Two options are available to create requirements: Header level or component level. For our computer business scenario, choose the CREATE REMAINING REQUIREMENT AT HEADER LEVEL option, which allows two-step ATP checks to be performed at the header and component levels.

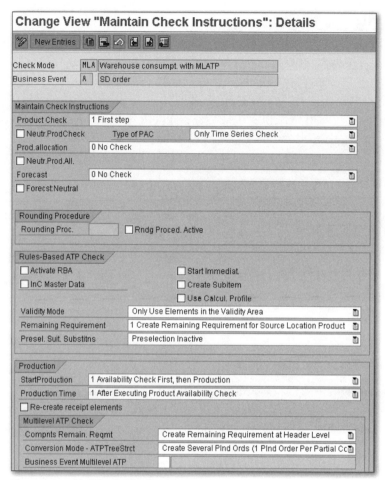

Figure 10.5 Multilevel ATP Check Instruction

▶ CONVERSION MODE – ATPTREESTRCT

In this field, define the type of sales order confirmations (full or partial) for which you want the planned orders to be created in PP/DS after the ATP tree structure is converted. The ATP tree structure is only created after both the steps of multilevel ATP are confirmed. The first step determines the requirement date and quantity for the components to be checked in the second step. For our computer business scenario, you can choose to have planned orders created even for the partial confirmation of the sales order.

▶ BUSINESS EVENT MULTILEVEL ATP

Here, you can use the special business event for multilevel ATP to distinguish between the check control for the components and the check control for the finished product; the combination of the business event and check control defines the scope of check for the ATP check. This field is used when the scope of check differs between the finished product and components. For our scenario, we have kept the scope of check similar for both finished goods and component.

10.3.3 Global ATP: Rules-Based Multilevel ATP

For our computer business scenario, we want to build business rules for inventory being searched in multiple production locations, and, if not available, the critical raw materials can be substituted by alternative component items. To suit this requirement, we need to configure the rules-based ATP for alternative location or alternative components check during the multilevel ATP check. In this section, we have provided a list of configuration steps and screenshots to mark your progress.

1. Define the condition table for product and internal product (finished product and component of PC assembly). Select the two fields for the finished product and components from the list of available field catalogs, and generate them before saving the condition table.

2. Define the ACCESS SEQUENCE, and assign a condition table to it. This configuration defines the selection criteria for the PC manufacturing condition table maintenance. Figure 10.6 shows the combination of the access sequence and previously configured condition table.

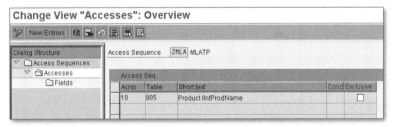

Figure 10.6 Access Sequence Definition for Multilevel ATP

3. Define the CONDITION TYPE (in our example, ZMLA), and assign the access sequence to it to combine the condition table and access sequence.

4. Define the RULE STRATEGY, and assign the condition type to it. Here, you can define the number of access sequence and condition type, which can be incorporated in the same rule strategy.

5. Define the rule strategy sequence (RULE STRAT SEQ.), and assign the rule strategy to it. Figure 10.7 shows the three steps of rules strategy that are defined with rules-based and multilevel ATP checks.

Figure 10.7 Rule Strategy Sequence for Multilevel ATP

6. Assign the rule strategy sequence to the specified combination of technical scenarios, business events, and action types as shown in Figure 10.8.

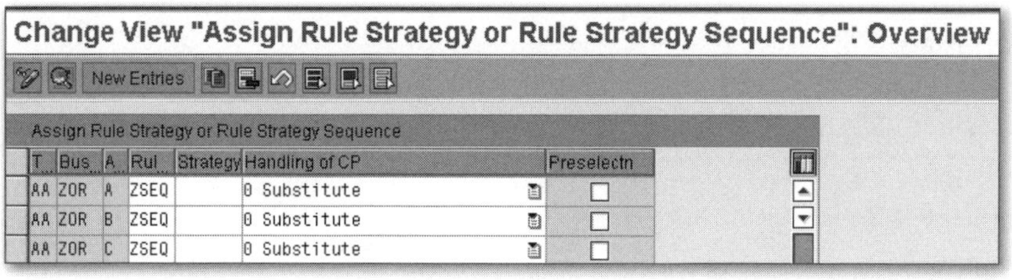

Figure 10.8 Assignment of Rule Strategy Sequence to Technical Scenario, Business Event, and Action Type for Multilevel ATP

10.3.4 Production Planning and Detailed Scheduling: Global Settings

SAP APO PP/DS is used to create production orders in the system. PP/DS uses an algorithm in the form of heuristics and master data to create the planned orders. For multilevel ATP, you use PP/DS to create planned orders from the saved ATP tree structures, which helps with system performance.

The global settings define the basic setup for PP/DS to create and schedule production orders. Depending on the global setting configuration or master data settings, you can convert planned orders for the computer business scenario. This setting is maintained in the PP/DS configuration global settings or in the product location master data. The scheduling horizon defines the time horizon for which you need to convert the ATP tree structure into planned orders. The conversion of the ATP structure to a planned order depends on one of the following settings:

▸ PP/DS horizon maintained in the product master

▸ PP/DS horizon maintained in the planning version (Transaction /SAPAPO/ MVM)

▸ Customizing of global settings of PP/DS (Transaction /SAPAPO/RRPCUST1).

The number of days you specify in the SCHEDULING HORIZON IN DAYS field is used to immediately convert the ATP tree structure into the procurement proposal example panned order. The duration of the scheduling horizon is defined in calendar days. If none of these conditions are met when the sales order is saved, the system saves the ATP tree structure. You can convert the ATP tree structure with requirement dates outside the scheduling horizon (PP/DS horizon) using the following transactions:

▸ **Transaction /SAPAPO/RRP_ATP2PPDS:** Conversion of ATP tree structures by maintaining the offset to the scheduling horizon.

▸ **Transaction /SAPAPO/ATP2PPDS:** Conversion of ATP tree structures in the background can be used to convert ATP tree structures into planned orders or STRs in the background.

To convert ATP tree structure conversion to PP/DS planned orders, maintain the scheduling horizon in calendar days and set the STRATEGY PROFILE for forward/ backward scheduling strategy (refer back to Figure 6.21 in Chapter 6). To do this, follow the IMG path SPRO • ADVANCED PLANNING AND OPTIMIZATION • SUPPLY CHAIN PLANNING • PRODUCTION PLANNING AND DETAILED SCHEDULING • GLOBAL SETTINGS • MAINTAIN GLOBAL PARAMETERS AND DEFAULT. We have maintained the CALENDAR DAYS value as 40, and the strategy profile as SAP002 for the scheduling of the planned orders.

Additionally, use Transaction /SAPAPO/ATREE_DSP (see Figure 10.9) to display all of the active tree structures that are waiting for PP/DS order conversion. The receipt and requirement element details are seen for each order confirmed during the multilevel ATP check.

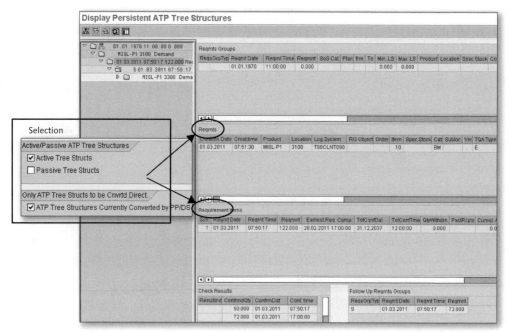

Figure 10.9 ATP Tree Structure Display

10.3.5 Demand Planning (SAP APO DP): Planning Area and Planning Book

The next configuration element focuses on the demand planning of the computer finished goods using the characteristics-based concept in SAP APO DP. Based on historical sales order data in the planning books for the computers, a forecasting model can be built to perform statistical forecasting for the finished goods.

The business process is supported by characteristics-based forecasting (CBF), which is a functionality in DP that is used to forecast products with different attributes, as well as perform the BOM explosion for the components. The configuration requirement to activate the CBF in SAP APO DP to support this functionality is done with the CHARSTC-BASED FORECASTING indicator at the basic planning object structure (accessed via Transaction /SAPAPO/MSDP_ADMIN), which is illustrated in Figure 10.10.

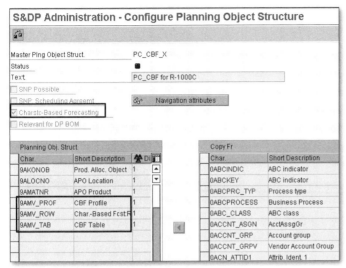

Figure 10.10 Characteristics-Based Forecasting in SAP APO Demand Planning

Figure 10.11 shows the design configuration to set up a planning book in SAP APO DP. The planning books serve as a user decision supporting tool to slice and dice the DP data at different characteristics levels for a given bucket (e.g., monthly). The demand planner views or simulates the sales order, forecast, and any changes for the computer products in the planning book.

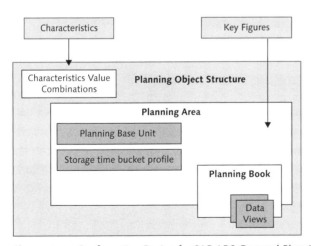

Figure 10.11 Configuration Design for SAP APO Demand Planning

An example configured planning book (accessed via Transaction /SAPAPO/SDP94) for CBF is shown in Figure 10.12.

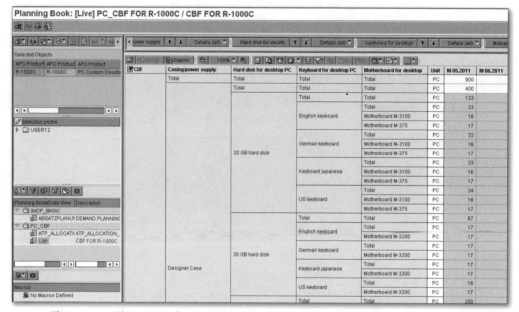

Figure 10.12 Planning Book in SAP APO Demand Planning for CBF

Now that we've discussed the configuration objects for global ATP, PP/DS, and DP, let's look at the master data requirement to make this integrated scenario work.

10.4 Basic Master Data Rule Requirements

The master requirements for multilevel ATP revolve around variant configuration, production, and DP. The configurations are represented by characteristics values. During the sales order processing, these characteristics values need to be input for planning and execution processes. Multilevel ATP master data maintenance is done in SAP ERP and SAP APO.

In the following subsections, we will discuss the most relevant master data for multilevel ATP.

10.4.1 SAP ERP Variant Configuration

Variant configuration is used when you have a configurable material such as a computer (made up of components such as a processor, monitor, keyboard, etc.). These components are called *characteristics* in variant configuration. If variant configuration is used in SAP ERP, master data in the form of super BOM, super routing, class, characteristics, object dependencies, and configuration profile are required. The relation and interdependencies between these master data objects is shown in Figure 10.13.

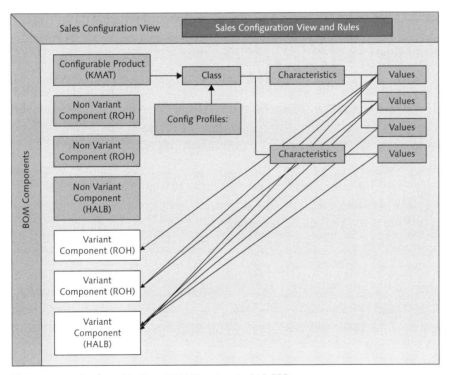

Figure 10.13 Configurable Item BOM Structure in SAP ERP

In the following list, we describe each of these master data objects briefly:

▶ **Super BOM**
The super BOM contains all of the components (both variant and nonvariant parts) needed to produce the configurable product.

▶ **Super routing**
Describes the production process for all variants of a product. Instead of creating a routing for each variant of a product, you can create operations for one routing or a "super" routing. It is also possible to maintain object dependencies for sequences, operations/suboperations, and production resource/tool assignments in super routing.

▶ **Characteristics**
These are used to define the features of a configurable material. To enable the system to use characteristics to configure a material, assign the material to a class of class type 300 in Transaction MM02, and then choose the CLASSIFICATION tab in the material master.

▶ **Variant class**
The variant class is used to hold, or contain, the characteristics that describe the configurable material. The class type determines which object types can be classified. Class is used in variant configuration if the class has a class type that supports variant configuration. In customizing for classification, the VARIANT CLASS TYPE indicator must be set for the class type. In the standard system, this is class type 300.

▶ **Object dependencies**
Used to restrict the combinations of characteristics options, and selects the correct BOM components and operations to produce a variant. The following functions are performed by object dependencies:

  ▶ Describes the interdependencies between characteristics and characteristic values.

  ▶ Controls which components are selected from a BOM and which operations are selected from a task list.

  ▶ Changes the values of fields in BOM items and operations during configuration.

▶ **Configuration profile**
The configuration profile controls the configuration process in the sales order. The configurable profile is also used to define central settings for configuring the object. Using this profile via Transaction CU43 (Figure 10.14), it is possible to hide some of the characteristic values that are defined during characteristic creation. Based on this configuration profile during the sales order creation (via Transaction VA01) for computer finished goods, the profile will be prompted to enter all the characteristics value defined (e.g. casing, keyboard, hard disk, etc.) as shown in the figure.

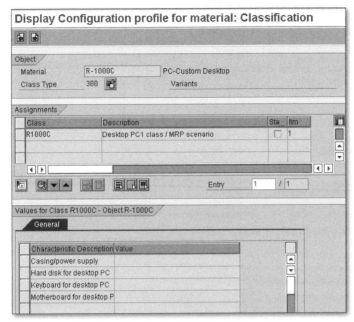

Figure 10.14 Configuration Profile Definition in SAP ERP

10.4.2 SAP APO Demand Planning: Characteristics-Based Forecasting

You can use SAP APO DP for statistical forecasting and promotion planning based on the historical data and forecast model as input. Because the computer business scenario has many characteristics variants, SAP recommends using characteristics-based forecasting (CBF).

The master data needed for SAP APO DP are CBF profile, CBF table, and characteristics value combinations (CVCs). The dependencies between these three master data sets in SAP APO are shown in Figure 10.15.

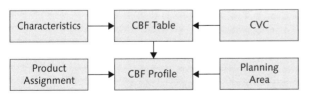

Figure 10.15 SAP APO Demand Planning – CBF Master Data Relationships

These elements help in the forecasting process and the subsequent release of the forecast to SAP APO PP/DS. The CBF profile assigned to the configurable product is maintained in the CBF profile and consists of the CBF table and characteristics values. The forecasting is done on these characteristics values and is also relevant for the ATP check and forecast consumption process. The following list describes the master data objects briefly:

► **CBF table**
Accessed via Transaction /SAPAPO/IPM01, the characteristic table is a planning object that contains characteristic combinations (keyboard, hard disk, motherboard, etc.).

► **CBF profile**
Accessed via Transaction /SAPAPO/IPM01, the planning profile contains characteristic tables for a configurable material. As shown in Figure 10.16, the valid characteristics combination for computer parts is generated for a particular configurable item.

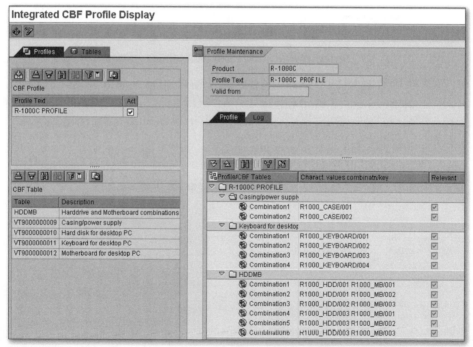

Figure 10.16 CBF Profile Maintenance in SAP APO Demand Planning

▶ **Characteristics value combinations (CVC)**
Accessed via Transaction /SAPAPO/MC62, this defines the combinations by which the configurable product can be forecast and planned.

10.4.3 SAP APO Product Location Master

You can access the SAP APO product location via Transaction /SAPAPO/MAT1 and click different tabs to maintain the master data in the ATP, DEMAND, and PP/DS tabs. The master data that is maintained in these tabs helps in the ATP check and forecast consumption process. The tabs and the fields maintained in them are listed here:

▶ ATP
Define the CHECK MODE and ATP GROUP. You can define the values separately for finished goods or components depending on the scope of check. For our business scenario, the same check mode (02) is maintained for both finished and complete.

▶ DEMAND
Define the forecast consumption for the components items. The dependent demand generated from finished goods sales orders is consumed by the CBF forecasts (shown in Figure 10.17). For the forecast consumption process to work, the ASSEMBLY PLANNING flag needs to be checked for the finished goods to trigger the forecast consumption. The proposed strategy of planning with assembly needed for forecast consumption is transferred from SAP ERP via CIF.

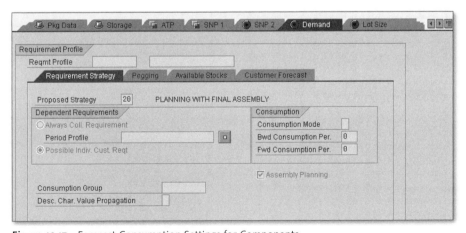

Figure 10.17 Forecast Consumption Settings for Components

▶ PP/DS

Define the PP/DS HORIZON for the ATP tree structure conversion to planned orders and the plan explosion for PDS. For our business scenario, you can maintain 30 days (short term) for the conversion because the planning is done at the daily bucket. For medium- to long-term (more than 30 days), the planning is done in monthly buckets.

10.4.4 SAP APO Production Data Structure

The production version (routing and BOM) is transferred via CIF to SAP APO in the form of the production data structure (PDS) or production process model (PPM). The use of the PDS is mandatory for the integration of object dependencies from SAP ERP. Similar to the object dependencies check in SAP ERP, it is possible to simulate the impact of a configuration within the PDS display via Transaction /SAPAPO/ CURTO_SIMU. Figure 10.18 shows the PDS structure of the finished goods with BOM components and characteristics values for the components.

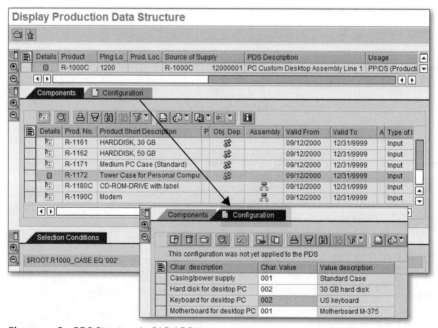

Figure 10.18 PDS Structure in SAP APO

10.4.5 Rules-Based Condition Record

A condition record is defined to maintain the rules-based master data for the location or component substitution business rules. You can access the table via Transaction /SAPCND/AO11 and input the related condition type as configured earlier in Section 10.3.3.

Now that we've completed the configuration and master data maintenance for global ATP and PP/DS, we can begin business scenario testing.

10.5 Key Steps in Scenario Testing

Two scenarios are shown in this section. In the first scenario, the sales order characteristics value is transferred to SAP APO. Based on these characteristics values for the computer, the components are checked for availability. In the second scenario, we demonstrate the integration of rules-based ATP with multilevel ATP whereby the computer components can be substituted if the primary components are not available.

10.5.1 Scenario 1: Multilevel ATP

During the sales order creation (shown in Figure 10.19), the sales order requests the characteristics value assignment for the component items. The sales order item category is TAC (variant configuration). During the sales order processing, the finished good (and components) availability check is done with the multilevel ATP check, and the corresponding planned order is created in SAP APO.

The Receipts Chars and Requirements Characteristics for pegged elements are shown in the Pegging Overview tab in the SAP APO Product View screen of Transaction /SAPAPO/RRP3 (Figure 10.20). The characteristics valuation for the planned order and sales order can be seen by clicking the green triangle icons. The confirmation of the configurable product is based on the component availability dates.

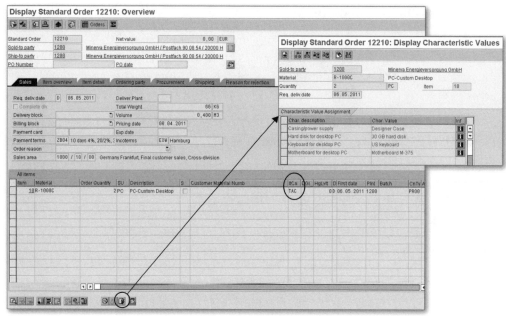

Figure 10.19 Variant Configuration Sales Order Creation in SAP ERP

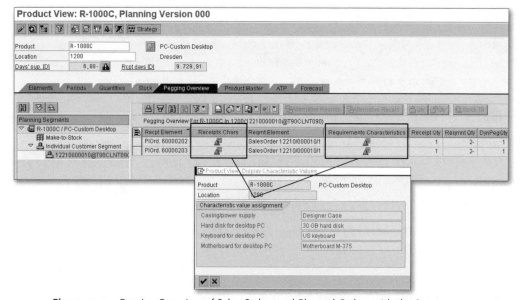

Figure 10.20 Pegging Overview of Sales Orders and Planned Orders with the Same Characteristics Values

The planned order details are shown in the Context for Planned Order screen shown in Figure 10.21 (accessed via Transaction /SAPAPO/RRP3). Along with the displayed planned order details, you can click the Context button for more drilldown details. All the dependent demand of the component element is shown pegged with the corresponding receipt elements.

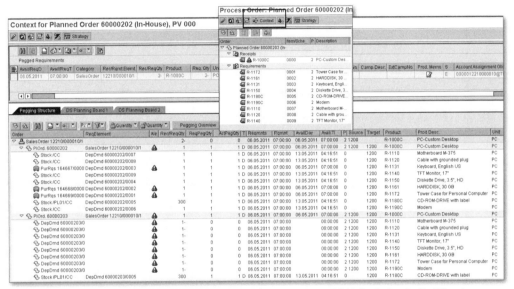

Figure 10.21 Planned Order Context View Showing the Component BOM Explosion in Multilevel ATP

If you increase the sales order quantity, an additional planned order is generated.

10.5.2 Scenario 2: Multilevel ATP with a Rules-Based Check

In our second example, we create the sales order in SAP ERP. Following this step, the multilevel ATP check is triggered automatically for the computer finished goods and component items during the sales order creation process. The confirmation of the sales order is based on the component availability date.

The planned order is created later, after saving the sales order, using SAP APO PP/DS due to performance reasons. An ATP tree structure is created in the background, which will be used later for the conversion to the PP/DS planned order.

You can display the ATP tree structure with Transaction /SAPAPO/ATREE_DSP to view all the sales orders that have undergone the multilevel ATP check and are waiting for the PP/DS planned order conversion. Use Transaction /SAPAPO/ ATP2PPDS within the PP/DS horizon defined in order to initiate the conversion to receipt element planned order. Upon conversion, the multilevel ATP planned order is created with a status of CF (confirmed fully), which you can see in the Product View screen (shown in Figure 10.22).

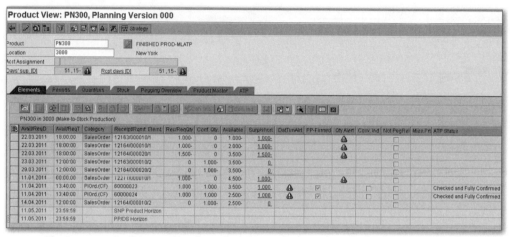

Figure 10.22 Confirmation Based on the Multilevel ATP Created Planned Orders

The multilevel ATP planned order created (shown in Figure 10.23) will have PDS or PPM exploded. Note that the quantity cannot be changed manually.

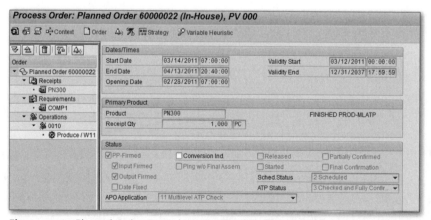

Figure 10.23 Planned Order Created as a Result of Multilevel ATP

During the second step of the multilevel ATP check, the dependent demand for the component (Figure 10.24) is automatically checked with the available receipts elements. The second step for the component check is automatically triggered after the computer finished good availability check.

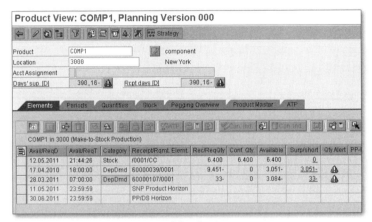

Figure 10.24 Dependent Demand for the Component

Another business rule that can be modeled is component substitution. Based on the rules-based ATP check, a component can be substituted if the primary component is not available. As seen in Figure 10.25, multilevel ATP checks the availability of component 1 while performing the availability check for the finished goods. Component 1 is not available and is being substituted by component 2.

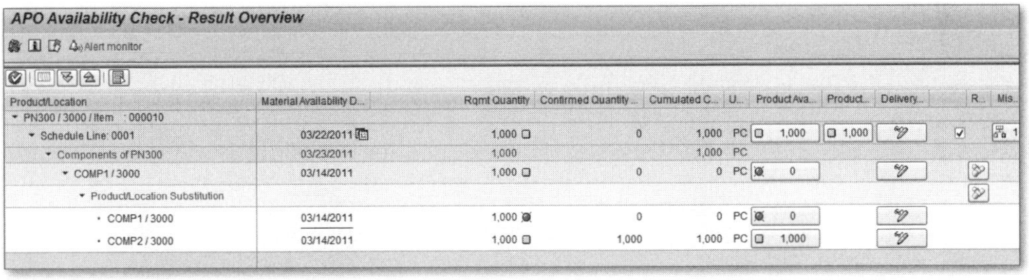

Figure 10.25 Rules-Based Component Substitution in Multilevel ATP

The second step of multilevel ATP again searches for the availability of receipt elements for the substituted component. If applicable, the finished goods planned order CONTEXT view shows the substituted component.

10.6   Summary

Multilevel ATP functionality is best suited for the make-to-order or configure-to-order scenarios, using the variant configuration concept. Using the computer manufacturing company as our example business scenario, we learned the configuration and master data setup that is required to model the multilevel ATP check. The functionality using characteristics-based planning helps in performing the component availability check before confirming the customer sales orders. In this advanced ATP check, both the planned order duration and the object dependencies are factored. Unlike CTP, multilevel ATP assumes that production capacity is not bottleneck, and can be combined with rules-based ATP to provide component or location substitutions.

The next chapter shows how you can integrate global ATP with different modules of the supply chain planning processes. This integration is required for the end-to-end business process in order for fulfillment and supply chain planning to work seamlessly and provide process visibility.

Global ATP integrates with supply planning processes for effective order fulfillment. By integrating with SAP APO capable-to-match and transportation planning and vehicle scheduling modules, we show you how global ATP capabilities meet the business objectives of integrating supply chain planning with order fulfillment.

11 Integrating Global ATP with Supply Planning

Companies try to improve delivery performance (and thus customer satisfaction) by tightly integrating order fulfillment with supply planning. This helps companies keep their inventory in control and also reduce overall supply chain cycle time.

The objective of this chapter is to explain the integration points between supply planning and order fulfillment, as well as how the overall end-to-end business process works. This chapter presents the supply planning and global ATP integration concepts and gives examples from supply chain planning, as well as transportation planning and scheduling, to show the execution integration aspects. The examples we have included show how you can integrate the global ATP functionality with other components of SAP ERP.

11.1 Integration between Supply Planning and Order Fulfillment

Global ATP integrates closely with supply planning for the order-fulfillment process and commits to customers' orders based on the input information provided by the supply planning receipts elements. Figure 11.1 illustrates the integration between global ATP and supply planning.

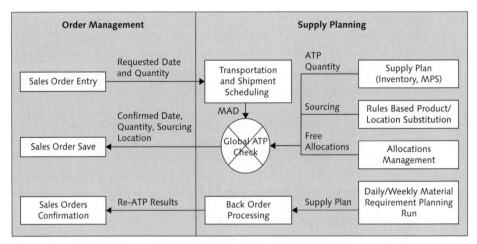

Figure 11.1 Integration between Order Management and Supply Planning

As shown in the figure, the following are the main integration features:

▸ Transportation shipment and scheduling to calculate the material availability date (MAD) based on the lead time of business activities before the global ATP product availability check (refer to Chapter 5).

▸ Current available stock and future supply plan receipts as ATP quantity input to global ATP calculation.

▸ Rules-based ATP checks for determining product or location substitutions based on supply chain business rules (refer to Chapter 6).

▸ Allocation management to distribute and sell products to key customers during a supply shortage. Allocation can also be termed as quotas for distribution of available inventory (refer to Chapter 7).

▸ Backorder processing (BOP) takes the latest supply planning run inputs to re-ATP all the backlog orders to calculate a new MAD and commit to new delivery dates (refer to Chapter 8).

The seamless integration between supply chain planning and order fulfillment increases the quality of the customer service level and provides tight inventory control in the supply chain. The integration provides valuable inputs to the company's sales and operation planning process toward demand versus supply balancing.

Global ATP serves as a corrective tool during the execution process by not only optimizing the supply network inventory by searching stocks from multiple locations but also by triggering the manufacturing process when imbalances occur in the demand and supply plans. Global ATP—with its capable-to-promise (CTP; refer to Chapter 9) and multilevel ATP (refer to Chapter 10) capabilities of checking production capacities and key component availabilities—connects the sales order and manufacturing processes on near real time.

Now that you have an overview of the integration, let's look at the first example, which uses the combination of supply planning (using a CTM algorithm) and the global ATP rules-based approach to solve a business scenario.

11.2   Integrating Rules of Global ATP in the Capable-to-Match Planning Run

Capable-to-match (CTM) is a supply planning engine that performs iterations processes to match demand with supplies according to the search strategy defined. This engine is primarily used to prioritize demand elements (sales orders, rush orders), customer priority (key accounts), and product priority (high margin).

Global ATP can be integrated with CTM to support *down binning* scenarios (substitution of lower-quality products by higher-quality products), which are often found in the high-tech industries (e.g., in the semiconductor business). In this scenario, rules-based global ATP using product substitution is combined with the CTM planning engine. Let's take a semiconductor industry example, for instance, where primary products are often replaced or substituted by another co-product to keep the manufacturing process progressing. Using the rules-based feature, you can specify substitutions that the system can use so that a higher-quality product can be used to fulfill the demand for a lower-quality product. This scenario is common when the demand is more than available inventory for the primary product.

In the CTM planning run, the system uses the available receipts and supplies the higher-quality product as replacement stock. During the production step, the system simultaneously includes generated co-products directly in the quantity conversion for covering the requirement. At the same time, the system distributes the desired requirement quantity across the receipt elements in the planned order for the original product and the co-products, in accordance with the output quantity relationships given in the in-house production source of supply. The system also performs this distribution if you have only defined substitutions for one part of the co-products. The system uses the available receipts for co-products immediately in a product substitution order to cover the requirement for the original product.

CTM planning always performs a down binning scenario when the following prerequisites have been fulfilled:

▶ An in-house production source of supply, with co-products, exists for the original product.

▶ Substitutions have been defined that the system can use for an original product with co-products that have the same in-house production source of supply.

Next, let's look at the configuration and master data setup to model this scenario in the system. The configurations need to be completed in both global ATP and CTM to enable the supply planning run. The master data involves maintenance of the supply planning run scope and the profile to define the demand and supply constraints/priorities.

11.2.1 Configuration for Rules-Based ATP Integration with CTM

For CTM, follow the path to define the parameter values (the resulting screen is shown in Figure 11.2): IMG • ADVANCED PLANNING AND OPTIMIZATION • SUPPLY CHAIN PLANNING • MULTILEVEL SUPPLY AND DEMAND MATCHING • MAKE SETTINGS FOR RULES-BASED PLANNING.

Next, define the rules-based condition customization:

▶ **Access sequences**
Follow the IMG path IMG • ADVANCED PLANNING AND OPTIMIZATION • SUPPLY CHAIN PLANNING • GLOBAL AVAILABLE-TO-PROMISE • RULES-BASED AVAILABILITY CHECK • MAINTAIN ACCESS SEQUENCES to maintain the ACCESS SEQUENCE with one condition field ("Product Number") as shown in Figure 11.3.

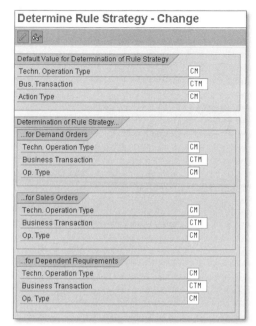

Figure 11.2 Capable-to-Match Configuration for Rules-Based ATP Check

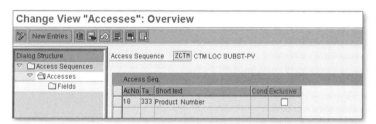

Figure 11.3 Access Sequence for Capable-to-Match Rules-Based Planning

▶ **Condition type**
Define the condition type CTM, and input the access sequence configured in the earlier step. To do this, follow the path IMG • ADVANCED PLANNING AND OPTIMIZATION • SUPPLY CHAIN PLANNING • GLOBAL AVAILABLE-TO-PROMISE • RULES-BASED AVAILABILITY CHECK • CONDITION TYPE.

▶ **Rule strategy**
Define the RULE STRATEGY with the earlier configured condition type (as shown in Figure 11.4). Follow the path IMG • ADVANCED PLANNING AND OPTIMIZATION • SUPPLY CHAIN PLANNING • GLOBAL AVAILABLE-TO-PROMISE • RULES-BASED AVAILABILITY CHECK • RULE STRATEGY.

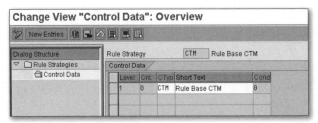

Figure 11.4 Rule Strategy for Capable-to-Match Rules-Based Planning

▶ **Assign rule strategy**

Define the TECH. SCENARIO, BUSINESS TRANS., and ACTION TYPE as configured earlier for CTM (see Figure 11.5). This configuration provides the technical link between global ATP and CTM. The global ATP configuration of the technical scenario/business transaction/action type combination should coincide with the CTM configuration of the technical operation type/business transaction/action type combination. To do this, follow the path IMG • ADVANCED PLANNING AND OPTIMIZATION • SUPPLY CHAIN PLANNING • GLOBAL AVAILABLE-TO-PROMISE • RULES-BASED AVAILABILITY CHECK • ASSIGN RULE STRATEGY OR RULE STRATEGY SEQUENCE.

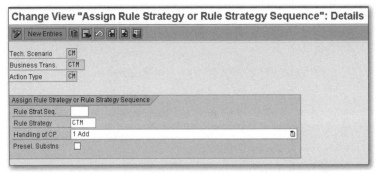

Figure 11.5 Rule Strategy for Capable-to-Match Rules-Based Planning

11.2.2   Master Data for Rules-Based ATP Integration with Capable-to-Match

The master data steps for our business scenario consist of maintaining the global ATP rule maintenance and condition table, while maintaining the CTM profile.

The global ATP rule maintenance specifies the business rule for the product substitution, while the condition table connects the product with the rule for the global ATP check. In the CTM profile, we mention rules-based planning for the supply planning run.

▶ **Rule maintenance**
You can access this step via Transaction /SAPAPO/RBA04. Maintain the rule with location product substitution (shown in Figure 11.6). Create a user-defined rule, and then under LOCATION PRODUCT SUBSTITUTNS, maintain the primary products and co-products that need to be substituted.

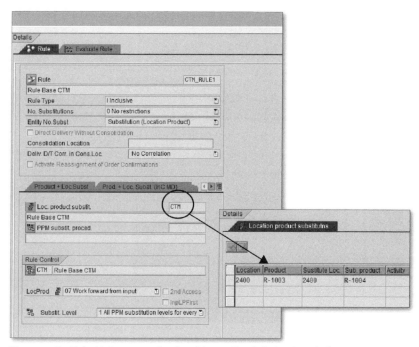

Figure 11.6 Rule Maintenance for Capable-to-Match Rules-Based Planning

▶ **Maintain rule condition table**
Access this step via Transaction /SAPCND/AO11, and maintain the rule condition table (shown in Figure 11.7). In the rule condition table, assign the product with the rule created in the prior step.

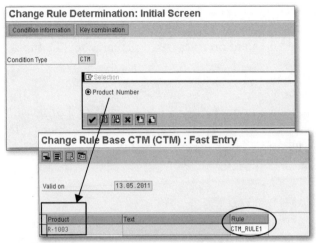

Figure 11.7 Rule Condition Table

▶ **CTM profile**

Access this step via Transaction /SAPAPO/CTM. Maintain the CTM profile to include the rule definition under the SPECIAL STRATEGIES tab as shown in Figure 11.8. In the SUBSTITUTION area of the tab, select the FIND AND USE RULE ACCORDING TO DEMAND option in the RULES field.

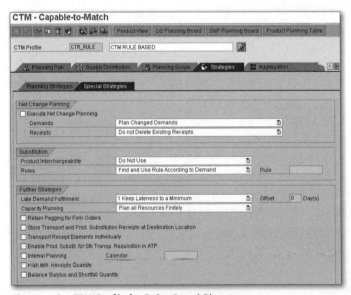

Figure 11.8 CTM Profile for Rules-Based Planning

Now that the configuration and the master data are complete, you can start the simulation run. The simulation run provides a good indication that the master data rule is picked. After the rule is picked, the item substitution should also occur for the supply shortage scenario. As shown in Figure 11.9, the simulation run displays the substituted item as supply element for the primary product demand (requirement).

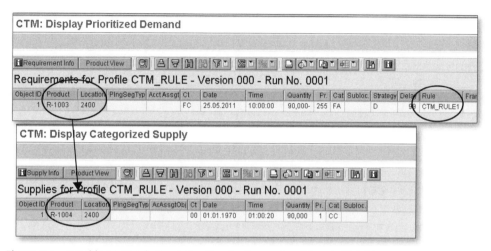

Figure 11.9 Capable-to-Match Simulation Run for Demand and Supply Matching

Now that we've looked at the supply planning run integration with global ATP, let's discuss the execution with transportation planning and vehicle scheduling (TP/VS). This functionality provides a feature named dynamic route determination (DRD), otherwise known as a routing guide), which is integrated with global ATP. We will discuss DRD and its integration with global ATP in the next section.

11.3 Integrating Global ATP in Transportation Planning and Vehicle Scheduling

Dynamic route determination (DRD) is a functionality within transportation planning/vehicle scheduling (TP/VS) that integrates with global ATP during order processing. This functionality enables you to determine the dynamic routes during the sales creation. During the sales order entry, route determination and scheduling is determined by taking into account carrier allocation and resource capacity. Figure

11.10 illustrates what happens when global ATP is triggered during the sales order creation in SAP ERP.

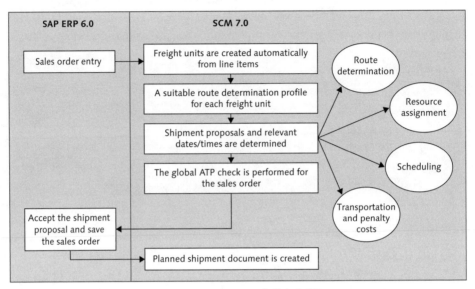

Figure 11.10 TP/VS Dynamic Route Determination and Global ATP

A computer manufacturer markets its products worldwide and has a globally distributed supply chain, where multiple sales orders are received from overseas customers and a shipment is consolidated with all these sales orders for shipping the goods via sea. Following are the DRD process steps for how the transaction progresses from SAP ERP to SAP Supply Chain Management (SAP SCM) and global ATP integration:

1. During the sales order creation of these multiple orders in SAP ERP, all the sales order line items are converted into freight units, and a temporary shipment is created in SAP SCM.

2. A DRD profile is identified, which defines the planning constraints. Also in this step, the suitable routes are determined, the resource is assigned for capacity reservation, MAD is determined via scheduling, and the transportation and penalty costs (based on the cost profile) are calculated. The routes are identified based on the customer and material master data; the orders are then scheduled based on the resource (shipping vessel) available capacity.

3. The system displays proposal shipments (shown in Figure 11.11), and the global ATP check is then performed based on MAD to determine the delivery dates on customer orders. The user accepts the delivery proposal on the shipment. The business has options to consolidate the freight units based on different transportation criteria (transportation cost, lead time, etc.).

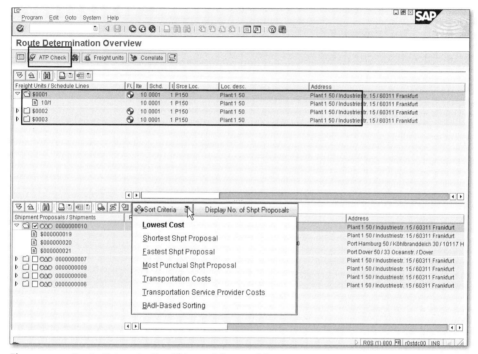

Figure 11.11 Route Determination Shipment Proposal Screen

4. After the shipment proposal is selected by the business users, and the sales order is saved in SAP ERP, a planned shipment is created in TP/VS.

11.3.1 Dynamic Route Determination (DRD) Profile

The DRD profile is used to model the business supply chain constraints related to transportation. The shipment proposal created in TP/VS is based on this profile. The profile contains control parameters in terms of transportation duration, planning horizon, windows, and resource assignment for DRD. The route determination profile defines the steps that the route determination is to execute and for which orders. The following parameters are defined in the route determination profile:

▶ STRATEGY

The strategy controls the steps that DRD performs. SAP SCM delivers a standard strategy that will be used. DRD performs the following steps with strategy 50_DEFAULT:

   ▶ 50_DND: Geographical determination

   ▶ 50_RSE: Assignment of vehicle resources

   ▶ 50_SCHD: Scheduling

   ▶ 50_CAPA: Check of transportation allocations of transportation service providers (TSP)

   ▶ 50_CCAL: Determination of transportation and penalty costs

▶ FIXED TRANSPORTATION DURATION

This specifies whether the system is to use fixed transportation duration or is to take into account the transportation lane as the basis for determining material availability date via scheduling for global ATP check. In our case, the transportation duration maintained on the transportation lane will be considered. For distances between locations within transportation zones/discharge port regions, an average transportation duration and distance is maintained.

▶ PLANNING HORIZON

This parameter is used to define the time period in which the system can schedule shipments. When DRD is called from the TP/VS planning view (Transaction /SAPAPO/VS01), the system takes into account the orders and shipments within the planning horizon.

▶ WINDOW FOR DELIVERY DATE/TIME

Pickup and delivery windows will be used during the DRD run to plan departure and arrival dates based on the customer-confirmed delivery date via backward scheduling.

▶ COST PROFILE

This parameter defines which relevant costs and constraints should be considered during automatic planning.

▶ RESOURCE ASSIGNMENT

The assignment of resources is done by selecting the one defined means of transport that automatically preselects all maintained resources for transportation costs.

Figure 11.12 shows an example of a DRD profile (accessed via Transaction /SAPAPO/ VS16), that contains the strategy, condition name to define the scope of planning, planning horizon for the planning needs to run, cost profile for the transportation cost calculation, and the time window for the execution. Different profiles can be maintained by the computer manufacturer business users per different transportation routes (a source location serving a target location with a specific means of transport) in the supply network. For example, if the computer manufacturer has the option to transport the goods via road, sea, or air, three profiles per transportation model are available for the business user to select. The simulation mode is also available in DRD with Transaction /SAPAPO/VS18.

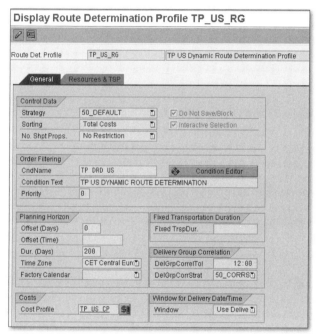

Figure 11.12 Dynamic Route Determination Profile

The business user has to model these hard and soft constraints, which are defined as limitations for particular distribution models. The planning engine of TP/VS considers these constraints while performing the DRD and global ATP checks. The major planning constraints are listed here:

▶ Compatibility of resources to the freight units (hard constraint). For example, particular goods can only be shipped in specific vehicle (resource) types.

- Loading capacities of a vehicle resource. A DRD run can only schedule orders within existing transportation capacities (hard constraint).
- Early pick up based on window (soft constraint).
- Late delivery and nondelivery (hard constraint).
- Requirement date violation (soft constraint).

Transportation and penalty costs are also calculated based on cost profile definitions during DRD.

11.3.2 Activation of Dynamic Route Determination

DRD needs to be activated in both the SAP ERP and the global ATP systems by following these guidelines:

- In SAP ERP, use Report ATP_BASIC_SETTING to activate DRD. Before executing the report ([F8]), check the two available options:
  - GROUP CHECK WITHOUT DELIVERY GROUP: Selecting this allows construction of cross freight units.
  - RE-TRANSFER ATP DESIRED DATES: Selecting this allows the DRD results to be used for order confirmation.
- In the SAP SCM system, follow the path IMG • ADVANCED PLANNING AND OPTIMIZATION • TRANSPORT PLANNING AND VEHICLE SCHEDULING • DYNAMIC ROUTE DETERMINATION • ACTIVATE DYNAMIC ROUTE DETERMINATION. On the resulting screen, activate the DRD for the SAP ERP logical system and order type.

11.4 Summary

The integration of global ATP and supply planning aims to resolve any demand and supply plan disparity in the supply chain. The integration helps in inventory reduction, improves cycle time, and increases customer satisfaction level. Not only can global ATP search inventory across supply networks, but it can also gauge the availability of manufacturing capacities and critical components before committing to customer orders.

In this chapter, we gave an overview of the integration between supply planning and order fulfillment and how a specific business scenario can be modeled using other planning engines (CTM, TP/VS). Global ATP offers a great flexibility in modeling supply chain constraints, and the tight integration with supply planning is its one of the core capabilities.

The next chapter shows how SAP Customer Relationship Management (CRM) can be integrated with global ATP to provide better customer order visibility.

The integration of SAP Customer Relationship Management with global ATP improves online order processing and visibility. By using customization, CRM master data mobile, and Internet, customers can immediately get the confirmed delivery date for orders using global ATP.

12 Integrating the SAP Customer Relationship Management System with Global ATP

SAP Customer Relationship Management (which we'll call CRM) is a business suite that focuses on the overall sales cycles with a company's customers. Besides the introduction of mobile, Internet, and interaction call center order processing, the business suite also helps with key account management and account planning. With the recent revolution of CRM usage in the form of a customer interaction center and Internet sales (portal), it is becoming increasingly important to understand the integration of the CRM (order taking) system with global ATP. The real-time integration between CRM and global ATP helps businesses provide near real-time commitment of delivery dates to customer orders. This in turn improves the customer collaboration and customer satisfaction level in order fulfillment.

This chapter uses an example from a paper company that recently implemented CRM and now wants to integrate the ATP solution with the rules-based ATP check method. Three integration business scenarios—kit-to-order, special dynamic safety stock, and third-party order processing—are also explained briefly.

12.1 Overview of SAP CRM with Rules-Based ATP

Some of the key benefits that a business can realize using the CRM system include improved on-time delivery, reduced cost with better visibility of order status via the *touchless* (no changes after initial customer order creation) order-entry approach, and better sales forecasting.

These benefits are realized with proper estimation of delivery dates via the ATP check. The rules-based availability check with location or product substitution offers better results for order fulfillment. The sales order from CRM directly calls SAP APO global ATP to determine a delivering plant for performing the ATP check. You can then use global ATP with CRM to source a product from multiple locations, based on the rules-based availability of the stock. CRM uses BAPI_APOATP_CHECK for the online product availability check in SAP APO.

When a sales order is created in CRM, the requirements from the sales order create temporary quantity assignments (TQAs) in SAP APO global ATP. As soon as the sales order is saved, these TQAs are deleted from SAP APO.

Business Case Study

A paper company has recently implemented CRM using Internet sales (portal) to capture sales orders from different sales channels. The company has multiple distribution networks and wants to source its paper products from multiple locations to its customers when there is shortage of its paper products at the default plant. The company has specified business rules in global ATP to determine the delivering plant based on geographical or other business operations factors. They use the combination of product and/or location substitution to match the market demands.

Next, let's look at the SAP CRM and global ATP system configuration for setting up this business scenario.

12.2 Basic Configuration in the SAP CRM System

Because the sales order transactions are all integrated within three systems—SAP ERP, SAP CRM, and global ATP—and to ensure inconsistency on the sales order transaction publication, the configuration objects are mapped for consistency. One of the prerequisites for the CRM configuration is the transfer of specific objects from SAP ERP to the CRM system. Figure 12.1 displays the various objects that are mapped across systems. For example, the order type in SAP ERP is mapped with the transaction type in CRM. Similarly, the ATP profile in the CRM system needs to have the same naming convention as the requirements profile in the global ATP system.

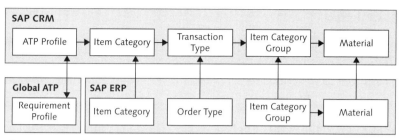

Figure 12.1 Configuration Objects for CRM

12.2.1 ATP Profile

In the CRM system, we will first define an ATP profile for the availability check of an item. The ATP profile is a numeric key (e.g., 110 as shown in Figure 12.2) that is assigned to the item category of a sales transaction item to control whether an availability check takes place for this item. For our paper company scenario where the sales order is created in CRM, the availability check is performed in global ATP. The paper sales order in CRM recognizes the ATP profile configuration, which is further mapped with the requirements profile in global ATP. The naming convention of the requirements profile in global ATP needs to be similar to the one mapped to the ATP profile in CRM online to carry out the following functions in global ATP:

▶ ATP product availability check

▶ Transfer of requirements for ATP calculation purposes

▶ Delivery scheduling for determining the customer delivery date

▶ Transportation scheduling for determining the material availability date (MAD) for the ATP check

The path to define the ATP profile is IMG • CUSTOMER RELATIONSHIP MANAGEMENT • BASIC FUNCTIONS • AVAILABILITY CHECK • AVAILABILITY CHECK USING SAP APO • DEFINE ATP PROFILE.

Figure 12.2 ATP Profile in SAP CRM

12.2.2 Item Category

The next step is to assign the ATP profile to the item category, as shown in Figure 12.3. Assigning the ATP profile to the item category for the paper company sales orders in CRM makes that item category relevant for the availability check in global ATP.

The path to assign the ATP profile is IMG • CUSTOMER RELATIONSHIP MANAGEMENT • BASIC FUNCTIONS • AVAILABILITY CHECK • AVAILABILITY CHECK USING SAP APO • ASSIGN ATP PROFILE TO ITEM CATEGORY.

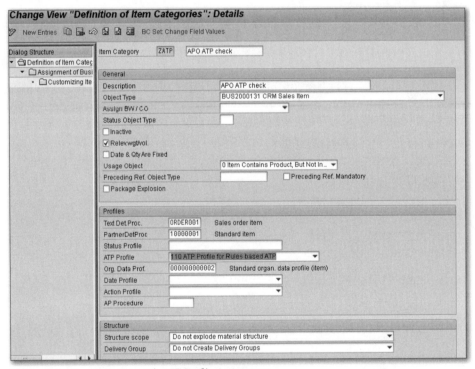

Figure 12.3 Item Category with ATP Profile Assignment

12.2.3 Item Category Determination

The paper company will be using Internet sales to create a customer sales order in SAP CRM. After the availability check is performed in global ATP and the order is saved in CRM, the order can flow to SAP ERP for the delivery process. This online flow is achieved by maintaining the CRM transaction type corresponding to the order type in SAP ERP. To configure this, follow the menu path IMG • Customer Relationship Management • Basic Settings • Define Transaction Type. Then, you can maintain the item category with path IMG • Transactions • Basic Settings • Define Item Categories. For the paper industry business scenario, maintain the transaction type as "TA" for telesales. This corresponds to the SAP ERP TAN item category.

Last, you need to assign the item category to the transaction type by accessing the configuration screen via the menu path IMG • Customer Relationship Management • Basic Settings • Define Item Category Determination.

In the CRM system, when a sales order line item does not completely confirm quantities from a default location that is based on the rules configured in global ATP at that time, location substitution or product substitution may occur. During this process, subitems are created where the main item holds the original demand, and the subitem receives the confirmation results from SAP APO. The configuration for this scenario is again performed in the menu path IMG • Customer Relationship Management • Basic Settings • Define Item Category Determination, where you create two entries for item usage as displayed in Figure 12.4. The first entry is for the main item rules-based ATP check, while the second entry is for the subitem substitution with item category "TAPA".

Trans.type	Desc.Tra...	ItmCtyGrp	Item usage	MainItmCty	Desc. Itm...	Desc.ItmCty	Alt. IC 1	Desc. alt. IC 1
TA	Telesales	ZATP CRM+ATP Check ▾	▾			APO ATP check	TAN	Sales Item
TA	Telesales	ZATP CRM+ATP Check ▾	AP01 RBA Main Item ▾			CRM Rule-Based ATP		
TA	Telesales	ZATP CRM+ATP Check ▾	AP02 RBA Item ▾	TAPA		CRM Rule-B.APO ATP check		

Figure 12.4 Item Category Assignment to Transaction Type

The rules-based logic in SAP CRM has two Item Usage categories defined as explained earlier, and these values are hardcoded in the availability check program:

▸ APO1 RBA Main Item: To determine the item category of the main item.

▸ APO2 RBA Item: To determine the item category of the subitem.

12.2.4 Business Partner Assignment

The delivering location in SAP APO global ATP is stored as a business partner in an SAP CRM system. The mapping of the SAP APO global ATP location to a business partner in CRM is important for both systems to recognize the primary location for the supply because the location is unknown during the sales order creation in CRM. Figure 12.5 displays this maintenance; the assignment is done via menu path IMG • Customer Relationship Management • Basic Functions • Availability Check • Availability Check Using SAP APO • Assign Location in SAP CRM to Location in SAP APO.

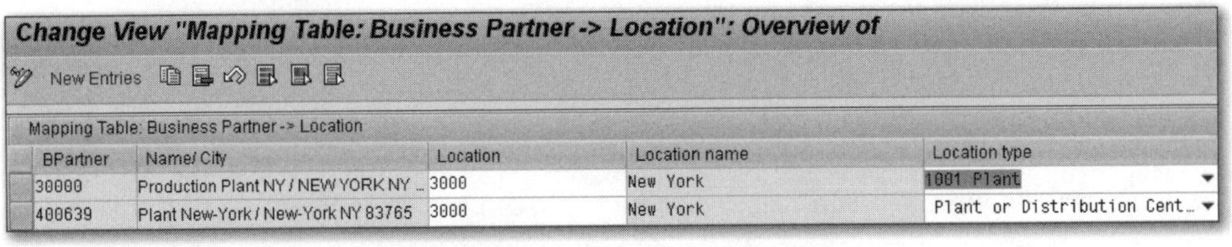
Change View "Mapping Table: Business Partner -> Location": Overview of
New Entries
Mapping Table: Business Partner -> Location
BPartner
Name/ City
Location
Location name
Location type
30000
Production Plant NY / NEW YORK NY ...
3000
New York
1001 Plant
400639
Plant New-York / New-York NY 83765
3000
New York
Plant or Distribution Cent...

Figure 12.5 Assignment of Location to Business Partner in CRM

Now that we've completed the SAP CRM configuration, let's look at the configuration steps you will need to set up SAP APO global ATP.

12.3 Basic Configuration in Global ATP for CRM Integration

The basic configuration in global ATP for our business scenario focuses primarily on the requirements profile and rules-based ATP customization. The configuration helps the paper company perform the product availability check for its paper orders created in CRM and also perform rules-based ATP check for location and/or product substitutions if the primary products are not available in the default location. To display the ATP results properly, you need to add the user parameter APO_ATP_PARA in the user settings. Assign the following two values in the CRM system (accessed via Transaction SU01):

- **5:** The ATP screen will always appear when the user presses `Enter` for each sales order item.
- **6:** To call up the ATP screen, the user must select the sales order item and choose Availability.

12.3.1 Requirements Profile

The first step in your basic configuration is to set up the requirements profile with a similar naming convention as used in the ATP profile in the SAP CRM system.

Using the requirements profile, the paper company can integrate CRM orders with global ATP for the availability check. The requirements profile specifies the scope of the CRM orders in the order type, business event, check mode, and rule strategy that the paper company wants to integrate with CRM. The requirements profile contains parameters at the requirements level that are relevant to the availability check, the transfer of requirements, and transportation and delivery scheduling. The profile will help the paper company determine the MAD for the ATP check.

You maintain the requirements profile via the menu path IMG • ADVANCED PLANNING AND OPTIMIZATION • GLOBAL ATP • GENERAL SETTINGS • MAINTAIN REQUIREMENTS PROFILE. The requirements profile is a numeric key. The value of the requirements profile is transferred to the CRM connected system during runtime. As shown in Figure 12.6, you need to assign CATEGORY "BM" (sales order), BUSINESS EVENT "AC" (checking rule in SAP ERP), and TECH. SCENARIO "AA" to the REQMTS PRFL "110" to integrate the CRM orders with the global ATP system. The two important parameters in the profile are BUSINESS EVENT and TECH. SCENARIO:

▶ BUSINESS EVENT
   A selection of defined operations within a business. The selected business event initiates the ATP check. "A" is used for sales order of make stock materials, "AE" is for make-to-order (MTO) materials, "RP" is for stock transport order (STO), and so on.

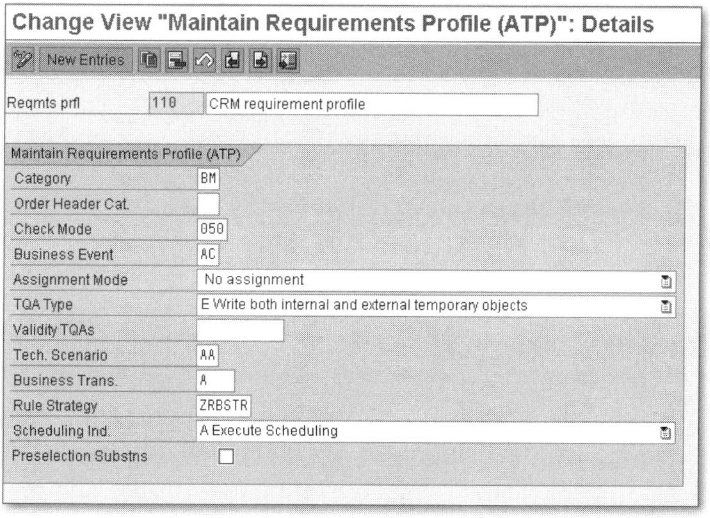

Figure 12.6 Requirements Profile in Global ATP

▶ TECH. SCENARIO
An activation parameter that is used for determining the rule strategy or the rule strategy sequence. The technical scenario corresponds to the communication technology, which triggers a rules-based availability check. Examples of technical scenario are online dialog ("AA"), batch input ("BB"), and EDI ("DD").

12.3.2 Rules-Based ATP

In CRM, there is no location connection with the sales organization and/or material. Using the rules-based ATP check in global ATP, the paper company can determine the supply location for the customer orders. The rules-based ATP check that is performed for CRM paper orders is a two-step activity:

1. The first rule is to determine the primary ATP check location.

2. The second rule is for location substitution and/or product substitution.

You can create a rule strategy or rule strategy sequence using the condition technique. The condition technique is widely used in SAP ERP to determine the value of a record using a search sequence from specific to general (refer to Chapter 6 for more detail on condition technique customization). To determine the rule for a business transaction, you assign a rule strategy to a technical scenario and an action type.

Because the CRM sales order does not pass any business transaction, you keep it blank in the configuration. The configuration path in global ATP is IMG • ADVANCED PLANNING AND OPTIMIZATION • GLOBAL AVAILABLE-TO-PROMISE (GLOBAL ATP) • RULES-BASED AVAILABILITY CHECK • ASSIGN RULE STRATEGY OR RULE STRATEGY SEQUENCE. The rule strategy is also assigned to the previously configured requirements profile.

This completes the configuration for both global ATP and CRM. We will now discuss the master data maintenance that is needed for the business scenario.

12.4 Master Data Maintenance

After the configuration steps are completed, the paper company business user needs to maintain master data involving integrated rule maintenance and the condition record in the global ATP system. Rule maintenance helps the paper company define the business rule for the location substitutions, and the condition record helps connect the products with the rule. These rules are created for both source determinations and locations and/or product substitution. Rules are created in global ATP using Transaction /SAPAPO/RBAO04 (Integrated Rule Maintenance). The menu path is ADVANCED PLANNING AND OPTIMIZATION • MASTER DATA • RULE MAINTENANCE • /SAPAPO/RBA04 - INTEGRATED RULE MAINTENANCE.

Figure 12.7 displays the resulting rule maintenance for the CRM business scenario. The procedure type in the rule determines how a procedure is valuated, which determines how location determination or product substitution is performed during the ATP check. We will use procedure type 3 for location determination for CRM. Procedure type 3 allows a single location for initial location determination for the availability check from the CRM system.

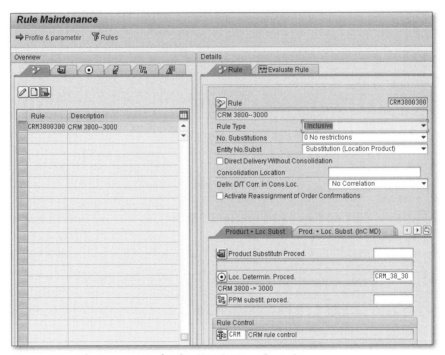

Figure 12.7 Rule Maintenance for the CRM Business Scenario

The condition record is another master data element that is required for our paper company business scenario to map the products with the defined rule. Maintain the rule value (defined earlier in this section) to the CRM product using Transaction /SAPCND/AO11, as shown in Figure 12.8.

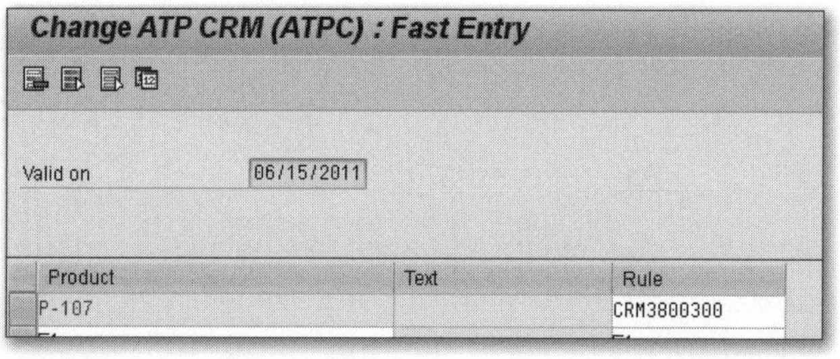

Figure 12.8 Condition Record

Now that we've completed the master data maintenance, we can perform the business scenario testing.

12.5 SAP CRM Business Scenario Testing

In this section, we'll discuss how the CRM customer order integrates with global ATP during the product availability check. Figure 12.9 displays the CRM sales order with location substitution performed. As displayed in the figure, there are two schedule lines: the first line with the default ITEM CAT. (TAPA), and the second line with the substituted ITEM CAT. (ZATP). A message is also displayed stating that the ATP check has been performed with substitution. The steps to replicate this in CRM system are as follows:

▶ We will first create a transaction for a sales order in the SAP CRM system. Use Transaction CRMD_ORDER, and then press ⌷F5⌷ on the keyboard to create a new transaction (sales order). The following three automated steps via configuration take place after you create the order.

▶ The SAP CRM system passes the material and action with the ATP profile to the global ATP system. The ATP profile finds the requirements profile in global ATP from which the rule strategy is determined.

▶ The rule strategy provides the first rule for the primary source location. The location determination occurs in global ATP, using the condition technique. If the stock of a product is not available at the primary location, then global ATP will create a subitem in the sales order based on the rules.

▶ The subitems appear based on the configuration settings in the SAP CRM and SAP APO systems and are indicators of location or product substitution.

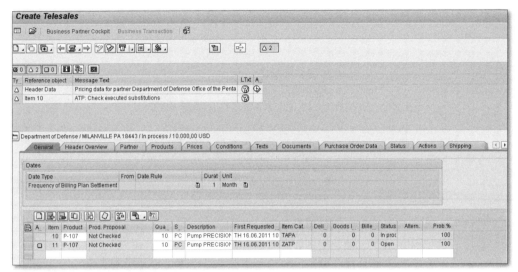

Figure 12.9 CRM Sales with Location Substitution

Figure 12.10 shows the rules-based location substitution during the CRM sales order where the primary location is replaced by the substitution location. The CRM order checks the primary location defined in global ATP, and if no stocks are available, it searches for inventory in the next location defined in the global ATP rule maintenance master data.

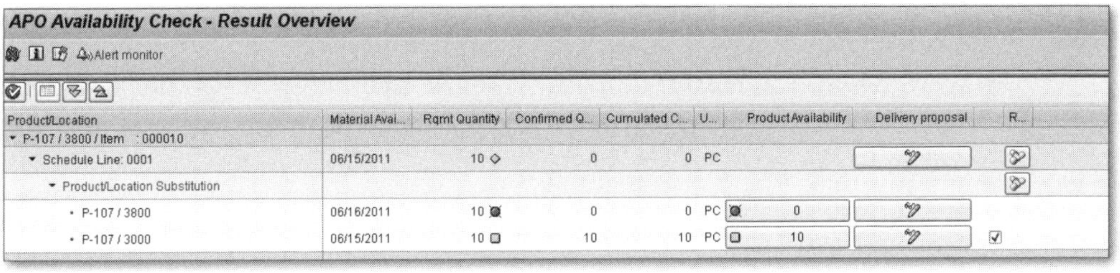

Figure 12.10 Rules-Based Location Substitution

The requirements generated by a sales order created in SAP CRM will trigger TQA generation in SAP APO. When you save the sales order, the TQAs (which are visible in Transaction /SAPAPAO/AC06) are deleted and saved in a time series in SAP APO. This sales order is transferred back to the CRM system through a middleware interface and saved as business documents in CRM.

SAP provides enhancement opportunities in CRM (related to global ATP) if the standard functionality does not support the business requirements. Some of these enhancement examples are explained in the next section.

12.6 Enhancements in CRM for Global ATP

SAP ERP has provided BAdIs (business add-ins) to enhance the availability check from CRM to SAP APO. A company can use the following BAdIs to fulfill any specific business requirement not supported by SAP standard functionality for the availability check, which are otherwise not possible using standard configuration:

▶ **CRM_ORDERADM_SCENARI**
This is the BAdI for posting requirements in SAP APO. In the standard system, the requirements from CRM are not transferred to the SAP ERP system when a sales order is created. The sales order is replicated in the SAP ERP system to create the delivery document. If a company does planning in the SAP ERP system, then this BAdI can be used to transfer the demand from the sales order to SAP ERP.

▶ **CRM_CONFIRM_01**
This is the BAdI to change the field catalog for SAP APO. This BAdI can be used to enhance the field catalog for SAP APO by adding custom fields that are not defined by SAP ERP in CRM.

▶ **CRM_AV_CHECK_APO_01**
This is the BAdI to change data that is transferred to SAP APO. This BADI can be used to manipulate the data coming back to CRM from SAP APO after the availability check.

12.7 Integration Scenarios with CRM

As a company looks for ways to improve its order-management business process via innovative processes, integrating CRM with global ATP becomes increasingly important to provide reliable information to customers. In the following subsections, we provide some business scenarios that are supported by CRM with its global ATP integration. Currently, all these business scenarios supported in CRM require integration with global ATP for the product availability checks.

12.7.1 Kit-to-Order

This feature allows a business to check the availability for a set of items in a kit included as BOM components. The kit-to-order is common, for example, during a new product launch or a sales promotion launch where multiple finished goods are kitted together to form a new product package. The availability check needs to be performed for all the kit items to confirm the customer's order fully. All of these items are collectively processed during the warehouse activities (pick and pack).

You can combine rules-based ATP for component substitution to provide flexible options if a few of the items in the kit inventory are not available for supply. There is no production involved in this process because the header item passes the requirements to the BOM kit components. An addition to this business process can be the palletized shipment of the kits to the customers. To achieve the palletized shipment, you can use the rounding lot size feature, which will propose ATP results based on rounding quantities. Activate the rounding feature in Transaction /SAPAPO/AC12, where you can specify different parameters, for example, package size per location or rounding direction (upward or downward) to control the ATP result.

12.7.2 Special Dynamic Safety Stock

Known as parameter-dependent ATP safety stock (PASS), this feature protects safety stock based on certain parameters. For example, you can specify a buffer of the safety stock for customer-order fulfillment for a sales order type parameter. In the SAP APO product location master data (Transaction /SAPAPO/MAT1), you can check an indicator that will cause the system to calculate and protect the PASS quantity during the availability check.

12.7.3 Third-Party Order Processing

This functionality, which is also termed *drop shipment,* is used in business scenarios when goods are shipped directly from the vendor (external partner) to the customer without coming to the company's warehouse first. The ATP check instruction configuration allows you to model this scenario in global ATP. External procurement of the requirement is done after checking against scheduling agreements or contracts if this procurement is per agreement.

Figure 12.11 displays the schematic process integration flow across four landscapes for third-party order processing (TPOP). The scenario helps optimize the supply chain cost by shipping the products directly to the customers from the source location. The business process is also tightly integrated with the vendors who provide the delivery schedule after the purchase order is received from the company.

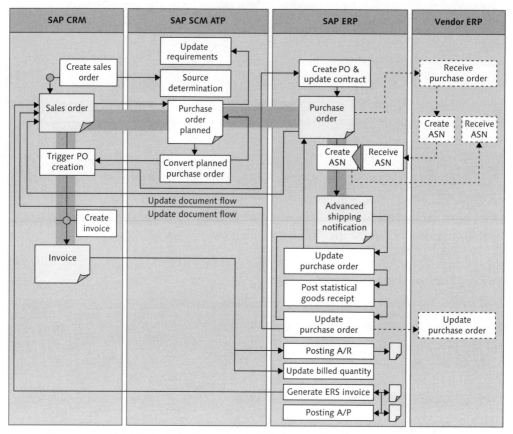

Figure 12.11 Third-Party Order Processing (TPOP) Process Flow (Source: *www.service.sap.com*)

As shown in Figure 12.11, after the sales order is created in SAP CRM, the order is ATP checked for source (location) and determination, and then requirement checked on stock availability in global ATP. After the sales order is confirmed, it triggers the creation purchase requisition/purchase order. The purchase order is sent to the vendor from the SAP ERP system, who might send the order acknowledgement on goods shipped to the customer directly. The subsequent finance process follows to complete the business process.

12.8   Summary

Increasingly, companies are implementing SAP CRM to realize the benefits of on-time delivery, cost reduction with better order status visibility, and portal usage. Global ATP plays an important role in providing the order confirmation after the ATP check.

After reading this chapter, you should understand how rules-based ATP can be combined with CRM Internet sales. The chapter explained the customization steps, master data, and enhancement opportunities in CRM for the global ATP process. Additionally, new integration business scenarios for kit-to-order, special dynamic safety stock, and third-party order processing were explained briefly. These new integration business scenarios help companies optimize supply chain costs and improve order fulfillment.

The next chapter looks at how global ATP can leverage the service oriented architecture (SOA) framework and concept to build a robust order management business process.

Service-oriented architecture (SOA) is now a mainstream architectural strategy for providing future proof integration to SAP and non-SAP systems. This chapter highlights the enterprise services available for modeling and designing the order-management business process.

13 Accelerate Your Global ATP Implementation with Service-Oriented Architecture (SOA) Packages

The SAP approach to service-oriented architecture (SOA) provides a platform for companies to relate information technology (IT) landscapes to changing business models. SAP provides packaged SOA templates in the area of global ATP, which allows businesses to model their ATP processes. SOA is founded on four basic pillars: service-oriented architecture, business context, enterprise services, and pragmatic application. SOA provides the technology architecture for ATP; the business context provides the ATP business logic and process integration. Enterprise services provide the flexibility to reuse ATP application functionality and the pragmatic application where it makes sense to deploy the enterprise services in ATP business processes.

After introducing SOA, this chapter dives into two of the enterprise bundles available: ATP check and backorder processing (BOP) in the order-fulfillment area. The package serves as a template for any industry to introduce and implement the concept of availability check. The chapter also provides an overview of the basic terminology used in SOA.

13.1 Introduction to Service-Oriented Architecture

SOA creates a collaboration platform with business partners, which makes integration viable for companies to create end-to-end business process visibility. A great example of SOA is the e-commerce platform, where the company and customers can collaborate with greater transparency on the sales order fulfillment information.

Even though the IT infrastructure may be different between the companies, SOA still provides a platform for communication and supply chain visibility. SOA is a blueprint for an adaptable, flexible, and open IT architecture for developing ATP based service-based, enterprise-scale business solutions in area of order fulfillment. With SAP NetWeaver as a technical foundation, SOA moves IT architectures to higher levels of adaptability—and moves companies closer to the vision of real-time enterprises by elevating Web services to an enterprise level.

SAP defines SOA as the following (*www.sdn.sap.com*):

> *SOA is a blueprint for services-based, enterprise-scale business solutions that are adaptable, flexible, and open. It enables innovation and standardization in a single environment, allowing businesses to deliver new innovative applications and packaged solutions with the speed and efficiency that the business requires to reduce the total cost of ownership (TCO).*

Several key characteristics allow businesses to enable SOA for an SAP Supply Chain Management (SAP SCM) application, which we will briefly discuss in the following sections.

13.1.1 Configuration Templates

Configuration templates in the ATP business process area allow enterprises to reduce implementation time by subscribing to common global business processes as reference, which can be adapted by businesses. A good example is the Web User Interface (Web UI) portal template for the product availability check, which can be implemented rapidly. These customers can log in, collaborate with their business partners, load master data, and plan collaboratively with suppliers. After the system or process has been set up, customers can execute processes.

13.1.2 Ease of Integration

To help customers leverage existing backend systems, software as a service (SaaS) solutions provide new platform on business process integration. SaaS provides business process libraries which contains list of application programming interface (API) for process integration. The intention is to allow customers and third-party solution providers to leverage this API as a supply chain platform. Although the SOA concept surrounds designing and building software, it is more of a manufacturing model for new business process improvement initiatives. It can, however, be used as an SaaS build application for its customers.

13.1.3 Business Process Library

To feed the configuration templates and to allow extension through the SOA API, there needs to be a set (or library) of process solutions and functional enhancements, such as self-service reporting. For example, business library might contain sample ATP business process templates.

SAP delivers SOA enterprise services, which are typically a series of Web services combined with business logic that you can access and use repeatedly to support a particular business process. Aggregating Web services into business-level enterprise services provides a more meaningful foundation for the task of automating enterprise-scale business scenarios. For example, you could use the ATP availability and BOP template for order fulfillment to automate the interactive and background ATP checks.

The architecture can be related to the IT landscapes of business models and can be reconfigured quickly to changing business needs. The SOA architecture delivers the following benefits:

- An integrated platform for enterprise services
- A mature business process management tool for process composition and orchestration
- An Enterprise Services Repository (ES Repository) from which business services can be called and composed into applications and processes
- As simple toolset and product mix with clearly defined roles

SAP ERP provides enterprise services bundles (ES bundles) that help to build the comprehensive portfolio of business scenario descriptions that are SOA enabled by solutions and enterprise services shipped by SAP today. Each ES bundle refers to a set of enterprise services that support a particular business process and are made available as part of the SAP enhancement packages for SAP Business Suite solutions. ES bundles help design composite applications using SAP NetWeaver enterprise services development and modeling tools. ES bundle documentation provides the following benefits:

▶ Use cases showing how enterprise services help implement certain business process steps

▶ Documentation of how to extend and reconfigure processes in a business scenario

▶ Explanations of the relevant business scenarios, processes, and roles involved

▶ Guidance about how to put the services to work

SAP ERP provides two related ES bundles for the logistics and order fulfillment management end-to-end business process:

▶ ATP check ES bundle

▶ Availability issue resolution and backorder processing (BOP) ES bundle

Logically, an enterprise service is a service operation that is derived from a standardized interface pattern, which contains operation names such as *create, read, update,* or *cancel,* and incorporates communication patterns. In terms of business processes, the service operation helps to perform the creation, update, or deletion of the transactional data in scope.

Now that we've discussed to SOA architecture, let's move on to how it can be implemented in the order management area. The ES bundles for each functional area can be leveraged in the design and implementation phase of a project.

13.2 Modeling and Designing the Order Management Process in SOA—Case 1: ATP Check Enterprise Services Bundle

The ATP check ES bundle (source: *www.sdn.sap.com*) provides a set of services for a user to check the availability of products. For example, in a call center when a consumer has expressed interest in a product, this ES bundle enables the staff to ascertain in real time the availability, quantity, and location of that product and make that information available to the sales representative. Additionally, the ATP check allows the sales clerk to reserve, order, or cancel a product in specific amounts and at predetermined times on behalf of a customer. The ATP check ES bundle supplies the enterprise services that connect customer service with one of the following options:

▶ SAP SCM (version 5.0 or later) to check availability using the global ATP functionality

▶ SAP ERP to check availability using the ATP functionality

Implementing the ATP Check ES bundle allows organizations to do the following:

▶ Improve customer service by extending access to SAP ERP data to a broader end-user base

▶ Use custom UIs for performing ATP checks

▶ Offer ATP checks in new scenarios fitting customer requirements

▶ Extend the ability to more users to perform ATP checks against SAP SCM or SAP ERP

Figure 13.1 shows the business activities in the ATP check ES bundle. The ES bundle tries to fix any rough spots in the seamless integration of product availability queries and reservation functionality.

Figure 13.1 ATP Check ES Bundle Business Process

The ATP check ES bundle offers a vital means of providing customers with accurate information in real time regarding the availability, quantity, and cost of products in which they have expressed interest. In addition, products may be reserved, ordered, or canceled at the customer's demand, in a variety of amounts and configurations. For example, a product that is not available at one location can be located and ordered from another location and then scheduled for delivery, in part or in whole, on one or more dates.

Table 13.1 illustrates the business process steps and corresponding enterprise services that are invoked during order processing.

Business Process Steps	Enterprise Service Invoked	Business Object
The sales representative triggers the system to search for product related information.	Find Material by ID and Description	Material (SAP SCM)
The sales representative searches for the location using the ID information from the search results.	Find Location by ID and Type Code and Description	Location (SAP SCM)
The sales representative selects the location from the search result.	Read Location	
The sales representative searches for the availability of the requested product at this location.	Check Requirement_V1	
If the product is not available in inventory, the sales representative can search for availability of the requested product at another location.	Check Requirement_V1	
If the requested product is available at another location, the sales representative can reserve the requested product.	Create Requirement_V1	Product Availability Requirement (SAP SCM)
The sales representative hands over the ID from the reservation and links it to the customer to get the reserved product delivered to the present location.	Create Customer Requirement Create Purchase Order	Customer Requirement (SAP SCM)
With the reservation ID, the order can be changed at a later date.	Change Purchase Order	

Table 13.1 ATP Check Use Case

Working through the steps in the preceding table, SAP ERP has designed a customized web based user interface (UI) away from traditional SAP GUI based Transaction /SAPAPO/AC04 (SAP APO Availability Check: Simulation). Figure 13.2 shows the interactive availability check UI that is composed with the Visual Composer in combination with the composite application framework. The screen hides the technical information and provides more business-related information to the user and aims for an easy intuitive experience for business users while performing a global ATP check on customer orders.

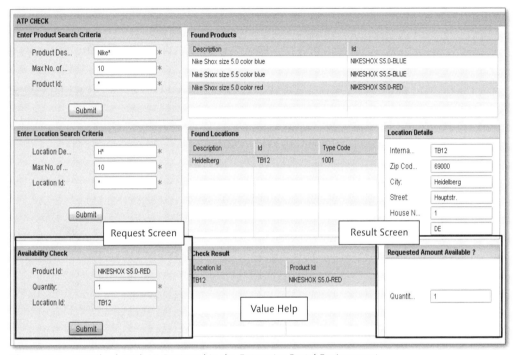

Figure 13.2 ATP Check Web UI Designed in the Enterprise Portal Environment

The backorders is another important part of the ATP check that needs to be processed with a re-ATP check for future customer delivery dates. The next section explains how BOP is provided in an ES bundle package.

13.3 Modeling and Designing Order-Management Process in SOA—Case 2: Availability Issue Resolution and Backorder Processing ES Bundle

The availability issue resolution and BOP ES bundle (source: *www.sdn.sap.com*) helps streamline the handling of backorders. By connecting those enterprise departments that handle backorders—departments with titles such as customer service, expediting group, backorder action services, or procurements service—with each other and the rest of the company, critical data that is necessary to ascertain the status of backorders or availability of products can be retrieved faster.

The bundle effectively enables companies to improve their fulfillment and backorder rates, substantially improving their overall service level.

The availability issue resolution and BOP ES bundle can be used to list backorders for the purpose of analysis and resolution by the user. A list of backorders for manual processing is created, and then specific entries are retrieved for processing. Sources for products can be located, and products (e.g., spare parts) can be shifted from one order to another, using services in this bundle.

Services in this ES bundle (see Figure 13.3) also check the availability of specific products.

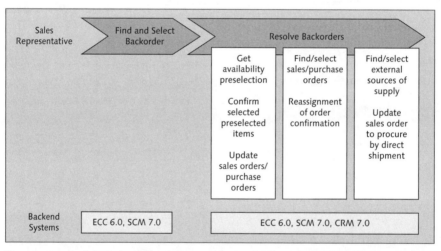

Figure 13.3 Availability Issue Resolution and Backorder Processing ES Bundle Business Process

Using this ES bundle, the business users can run the ATP check in a few different ways:

▶ First, it can provide a preselection functionality, in which the ATP check lists locations where a given product or possible substitutes are available, and then the user selects a product and location from this preselection to make a reservation. (Users can select multiple products or locations as well.) This preselection functionality is provided by the enterprise services in this ES bundle.

▶ Second, the ATP check can be run in such a way that the ATP check itself selects a location where the product is available in the specified quantity and based on date requirements. This second type of ATP check can be run in two ways: Normal and simulative. The normal ATP check will reserve the quantity. A simulative ATP check can be run instead, which simply checks availability without reserving the quantity.

▶ The backorder can be resolved in the following scenarios:

  ▶ By internal source (from different locations)

  ▶ By reassignment of order confirmation (emergency orders)

  ▶ By external source (third-party order processing)

This ES bundle is a cross-component bundle that integrates multiple applications for managing the BOP of orders to increase customer satisfaction. The deployment scenario will have a planning system (SAP ERP or SAP SCM) and execution system (SAP ERP or SAP CRM) in the system landscape.

Table 13.2 illustrates the business process steps and corresponding enterprise services that are invoked during the reprocessing of the backorders. The backorders are sales orders that didn't receive action on the requested date and need to be processed for future customer delivery dates.

Business Process Steps	Enterprise Service Invoked	Business Object
The composite application searches for backorders that are assigned to a particular sales representative.	Find List Property by Type Code	Order Due List (SAP SCM)
The composite application displays the backorder list for the user.	Read Order Due List	
Resolution by Internal Source		
The sales representative lets SAP SCM generate a preselection to show options for filing the backorder.	Create Preselection	Product Availability Preselection (SAP SCM)
The sales representative selects an option from the preselection list.	Create Preselection-Based Requirement	Product Availability Requirements (SAP SCM)

Table 13.2 Availability Issue Resolution and Backorder Processing Use Cases

SAP SCM modifies the sales orders to reflect the updated order information, invoking the appropriate service for the execution system.	Change Sales Order Product Availability Requirement Confirmations (SAP ERP/ CRM)	
Resolution by Reassignment of Order Confirmation		
The sales representative looks for other sales orders to fill the backorders.	Find List Item by Material ID and Supply Planning Area ID	Order Due List (SAP SCM)
The sales representative selects both orders and creates a temporary worklist item that includes them.	Create Order Due List Worklist item	Order Due List (SAP SCM)
The sales representative reassigns the item confirmation.	Execute Order Due List Reassignment	
Resolution by External Source (CRM as Execution System)		
The sales representative looks for third parties that can fulfill the backorder.	Find Source of Supply by Elements	Source of Supply (SAP SCM)
The sales representative selects the best source of supply.	(No enterprise service operation invoked in this step)	
The sales representative arranges to have the product shipped to the customer.	(No enterprise service operation invoked in this step)	
The sales representative changes the sales order accordingly.	Update Sales Order (CRM)	

Table 13.2 Availability Issue Resolution and Backorder Processing Use Cases (Cont.)

Now that we've discussed the two cases of SOA modeling in the order management area, let's drill down further on the components that consitute the SOA architecture.

13.4 Understanding SOA by Design

SOA is comprised of many components, and this section provides the key definitions for the modeling process. Enterprise services are identified at the business level to support a specific business process.

Figure 13.4 shows the breakdown of the many components that make up SOA, as well as the interaction among the components.

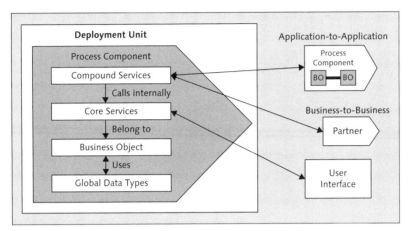

Figure 13.4 SOA by Design

The definitions of these components are as follows:

▸ **Deployment unit**
This software package can be operated on a separate physical system, isolated from other deployment units. It contains a set of process components.

▸ **Process component**
This software package realizes a business process and exposes its functionality as services. These are the building blocks of the SOA solution and are modular and context independent. For example, the SAP ERP Sales Order Processing component provides the Manage Sales Order In service interface, among others. From this interface, you can access the Create Sales Order service operation.

▸ **Service operation (compound services)**
The smallest, separate callable function within the service interface, described by a set of data types used as input, output, and fault parameters serving as a signature. A service operation is grouped by service interfaces. An example of service operation is Create Sales Order.

▸ **Service interface (core services)**
A named grouping of service operations, based on standardized interface patterns, such as create, update, or cancel. An example of interface is Manage Sales Order In.

▶ **Business object**
This is a logical object of significance to the business. It represents a class of entities with common characteristics and common behavior that describes well-defined business semantics. Business objects are used to model a business process. They represent a specific view on business content. A sales order is an example of a business object.

▶ **Global data types**
An SAP-wide defined data type with meaning, structure, and values based on industry standards.

▶ **Composite application**
Application that uses data and functions provided as services by underlying applications and combines these into user-centric processes and views, supported by its own business logic and specific UIs.

▶ **Services registry**
Located centrally within an SOA landscape, this registry for Web services contains entries for all services and service definitions in that landscape. The registered services are classified using semantic-rich classifications systems to enable browsing of services by classification.

Now that we understand the core components and how to model SOA in the SAP ERP environment, we can move on to talk more about the Enterprise Service Repository (ES Repository), which is the technical engine in implementing SOA in SAP ERP.

13.5   Enterprise Service Repository

The ES Repository stores the definitions and metadata of enterprise services and provides an integrated modeling environment for defining enterprise services, data types, and other design objects for SOA-based business processes (example: ATP business processes) in a standards-compliant manner. This central unified repository (shown in Figure 13.5) includes a governance process to define and model enterprise services. As shown in the figure, the new enterprise SOA forms a much more unified method of integrating business processes into the common platform of the repository. Unlike the earlier version of Web services, the repository serves as a technical focal point for delivering the end-to-end business process (e.g., order-to-cash business process).

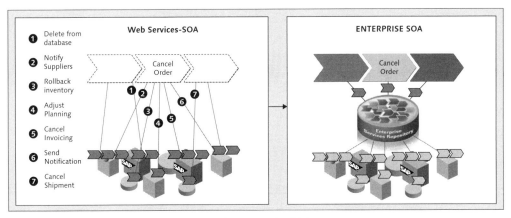

Figure 13.5 Enterprise Service Repository as the Engine for SOA

The repository provides end-to-end modeling support (shown in Figure 13.6) with a rich content database. Beginning from the design phase to the build and implementation phase, the repository supports the complete process with accelerators. For example, for the design phase, the business can leverage on the available integration scenarios, process components, business objects, and global data type definitions available in the area of global ATP.

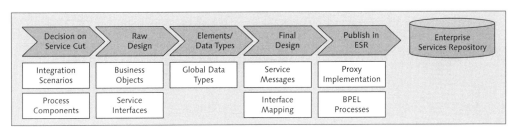

Figure 13.6 Enterprise Service Repository Components Library (Source: *www.service.sap.com*)

Similar for the build and implementation phase, the repository can support existing interface mapping and proxy implementation templates, which can leverage the implementation phase towards implementation of global ATP. For example, the repository contains the integration scenario library, which in turn contains the required SOA contents for the business process and high-level process integration points under the business process execution language (BPEL) library. Business Process Execution Language for Web Services (BPEL) is an XML-based language for standardizing business process description as well as standardization of interaction between business processes in a distributed environment.

To discover which enterprise services are available, you can call Transaction SOA-MANAGER (or old Transactions WSADMIN/WSCONFIG) in the SAP GUI. Expand the folder SOAP APPLICATION FOR XI PROXIES. This displays the technical names of all enterprise services that are available in the SAP Business Suite.

13.6 Summary

Service-oriented architecture (SOA) is a design foundation for software development, deployment, and maintenance for companies to gain competitive advantage in the marketplace. SOA offers companies opportunities to innovate and redesign their business process for customer service excellence. This chapter briefly introduced SOA and the capabilities it offers with its Enterprise Service bundles. In the area is global ATP, there are two SOA templates provided in the form of product availability (ATP) check and backorder processing (BOP). The templates for the ATP comes in form of Enterprise Bundle which provides use cases, preconfigured business scenarios, documentations on how to change or extend the existing customization, and available business user roles.

The last chapter shows how you can monitor and maintain a live productive global ATP environment. Also discussed in the chapter is the importance of having a disaster recovery plan for business continuity during unplanned system outages.

This chapter provides guidelines on proper housekeeping and maintenance best practices for running global ATP smoothly in a productive environment and creating a sustainable solution.

14 Maintenance and Monitoring Procedure for Global ATP

Monitoring and maintenance to ensure the smooth and reliable flow and handling of the global ATP business process are important, because global ATP plays a pivotal role in the order-fulfillment business process. The objective of this chapter is to provide insight into the production environment for monitoring procedures, error handling, and escalation management for the global available-to-promise (global ATP) system. You will also learn the key activities that you need to perform as part of the disaster recovery plan during system outages and how to ensure business continuity when the global ATP system goes down.

14.1 Monitoring and Maintenance

Global ATP monitoring tasks are done on a daily or weekly basis, and maintaining the routine is important to make sure that the global ATP results are accurate and that there is transactional data consistency between SAP ERP and global ATP.

14.1.1 Backorder Processing (BOP)

BOP functionality can be executed either via a background job using Report /SAPAPO/BOP or interactively using Transaction /SAPAPO/BOPI. The following recommendations are useful for BOP:

▶ Schedule the BOP background job to run once a day when the volume of sales order processing is less.

▶ Execute BOP in parallel background jobs by separating the product sets in the filter profile variant.

▶ Execute BOP after the supply planning run to take account of the quantity and date of the latest receipts.

▶ Run the BOP close to the warehouse goods receipt frequency for the latest inventory count.

▶ Use standard filter type SAP_NETCHANGE when SAP ERP production planning (PP) creates planning file entries, and you want BOP to account only for these products during the BOP run.

▶ Use the standard filter type SAP_ALERT if you have transportation planning and vehicle schedule (TP/VS) implemented and want to process at source/destination location hierarchy levels.

14.1.2   Temporary Quantity Assignment (TQA)

Temporary quantity assignments (TQAs) reserve (or lock) quantities that are allotted during an ATP check in SAP APO against opposing parallel ATP checks. These quantities remain locked until the order that triggered the ATP check is either saved or exited without saving. In both scenarios, the TQAs are deleted. All ATP basic methods (product availability check, product allocation, and check against planning) create their own TQAs. A frequent problem may arise in a production environment where the TQAs are still in the *<unknown>* hanging state. This might happen due to an inconsistency in the Core Interface (CIF) transfer between the SAP ERP and global ATP systems and must be corrected to avoid data duplications.

14.1.3   Persistent Quantity Assignment

A persistent quantity assignment, unlike a TQA, continues to exist after a transaction is ended. The persistent quantity assignment reserves quantities over a longer, unspecified period until they are deleted by another transaction. Persistent quantity assignment is commonly used in BOP, multilevel ATP, CRM scenarios, and third-party processing scenarios.

You can use Transaction /SAPAPO/AC06 to display and clean up selective TQAs (based on the product location combination as shown in Figure 14.1). This transaction needs to be monitored on a weekly basis to view the TQAs, and entries should be deleted where appropriate. Multiple executions, one for each type of TQA, can be executed.

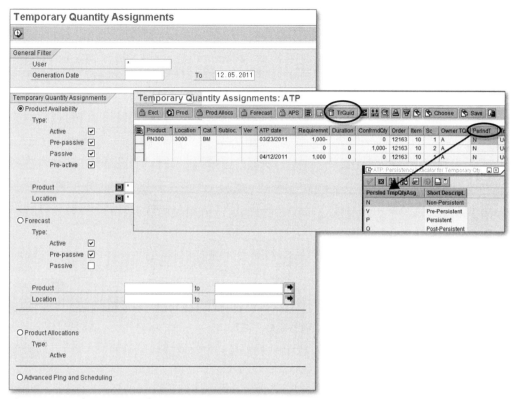

Figure 14.1 Deletion Report for Temporary Quantity Assignments

Entries that are more than a couple of days old can be deleted using Report /SAPAPO/OM_DELTA_REMOVE_OLDER. In this report, the BASIC METHOD section indicates the processes that were used to create the TQAs. We recommend selecting all types of TQAs, even though some may not be generated. The NON-PERSISTENT indicator is the only appropriate one and is the normal state for a TQA because it is generated only in this phase.

14.1.4 SAP ERP Database and SAP APO liveCache

For consistent global ATP results, the transactional data in the SAP ERP database needs to be in synch with SAP APO liveCache data. We have included a list of four reports in the following subsections that are available to ensure the consistency and correction between SAP ERP and global ATP.

Consistency Check Report

Perform the check using Transaction /SAPAPO/OM17 for the global ATP business objects. As shown in Figure 14.2, select the objects that are related to product location, sales, stocks, shipment, ATP time series, delivery schedule/confirmation, and product allocation for active version 000. SAP APO may contain both active version (000) and multiple simulation versions. Only the former interfaces with SAP ERP for the transaction data flow.

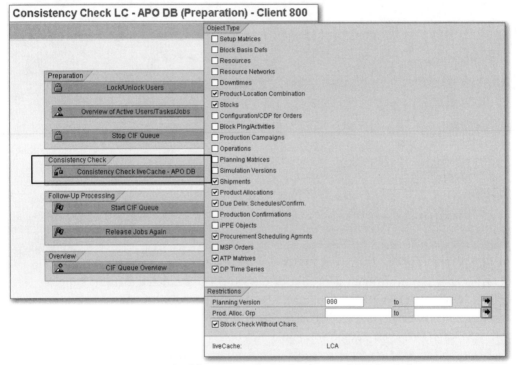

Figure 14.2 Consistency Check between SAP APO Database and SAP liveCache

Requirement Situation Correction

Use Report SDRQCR21 to rebuild the SAP ERP Table VBBE with order and delivery requirements. Only enter information in the MATERIAL and PLANT fields to execute on a subset of the data. If no material or plants are specified, then tick the PROCESSING PER MATERIAL box. Checking the DATA TRANSFER box executes an update of Table VBBE; leaving this box blank executes it in test mode. Checking the COMPARISON box ensures that the log report only shows the changed entries; leaving it blank reports all entries.

CIF Delta Report

This report is commonly used (Report /SAPAPO/CIF_DELTAREPORT3) to compare the transactional data from the SAP ERP database with SAP APO liveCache. The report can be scheduled to run in the background, and the log can be checked to for inconsistencies.

For correction, the report needs to be executed in online mode. To reduce the runtime when checking the sales orders, we recommend running the report with the checkboxes SALES ORDERS and USE TABLE VBBE flagged, which you can access under the DOCUMENTS TO BE CHECKED section. MATERIAL and PLANT fields can be entered to execute the report on a subset of the data only.

Correction Report for Sales Orders Requirements and Product Allocation

Report /SAPAPO/SDRQCR21 corrects all inconsistencies that may occur due to program errors or by queue entry deletion. This transaction is similar to /SAPAPO/CIF_DELTAREPORT3, but it checks and repairs additional tables.

Report /SAPAPO/SDRQCR21 corrects incorrect sales orders and delivery requirements in SAP ERP and SAP APO. In SAP ERP, you create requirements in the sales order via the schedule lines, and you create requirements in the delivery via the items. In SAP APO, these requirements are stored in SAP liveCache. Errors may arise due to program errors or deletion of queue entries.

This report should be implemented if the errors cannot be corrected using Report /SAPAPO/CIF_DELTAREPORT3. This affects the Sales & Distribution (SD) order tables in SAP APO in particular because for BOP to function without errors, the SD order tables have to be consistent and complete. This report ensures that this is the case. Report /SAPAPO/CIF_DELTAREPORT3 does not contain these checks. PRODUCT and LOCATION can be entered to execute on a subset of the data only.

In the DETERMINATION OF REQUIREMENTS IN ERP section, the READ REQMTS FROM TABLE VBBE option is set to use Table VBBE. The BUILD REQUIREMENTS FROM DOC. FLOW option is much slower because it rebuilds the date from the individual transaction documents. The CHECK SD ORDER TABLES checkbox should be checked to ensure that all the appropriate tables in SAP APO are included in the check.

14.1.5 Reorganization

You need to clean the global ATP-related tables to ensure data consistency and an accurate result by properly deleting obsolete transactional data, cleaning the old global ATP results, cleaning the ATP alerts, and running consistency checks between the time series and SAP liveCache objects.

Deleting SAP ERP Data No Longer Required in SAP APO

Using Report /SAPAPO/SDORDER_DEL, you can remove sales orders and deliveries that have been archived in SAP ERP (Table SDFIELD). The report helps to remove obsolete entries in Tables /SAPAPO/POSMAPN and /SAPAPO/SDFIELD. The report can be scheduled to run daily. The date variant shown in Figure 14.3 needs to have a dynamic date setting on the LAST CHANGED BEFORE field to only look at entries older than one month.

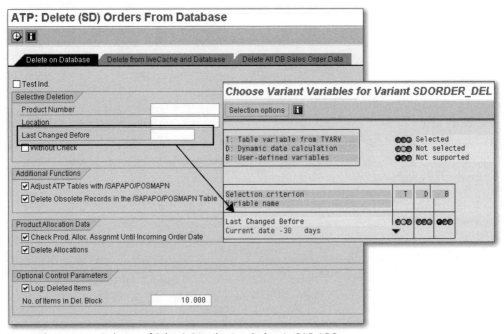

Figure 14.3 Deletion of Sales & Distribution Orders in SAP APO

Reorganization of ATP Characteristic Matrices

Using Report /SAPAPO/OM_REORG_DAILY, you can reorganize the sales order business objects daily in SAP liveCache. No input parameters are required when running this report.

Deleting Backorder Processing Runs

The saved BOP results can be deleted at regular time intervals using Report /SAPAPO/BOP_DELETE. BOP with the status update (U) can only be deleted online. The report can be scheduled to run daily with a recommended variant as shown in Figure 14.4.

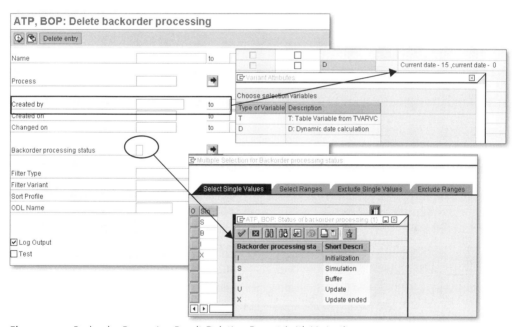

Figure 14.4 Backorder Processing Result Deletion Report (with Variant)

Deleting ATP Alerts

Shortage alerts are created during the product availability check or during the product allocation. The alert is also generated when the ATP ALERT indicator is selected in the check instruction configuration. Delete ATP-generated alerts from the database on a weekly basis using Report /SAPAPO/AMON_REORG. Remove the SIMULATION RUN flag to delete alerts from the database completely (see Figure 14.5.).

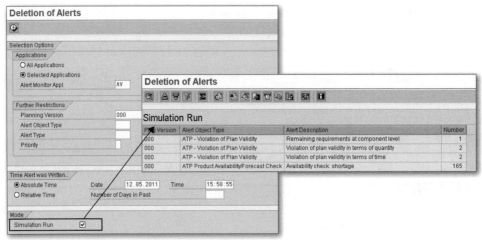

Figure 14.5 Deleting ATP Alerts in SAP APO

14.1.6 SAP APO Planning Area

If SAP APO demand planning (DP) is used for product allocation or characteristics-based forecasting (CBF) for multilevel ATP, the planning area must be maintained properly for SAP APO liveCache and time-series data consistency. Users can run the following reports for consistency checks:

▸ **Re-initialize product allocation planning areas for rolling time period**
Using Report /SAPAPO/TS_PAREA_INITIALIZE (see Figure 14.6), you can reinitialize the active planning areas for the appropriate rolling time period. Include the global ATP product allocation planning area, active version, and the rolling horizon where the time-series objects are future dated.

▸ **SAP liveCache consistency check**
Using Report /SAPAPO/TS_LCM_CONS_CHECK, you can clean up any product allocation inconsistent data in the planning area and planning book. The report constantly checks all series data in the product allocation planning area and corrects them. In the report selection, include the global ATP product allocation planning area, active version 000, and planning horizon that the time-series objects are valid in SAP liveCache. We recommend running this report in the background, as well as after any characteristics value combination (CVC) master data creation.

This report helps, for example, during the product allocation process where the sales orders that had product allocation gets deleted in SAP ERP. The sales orders are deleted in SAP APO via the CIF delta report in the database, but the data may still exist in SAP liveCache and be wrongly referenced in the planning book, or it may block the planning with the message "Invalid data status." Running this report corrects any existing data inconsistencies between the database and SAP liveCache.

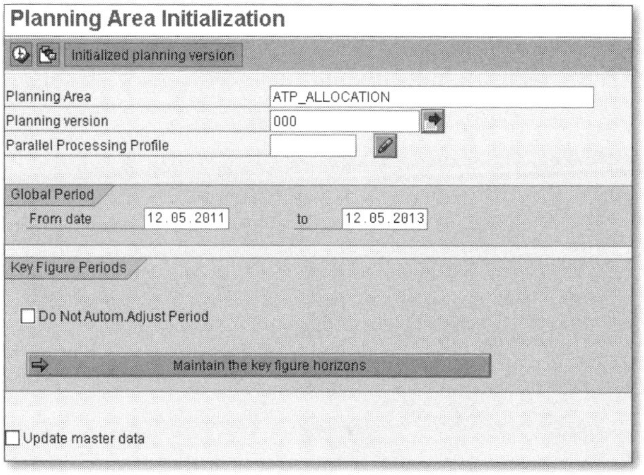

Figure 14.6 Planning Area Initialization for a Rolling Time Period

14.1.7 Product Allocation

Product allocation involves establishing a connection between the global ATP and DP. While DP sends the allocation quantity to global ATP and vice versa, global ATP sends the incoming sales order to DP. The data consistency between global ATP and DP ensures the ATP check and allocation accuracy. The following transactions need to be scheduled routinely for data consistency in the product allocation:

▶ **Transaction /SAPAPO/ATPQ_CHKUSG: Cleaning of Product Allocation Assignments**
  Allows for display and cleaning of product allocation assignments (see SAP Note 676128 for more information). This is a manual process that includes four checks (shown in Figure 14.7) and described here:

  ▶ Assgmt w/o Incoming Order Qty: Compares the incoming orders quantity assigned in the product allocation group with the orders that have product allocation assignments. This comparison is done at each characteristics combination level for every time bucket period.

311

▶ INCOMING ORD. QTY ASSGMNT: Also compares the incoming orders with product allocation assignments but only lists situations where the incoming orders quantity is greater than the orders total.

▶ ASSIGNMENT W/O ORDER ITEM: Lists incoming order quantity assignments where the corresponding order cannot be found. This assignment can be deleted but remain in the incoming orders quantity, or it can be removed completely and the incoming orders quantity reduced.

▶ ASSGMT W/O PRODUCT ALLOC. GRP: Lists orders that have a product allocation assignment but no product allocation group or characteristic combination (these may have been deleted after the order was created) and can be removed. Note: The specified product allocation groups are ignored with this option.

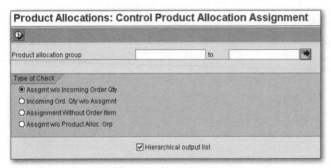

Figure 14.7 Product Allocation Housekeeping Transaction

▶ **Transaction /SAPAPO/ATPQ_KCGRP_U: Product Allocations: Update Assgmt** Similar to the prior transaction, the product allocation assignment can be cleaned by using Transaction /SAPAPO/ATPQ_KCGRP_U. This transaction can be scheduled as a background job to carry out the first option just described and automatically correct the incoming orders quantity. The main disadvantage of this transaction is that it has only one option, unlike the previous transaction that has four selection conditions. The advantage of this transaction is the horizon selection, which is useful if the earlier transaction runs into processing performance issues. The option with horizon selection helps define the scope of the run instead of all selecting all entries in ATP product allocation database.

Now that we've looked at the monitoring and maintenance activities in global ATP, let's consolidate the regular transaction and batch jobs that the global ATP technical engineer will use on a daily basis for system maintenance.

14.2   Regular Transactions and Batch Jobs

Businesses that use the global ATP system require routine batch jobs to be scheduled not only for the regular housekeeping (deletion) of past results but also to correct ATP results that are based on the current inventory. Table 14.1 lists the commonly used transactions and scheduled batch job for global ATP that help process any inconsistent transactional data, perform housekeeping on the data, and handle any errors blocking communication between the SAP ERP and global ATP systems.

Monitoring Object	Report/Transaction	Monitor Frequency	Monitoring Activity or Error-Handling Procedure
SAP APO: TQA	/SAPAPO/OM_DELTA_REMOVE_OLDER	Weekly	Deletes non-persistent entries daily that are older than two days.
SAP APO: External consistency check	/SAPAPO/CIF_DELTAREPORT3	Daily	Ensures that transactional data are reconciled between SAP ERP and SAP APO. The inconsistencies need to be corrected manually.
SAP APO: Sales order and deliveries archive	/SAPAPO/SDORDER_DEL	Monthly	Deletes sales orders and deliveries in SAP APO that are archived in SAP ERP.
SAP APO: TQA	/SAPAPO/AC06	Weekly	Displays and corrects any TQAs.
SAP APO: inbound queues	SMQ2	Alert notification via Report /SAPAPO/RCIFINQUEUECHECK	Monitors the inbound queues. Failed queues will have SYSFAIL status.
SAP APO: outbound queues	SMQ1	Alert notification via Report /SAPAPO/RCIFQUEUECHECK	Monitors the outbound queues. Failed queues will have SYSFAIL status.
SAP APO: product view	/SAPAPO/RRP3	Interactive	Global ATP availability overview (interactive).

Table 14.1 Global ATP Regular Batch Jobs and Transactions

Monitoring Object	Report/Transaction	Monitor Frequency	Monitoring Activity or Error-Handling Procedure
SAP APO: BOP result deletion	/SAPAPO/ BOP_DELETE	Daily	Deletes BOP results.
SAP APO: Alert reorganization	/SAPAPO/ AMON_REORG	Weekly	Deletes SAP APO ATP alerts from the database.
SAP APO: Incorrect assignment of sales orders and deliveries	/SAPAPO/ SDRQCR21	Weekly	Corrects sales order requirements and product allocation assignments in SAP ERP and SAP APO.
SAP APO: Interactive BOP	/SAPAPO/BOP	Interactive	Interactive BOP transaction.
SAP ERP: Sales order Table VBBE rebuild	SDRQCR21	Weekly	Recovery of sales and delivery requirements.
SAP ERP: Stock overview	MMBE	Interactive	Gives the stock overview for the type of stocks across multiple plants.
SAP ERP : Stock requirement list	MD04	Interactive	Displays the stock of the product for all MRP elements.
SAP ERP: Material document list	MB51	Interactive	Identifies incoming/ outgoing stock, including the non sales order/ delivery-related stock.
SAP ERP: Product availability check	CO09	Interactive	Availability check in SAP ERP if global ATP is not available or for products that are not related to global ATP in SAP ERP.

Table 14.1 Global ATP Regular Batch Jobs and Transactions (Cont.)

After summarizing the key transactions you need to maintain global ATP, let's now look at the disaster recovery plan that needs to be exercised for any unplanned system outages.

14.3   Disaster Recovery Plan

Before the global ATP functionality is placed in the production environment, it is imperative that a good business continuity and disaster recovery plan is simulated in a nonproduction environment. The concept of the disaster recovery plan is to maintain the business continuity in receiving sales orders from customers, performing basic product availability checks, and shipping goods to customers from the warehouse. The plan should also encompass bringing the situation back to normal after the SAP APO system is back up.

The concept calls for consistency on the basic ATP customization maintained in SAP ERP and global ATP. Making sure customization is the same for the requirement class and for scheduling will ensure that the basic availability check in SAP ERP Transaction CO09 or global ATP Transaction /SAPAPO/AC04 yields the same ATP result. Performing ATP in SAP ERP, however, does have some limitations:

▶ No check against the product allocation.

▶ No multilevel ATP checks.

▶ No rules-based ATP checks.

▶ No usage of capable-to-promise (CTP) functionality.

▶ Receipts planned in SAP APO (e.g., planned orders or purchase requisitions) are not published to SAP ERP to take into ATP calculations. This limitation depends on the checking horizon for the ATP checks. This horizon needs to be consistent with the SAP APO result publication to SAP ERP so you can perform ATP checks in SAP ERP while factoring in these published receipt elements.

The disaster recovery or business continuity plan can be divided into four main stages, which we discuss in more detail in the following subsections.

14.3.1   Switching the ATP Check from SAP APO to SAP ERP

When SAP APO liveCache or the database are down, messages appear saying "ATP check in system XYZ not possible, since SAP liveCache is not active" during the sales order creation or update to indicate that global ATP cannot be performed in SAP APO. The CIF queues in SAP APO Transaction /SAPAPO/CQ also display "Connection to SAP liveCache failed" entries. To switch the ATP check from SAP APO to SAP ERP, you must perform the following activities:

▶ Deactivate the integration model for the ATP check in SAP APO. This step is defined under a separate integration model using Transaction CFM3 or Report RIMODAC2.

▶ Sales order and deliveries should still be in an active integration model. During the recovery period, the system will generate STOP entries in the CIF queues. By maintaining the integration model active, the user can re-process the queues once the connection is established again between SAP ERP and global ATP.

▶ Delete all the BOP results in SAP APO that have not been processed during the outage period.

▶ Stop any related global ATP background scheduled jobs (e.g., BOP).

14.3.2 Performing an ATP Check in SAP ERP for the Interim

During the deactivation of ATP in SAP APO, Transaction CO09 in SAP ERP performs the basic product availability check in SAP ERP. During the local check in SAP ERP, the new or updated sales order is buffered in the CIF. The ATP check in SAP ERP will undergo the limitation of ATP functions as highlighted earlier in the section.

14.3.3 Switching the ATP Check Back from SAP ERP to SAP APO

After the SAP APO liveCache and database are restored, you must perform the following activities to switch the ATP check back from SAP ERP to SAP APO:

▶ Restart CIF queues to re-process the sales order and deliveries queues that were failing with "STOP" status.

▶ Perform a consistency check of the SAP APO database and SAP liveCache using Transaction /SAPAPO/OM17.

▶ Check and fix IDocs if there are interfaces built for sales orders and deliveries.

▶ Reactivate the ATP check integration model for the global ATP check in SAP APO.

▶ Perform an external consistency check between SAP ERP and SAP APO for all the transactional data using Transaction /SAPAPO/CCR. While running the CIF delta report (/SAPAPO/CIF_DELTAREPORT3), monitor the CIF queue for any failures. Ensure all of the transactional data (requirements and receipts) are synched between SAP ERP and SAP APO.

14.3.4 Postprocessing Sales Orders in Global ATP

To ensure that the global ATP functions are reflected in the sales order, a re-ATP exercise needs to be performed for all the affected sales orders during the outage period. BOP should be triggered in the background and possibly done in a parallel processing way, depending on the transactional data volume. This is a mandatory step to avoid any negative global ATP situation on the sales orders because the orders may have been fully confirmed during the outage period.

Besides the disaster recovery plan, another important control area for optimal use of global ATP system is performance. We will discuss this topic in the next section.

14.4 Performance

For global ATP, performance relates to the processing time to perform the ATP check either interactively or in the background. Keeping CIF integration models active, which serves as the communication channel between global ATP and SAP ERP, is also important. Any delay in order processing has a huge impact on business goals, as the customer order might not be confirmed (partially or fully).

The following list describes the four areas that can influence the performance of the system and need to be monitored closely. The performance symptoms can be long processing times for ATP checks or the background taking too long to process.

1. **BOP**

   Performing a re-ATP of the sales orders based on the correct stock situations is primarily done on a daily basis. The performance is driven by the volume of the transactional data to be processed and the CIF settings. We highly recommend that the work processes in SAP APO and SAP ERP are balanced enough for parallel processing to optimize the remote function calls (RFC) during the high transaction volume scenario. This ensures optimal global ATP performance and better CIF communication flow between the SAP ERP and global ATP systems.

2. **Table /SAPAPO/SDFIELD**

   This table is used in global ATP to a large extent. We recommend keeping the additional fields to a minimum so the table records can be read sequentially at a faster rate.

3. **ATP alerts**

   The SAP APO Alert Monitor allows for exception management. This implies that the business would be alerted only for ATP scenarios where there are supply chain issues (supply shortage, constraints, etc.). The alerts that are generated are primarily written in the database, and too many alerts can have a negative impact on system performance. We recommend restricting the amount of alerts per business needs.

Besides the Alert profile setup, also check the check instruction configuration for which business scenarios the alerts are generated. The check instruction configuration (accessed via Transaction /SAPAPO/ATPC07) contains the checkbox ATP ALERT ACT., which generates an ATP alert every time there is a supply shortage during the ATP check.

4. **Core Interface (CIF)**

   CIF plays a major role in communication between SAP ERP and SAP APO, but at the same time, it can be a performance bottleneck when the system load is considerable. CIF performance is primarily influenced during mass data processing. Such processes include initial data supply, BOP, and SAP ERP document background processing. Consider the following recommendations when managing CIF performance:

   ▶ Perform routine housekeeping of old transactional data from the database. The larger the table, the more time the system takes to find its relevant data in the tables. We recommend running the regular reorganization batch jobs as suggested in Section 14.2.

   ▶ Perform a weekly index of the ARFC tables (ARFCSSTATE and ARFCSDATA) that are used in the transactional remote function call (tRFC)/queued remote function call (qRFC) process. The tables hold the actual tRFC/qRFC data in the calling and receiving system.

   ▶ Perform system load balancing of the qRFC with outbound and inbound queues. Ensure that there are sufficient dialog work processes available on the receiving system if using inbound queues. Refer to SAP Note 416475 for more details.

   ▶ Make sure you have upgraded the plug-in version, qRFC version, gateway parameters, and R/3 kernel version components to the latest version.

The ATP application logs provide a good indication of what technical steps were executed during the ATP processing.

14.5   Application Log

The application log needs to be monitored routinely for any errors or warnings encountered during the ATP check processing. The global ATP application log (accessed by Transaction /SAPAPO/ATPLOG_DSP or Report /SAPAPO/ATPLOG_DIS-PLAY) is a message log generated during the availability check. Information regarding the customizing settings, technical details of the check, warnings, or errors that have occurred during the check are recorded and stored in database.

The log is divided into different areas: backorder processing (BOP), rule evaluation (EVR), product allocation (PAL), scheduling (SCH), and temporary quantity assignment (TQA). Every application's class area is again subdivided into problem classes that document the importance of a message. In the technical view of an application log, the problem classes are available as very important, important, medium, other, and additional information. In the application-oriented view, there are only the problem classes very important, important, and medium. Further numerous filter possibilities exist alongside the subdivided display of messages in applications classes and problem classes.

An application log can also be exported in different formats. It is also possible to delete individual logs from the database by selecting the log to be deleted and then clicking the DELETE button.

14.6   Sizing

The SAP Quick Sizer check helps determine whether there are enough hardware and application server resources in the SAP SCM system to handle the global ATP expected workload. This check is important to run because it prevents any severe performance problems that can be caused by underestimating the hardware requirements. The sizing of global ATP involves sizing the memory requirements of the ATP time series in SAP liveCache. The CPU sizing is determined by the different ATP checks.

The inputs to the Quick Sizer are some basic master data and transactional data volume from SAP APO and SAP ERP. The Quick Sizer tool can be accessed online via *service.sap.com\quicksizer*. The inputs from the SAP APO side (see Figure 14.8) are the LOCATION PRODUCT master data, number of ATP basic (product availability), and/or advanced (rules-based or CTP) REQUEST calls for a defined period.

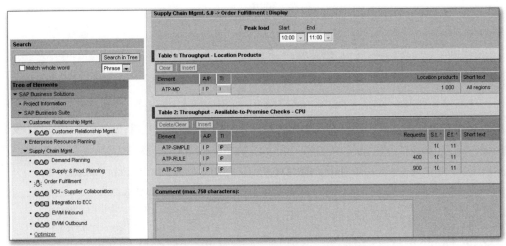

Figure 14.8 SAP APO Quick Sizer Input for Global ATP

The inputs from SAP ERP are on the transactional volume (sales orders, stocks, purchase orders), which will undergo ATP checks or will be used for ATP calculation for a defined period.

The Quick Sizer calculates (see Figure 14.9) CPU, disk, memory, and input/output resource categories based on throughput numbers and the number of users working on the global ATP application.

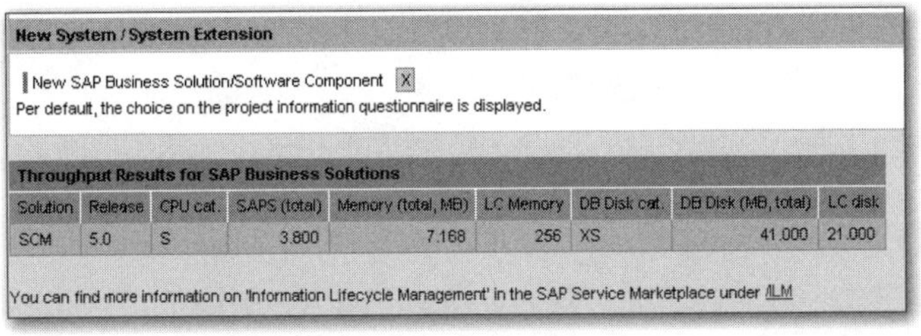

Figure 14.9 Quick Sizer Output

14.7 Summary

In this final chapter of the book, we looked at system administration and gave insights into the monitoring and error-handling procedures for global ATP. The maintenance procedures for routine deletion, hardware sizing, and scheduling the monitoring of batch jobs are imperative for better performance management and stability of global ATP. Companies implementing global ATP should have a well-defined disaster recovery plan for business continuity plan to be enacted during any unplanned system outages in the production environment to avoid any disturbance of the order fulfillment and execution processes.

Accurate delivery commitment for customer orders is an important factor for a company to maintain a strong relationship with its customers. Providing reliable and accurate information concerning when customer orders will be delivered increases customer satisfaction. This book demonstrated that global ATP, with its basic and enhanced capabilities across multiple industry scenarios, can provide a strong user-decision tool for the business community. You will now be able to model your specific order fulfillment business scenarios in global ATP with the business goal of lowering warehouse inventories, improving customer delivery reliability, and increasing your customers' satisfaction level.

Appendices

A Enhancements in Global ATP

This appendix discusses several technical enhancement techniques that are possible in global ATP. These enhancements (not supported within the standard SAP package) are used to customize customer-specific business requirements during global ATP implementation or during the support phase.

A.1 Minor Enhancement Scenarios in Global ATP

Minor enhancements in the global ATP business scenario primarily consist of smaller modifications during the sales order processing transaction or during the master or transaction data transfer from SAP ERP. Three areas support the minor enhancements: Core Interface (CIF), enhancement spots, and Business Application Interface Programming (BAPI).

A.1.1 Core Interface Enhancements

The Core Interface (CIF) communicates master and transactional data between SAP ERP and the global ATP system. During CIF communication, you can influence the master data (such as material master, customer, or plant) or transactional data (such as sales orders and purchase orders) to represent different corresponding data that are set to reflect their business process. An example of master data CIF enhancement is a publication of an additional field characteristics catalog from SAP ERP to the global ATP system. Similarly for transactional data, a business can use these enhancements to map receipts and stock elements from one plant to another consolidated plant where the ATP check is performed. You can activate the CIF enhancement in SAP ERP via menu path IMG • INTEGRATION WITH OTHER MYSAP.COM COMPONENTS • ADVANCED PLANNING AND OPTIMIZATION • APPLICATION SPECIFIC SETTINGS AND ENHANCEMENTS.

The CIF uses the user exit technique to transform the master or transactional data during the transfer from SAP ERP to SAP Event Management. The user exit helps in calling customer-specific ABAP codes so the standard functionality can be enhanced.

Table A.1 lists all of the enhancements that are available in SAP ERP and the corresponding enhancement in the global ATP system.

Enhancement	Exit Name in SAP ERP	Corresponding Exit Name in SAP APO
CIFMAT01	EXIT_SAPLCMAT_001 CIF to SAP APO: Enhancements to Material	EXIT_/SAPAPO/SAPLCIF_PROD_001 Inbound Processing: Products
CIFLOC01	EXIT_SAPLCLOC_001 Customer Exit for Initial Transfer of Plants	EXIT_/SAPAPO/SAPLCIF_LOC_001 Inbound Processing: Location
CIFLOC01	EXIT_SAPLCLOC_002 Customer Exit for Initial Transfer of Vendors	EXIT_/SAPAPO/SAPLCIF_LOC_001 Inbound Processing: Location
CIFLOC01	EXIT_SAPLCLOC_003 Customer Exit for Initial Transfer of Customers	EXIT_/SAPAPO/SAPLCIF_LOC_001 Inbound Processing: Location
	EXIT_SAPLCLOC_004 Customer Exit to Influence the SAP APO Location Type	
CIFPUR01	EXIT_SAPLMEAP_001 Customer Exit for Selection of Customer-Specific Purchasing Data	EXIT_/SAPAPO/SAPLCIF_PU_001 Inbound Processing: Purchase Order Documents
CIFLOC02	EXIT_SAPLCDC5_001 User Exit MRP Area Mapping	
CIFSLS02	EXIT_SAPLCSLS_001 User Exit: Inbound Processing of Sales Orders	EXIT_/SAPAPO/SAPLCIF_SLS_001 Inbound Processing: Customer Order
CIFSLS03	EXIT_SAPLCSLS_002 Customer Exit Immediately Before Dispatching Sales Orders	
	EXIT_SAPLCID3_001 Deltareport3: User Exit for Sales Order Comparison	

Table A.1 SAP ERP and Global ATP CIF Enhancement List

Enhancement	Exit Name in SAP ERP	Corresponding Exit Name in SAP APO
	EXIT_SAPLCID3_002 Deltareport3: User Exit for Comparing Purchase Orders and Purchase Requisition	
CIFSTK01	EXIT_SAPLCSTK_001 CIF to SAP APO: Stock Enhancements	EXIT_/SAPAPO/ SAPLCIF_STOCK_001 Inbound Processing: Stocks
CIFMAT02	EXIT_RCIFMTDE_001 Customer Exit Before Transfer of Deactivated Materials	

Table A.1   SAP ERP and Global ATP CIF Enhancement List (Cont.)

After the CIF enhancements are implemented, you need to perform corresponding developments in SAP APO as well so that during the reconciliation of transactional data (e.g., stock) between SAP APO and SAP ERP, no errors occur. The development can be done in the BAdI /SAPAPO/CIF_DELTA3 (Enhancements Comparison Report). Two examples for this BAdI development are:

▶ **Method RELEVANT_FOR_COMPARE_R3_STOCK: Filtering of R/3 stocks that are not relevant**
In this method, you can exclude the stock of a material in a particular storage location from comparison in Report /SAPAPO/CIF_DELTAREPORT3. If you do not exclude the material in this BAdI, then those materials keep on appearing in the reconciliation report.

▶ **Method RELEVANT_FOR_COMPARE_R3_SLS: Filtering of R/3 sales orders that are not relevant**
In this method, you can exclude sales orders of certain customers or customer groups from the comparison and reconciliation in Report /SAPAPO/CIF_DEL-TAREPORT3.

A.1.2 Enhancement Spot of ATP Check in SAP ERP

The enhancement spot is a technical modification of the transaction that is based on a specific business rule. For example, a business can be lead-time scheduling during the sales order process for a computer manufacturer. This means that the manufacturer receives normal sales orders but also sometime gets priority sales orders. In normal sales order types, the replenishment lead time is factored in, whereas for the rush order type, you don't want to consider the lead time for fulfilling the sales orders.

In standard SAP ERP functionality, the replenishment lead time is controlled by the checking group MTVFP, which is specified in a material master and cannot be changed in the sales order transaction processing without enhancement. This is where the enhancement spot provides a solution in the form of ES_SAPLATPC (Transaction SE18). In this enhancement, you can control the value of fields in the internal tables such as P_ATPCSX and P_ATPMATX. For a computer manufacturer, you can achieve the business requirement of not considering the lead time for rush order types by changing the value of checking group P_ATPMATX - MTVFP. You can change the value of the checking rule or business event P_ATPCSX - PRREG to change the overall ATP check control. The business benefit of implementing this enhancement is the order fulfillment of rush orders, which in turn increases customer satisfaction level. The enhancement spot can be readily accessed using Transaction SPAU_ENH.

A.1.3 Business Application Programming Interface (BAPI) Development

A Business Application Programming Interface (BAPI) is another mechanism provided by SAP ERP for inbound and outbound processing of sales orders, related master data, and transaction data. The BAPI serves as the communication standard interface for processing the business application objects either within SAP ERP or in external applications. The common use of the BAPI is on the data-conversion side, focusing on the master data loads during the project implementation phase. An example of a BAPI is BAPI_LOCSRVAPS_SAVEMULTI_30A, which can be used to create or change location data in SAP APO.

A.2   Major Enhancement Scenarios in Global ATP

Major enhancements consist of modifications done using BAdIs. SAP ERP offers flexibility in its standard program by providing explicit enhancement points where customers can put their ABAP code to modify the output result. For instance, a computer manufacturer might use backorder processing (BOP) of sales orders, where the business requirement may be to process only specific customer orders, which is not achieved by a standard filter type. The BAdIs for the BOP are based upon object-oriented programming (also known as ABAP code) and can be called multiple times. You will use Transaction SE18 to access a BAdI.

The next sections provide some examples of user exits that are used in conjunction with BAdIs. The BADI can internally call the function module where the ABAP code can be implemented.

User Exits for Backorder Processing

▸ **EXIT_/SAPAPO/SAPLBOP_100: ATP, BOP: Backorder Processing: Display List**
BOP results display information about the sales order line items processed by BOP. In this user exit, you can enhance the results of BOP, if the business requirement is to display certain custom fields such as sold-to (customer) name or delivery priority field in the BOP result. You can delete certain sales orders from display also if those orders are not checked by BOP.

▸ **EXIT_/SAPAPO/SAPLBOP_FILT_010: ATP, BOP: Backorder Processing: Filtering**
The BOP filter is used to list the sales order line items for the BOP run. A company can filter the sales orders by plant or by created date. In this user exit, you can add custom fields that are not provided as standard fields in BOP. SAP Note 376773 provides detailed instructions on how to add custom fields in the BOP filter.

▸ **EXIT_/SAPAPO/SAPLBOP_SORT_020: ATP, BOP: Backorder Processing: Sorting**
The BOP sort prepares the list for the BOP run in ascending order or descending order, based on the configuration settings. In this user exit, you can add new fields to sort the list of the sales orders in the BOP run. You can also add custom fields to the sort such as a customer group, and so on.

User Exits for Scheduling

▸ **EXIT_/SAPAPO/SAPLVCRM_001: Scheduling: Inbound Interface**
This user exit can be used to change the scheduling proposal and is commonly used with another SAP ERP user exit: FM APO_SCHEDULING.

User Exits for Rules-Based Product or Location Substitution

▸ **BAPI_RULESRVAPS_SAVEMULTI: Create or Change Substitution Rules**
A global company with multiple products and location combinations can have many rules for product or location substitution. Sometimes in constantly changing scenarios, it becomes difficult to maintain these rules. Using BAPI_RULES-RVAPS_SAVEMULTI, you can create or change rules. You can use BAPI_LSPSRVAPS_SAVEMULTI to create or change the location determination procedure. Similarly, you can use BAPI_PSPSRVAPS_SAVEMULTI to create or change the product substitution procedure.

▸ **EXIT_/SAPAPO/SAPLATPR_002: Processing: Result of Rules-Based ATP**
A global company can source products from multiple locations to its customers. Often, the time difference between two locations is very large; for example, the time difference between the United States and China is 17 hours. When a location substitution occurs from the United States to China, the transportation scheduling does not take the time zone offset into account. In this exit, you can calculate the correct offset and adjust the material availability date (MAD) on the substituted location. SAP Note 377780 — RBA: Use of User Exit APORB001 — provides more detail.

A.3   Enhancements in SAP ERP Field Catalog for SAP APO Global ATP and Product Allocation

For rule-based ATP and product allocation, we often have business requirements to include certain custom fields that are not available as SAP ERP standard characteristics fields.

In the INCLUDE FV45VFZY_USEREXIT_CATALOG_VALU, you can define custom fields such as ZZCUSTCLASS. In this way, the custom field can be mapped to SAP APO in the field catalog user exit. You can use the code snippet as shown in Listing A.1:

```
data : w_dacustclass (2) type c
*-- populate the values to ls_catalogue structure.
ls_catalogue-delnr          =    vbap-vbeln.
  ls_catalogue-delps        =    vbap-posnr.
  ls_catalogue-kfdna        =    'zzcustclass'.
  ls_catalogue-value        =    w_dacustclass.
  append ls_catalogue to itab_atpfield.
```

Listing A.1 Custom Field Catalog Code

Another example of modification in SAP ERP regards the field lengths that are defined in SAP ERP and global ATP. The length of the fields in SAP ERP sometimes differs with SAP APO fields. To map an SAP ERP field with an SAP APO field, you may have to convert the length in the user exit. Let's look at some examples:

▶ **The Material**
MATNR is an 18-digit field in SAP ERP, whereas in SAP APO, Material - /SAPAPO/ MATNR is a 40-digit field.

▶ **The Sold To (Customer)**
KUNNR is a 10-digit field in SAP ERP, whereas in SAP APO, Sold To /SAPAPO/ KUNNR is a 20-digit field.

To fix this problem, access the INCLUDE FV45VFZY_USEREXIT_CATALOG_VALU, and call function module CONVERSION_EXIT_ALPHA_INPUT to convert the length of a field to match the internal database format by adding leading zeros to the field.

A.4   Enhancements in SAP APO Field Catalog for SAP APO Global ATP and Product Allocation

Similar to the enhancements of the field catalog in SAP ERP, you can enhance the field characteristics in SAP APO. In brief, you need to enhance table /SAPAPO/ KOMGO to include all custom fields that are required in rules-based ATP or product allocation. You can do this by appending /SAPAPO/KOMGOZ and adding the append to /SAPAPO/KOMGO.

Another similar business scenario can occur in the product allocation master data during the creation of characteristics combinations. The business requirement may only be a few field lengths (e.g., 5 digits) from product hierarchy (PRODH). However, during the transfer, the complete 18-digit field is transferred from SAP ERP to SAP APO for the product master. This can be achieved using the user exit enhancement EXIT_/SAPAPO/SAPLATPQ_010 to initialize the parameter transfer and manipulate the field catalog characteristics prior to mapping the product allocation table.

B SAP Notes for Global ATP

Various developer notes exist for SAP Event Management. We have listed the most useful SAP OSS notes here to support the global ATP implementation and post go-live support issues.

B.1 General

SAP Note	Description
488725	FAQ: Temporary quantity assignments in global ATP
501446	List of all composite and FAQ notes about APO ATP
510533	CIF sales order integration: R/3 SD data consistency
495166	Tips and tricks for handling alert monitor
304501	Different customer requirements in R/3 and APO
1287255	/SAPAPO/ATP 112 when you delete temporary qty assignments
425825	Consistency checks, /sapapo/om17, /sapapo/cif_deltareport
894294	/sapapo/sdorder_del: Performance and advice
1284461	Release restrictions for SCM 7.0
444641	Correction of incorrect sales order requirements with APO
894294	/sapapo/sdorder_del: Performance and advice
1008133	Runtime for report /SAPAPO/SDORDER_DEL is too long
547508	FAQ: Schedule line overview and ATP

B.2 Rules-Based ATP

SAP Note	Description
909128	Stock transport orders with ATP with material substitution
1100874	Manual conditions for items with rules-based ATP check

SAP Note	Description
382195	Dates in R/3 sales order incorrect with rules-based APO ATP
321473	Error in RBA and condition controlled scheduling
1085147	TAPA/TAN - when is a subitem created?
502177	Integration: Rules-based ATP in sales
700386	FAQ: Rules-based ATP

B.3 CTP and Multilevel ATP

SAP Note	Description
426563	CTP: Settings, system behavior, and performance
480292	Multilevel ATP documentation
455421	Comparing multilevel ATP and CTP (documentation)
601813	FAQ: Characteristic evaluation in ATP check mode
520432	Consulting note: Determining dates in multilevel ATP

B.4 Scheduling Function

SAP Note	Description
604336	Shipment or transportation scheduling with APO ATP
1099818	Availability check and goods receiving hours
300951	Dates conversion after availability check in APO
481835	Analyzing the time zone settings
1287148	Integration PO to APO - Error "Invalid time interval"
547941	FAQ: Shipping and transportation scheduling in APO
719772	Performance in transportation and shipping scheduling
443500	R/3 versus APO: Dates in sales orders and deliveries

SAP Note	Description
526359	Time streams and APO shipment and transportation scheduling
1138721	Scheduling across year threshold is incorrect
833272	Change of delivery and transportation scheduling in SD

B.5 Backorder Processing

SAP Note	Description
563254	FAQ: Backorder processing
510912	BOP: Tip & Tricks
485085	Backorder processing: New rule evaluation
1130360	EDQA and ODL with sublocation
1105656	FAQ: Order due lists in SCM
635411	Performance: BOP reading filter in APO
519766	Consulting note: Backorder processing results display

B.6 Product Allocation

SAP Note	Description
445118	Transportation service provider selection
428102	Performance: Loading planning area version
705068	Performance: Loading data from an InfoCube
676128	Product allocations: Product allocation assignment check

B.7 Transportation Integration

SAP Note	Description
799787	Performance of scheduling and TP/VS
538147	APO: Process flow BOP - TPVS including monitor/functions

B.8 CRM Integration

SAP Note	Description
195884	Collective note: Link between CRM and APO
819744	Composite SAP Note: ATP in CRM
1142390	ATP; Inconsistent Customizing between R\3 and CRM
813662	Error message CRM_APO 203 for availability check with R/3
682613	FAQ: Local ATP from CRM
856727	Availability check with SAP R/3 as of CRM 5.0
1109473	FAQ: ATP: Availability check in Web UI
1071521	FAQ: ATP: Availability information with APO
1014337	APO available-to-promise from CRM: Location determination
872118	CRM5.0 ATP w/ APO: Collective note/settings/restrictions
315507	CRM-APO: Persistent temp. qty loads remain
445365	CRM-APO-ATP: Persistent temporary quantity loads are retained
328433	FM CRM_AV_CHECK_APO_GUID_CONVERT no longer effective
1071522	Settings and restrictions: Scenario A and APO-ATP

B.9 Enhancements

SAP Note	Description
376773	User exit EXIT_/SAPAPO/SAPLBOP_FILT_010

SAP Note	Description
385039	Transfer of additional fields via the R/3 APO interface
993452	Enhance field catalog for the ATP check in APO
174969	Rule determination does not work for numeric field values
377780	RBA: Use of user exit APORB001
379539	User exits in delivery and transportation schedulng
987299	Report /SAPAPO/SDRQCR21: Functional enhancements

C   The Authors

Sandeep Pradhan is an SAP solution architect in the field of supply chain management with more than 16 years of professional experience. He specializes in supply chain application advisory services and has achieved results by helping clients understand, architect, select, and implement the SAP supply chain solutions required to run their businesses. In his various roles (project manager, solution architect, supply chain manager), he has been responsible for providing thought leadership in supply chain strategy, business processes transformation, technology architecture, and business integration. He has worked on numerous full lifecycle SAP global ATP project implementations from the discovery phase through the implementation phase. Sandeep holds an MBA from Monash University, Australia, and is also author of the book *Implementing and Configuring SAP Event Management* (SAP PRESS, 2010). You can contact Sandeep Pradhan at *spradhan13@gmail.com*.

Pavan Verma is a certified SAP supply chain solution consultant with more than 17 years of professional experience. Pavan has expertise and a strong background in providing supply chain technical solutions as well business process reengineering solutions to clients. Pavan has been a team leader, architect, and consultant on global projects with Big Four consulting and leading companies. He has worked in the pharmaceutical, paper, high-tech, consumer packaging goods, and utility industries. Pavan has worked on numerous end-to-end lifecycle SAP global ATP project implementations. He holds a post-graduate Marketing Management diploma from Madurai Kamaraj University, India, and he is author of various white papers on *sdn.sap.com*. You can contact Pavan Verma at *pavanverma@yahoo.com*.

Index